Profound Parenting

There is something about this image of Twin Springs Plantation, where my family has retreated for five generations, that is for me, *profound.* The heavenliness that I feel as I see this familiar place cannot be denied. I am left with an unmistakable impression that the master of all creation is revealing a part of Himself to me. God's majesty is unspeakable and transcending and real, and I want to be as close as possible to that majesty as I walk through my life.

And that is what I have always wanted for my children. I wanted them to know the God that will speak to them. I wanted to be that person who would open the door for my children—the door that would profoundly influence the path of their lives.

> I am the door. If anyone enters by me, he will be saved and
> will go in and out and find pasture.
> John 10:9 ESV

Profound Parenting

A Southern Christian Mother
Answers Her Son's Request for a
Road Map to Parenting
It's Different. It's Radical. It Works.

Georgia Adams West

Cover Art by Caroline Kimbrough Moody

Joe West *loves* his grandchildren and he *loves* Auburn football!

For the love of my life, Joe West, who,
in living out before me the extraordinary life
that belongs to one who knows and loves Jesus,
introduced me to Christ.
The joy, peace, and love that was so evident in
his spirit was something I knew I wanted for myself.
Joe has given me more than he will ever know,
and has given our children more
than they could ever have asked for or imagined.

xi		Introduction Profound Parenting
1		Jonathan's Letter
3		Letter To My Children
5	Chapter 1	God Knew You Before You Were You
14	Chapter 2	Prayer
20	Chapter 3	Study Your Child
33	Chapter 4	How Your Children Will View You
37	Chapter 5	Your Voice, Your Countenance, Your Home, Your Goal
51	Chapter 6	Tell Your Children Who They Are
57	Chapter 7	The Critical Foundation
62	Chapter 8	Hide The Word In The Hearts

84	Chapter 9	No Formal Speeches Necessary
91	Chapter 10	Priorities
92	Chapter 11	Wisdom, Words, And Ways
110	Chapter 12	Teenagers
142	Chapter 13	Beware! Both Volunteering and Paying Jobs Can Preoccupy Your Mind and Your Heart
147	Chapter 14	Making Memories That Will Last A Lifetime
225	Chapter 15	Mind Your Manners
239	Chapter 16	Recognize the Truth and Act on It
249	Chapter 17	Your Southern Heritage
281	Chapter 18	A Letter To My Grandchildren

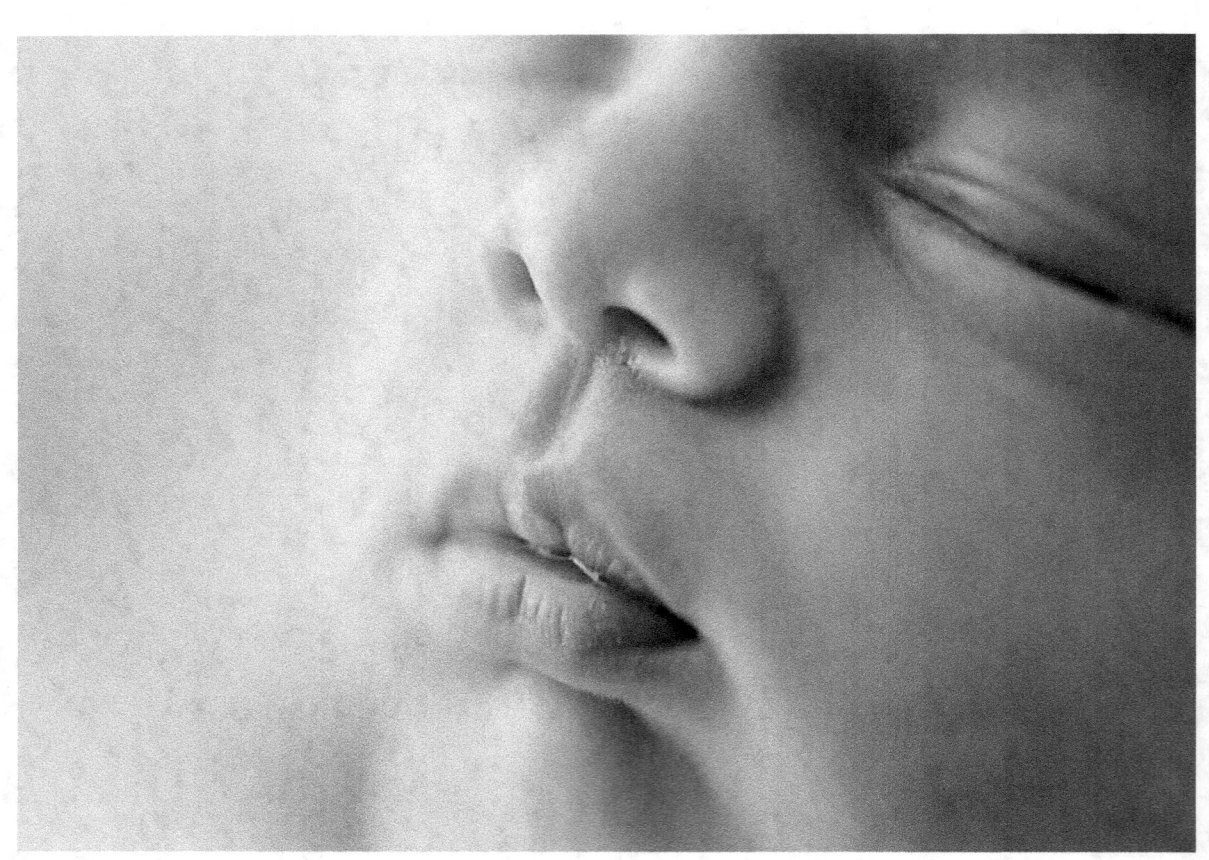

Margot

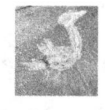

INTRODUCTION

Profound Parenting

I was shocked to find an email in my inbox from my middle child, Jonathan, asking me to write a book on parenting. He was in medical school at Emory and about to start his residency in interventional radiology at the University of Virginia. I couldn't imagine how he had even had time to think about asking me to do this, much less time to write a letter.

I took his letter seriously and began to ponder what had made his childhood different from anyone else's and what had made him ask me that same question. Then I realized that is was because my husband and I had an approach to parenting that was radically different from anyone I knew. Although Jonathan may not have known exactly what made it different, he knew that it was. And he knew that it was not perfect, but that *because of it* he found himself on a good path with good footing.

Our parenting was based on all of the things that the world now tells you to ignore. We live in a world that demands acceptance and tolerance of every way but God's way. It seems this world considers all parenting approaches acceptable, except the one that adheres to God's profound principles. On the face of this statement, you may think, "No! I know many people who parent with Biblical principles." However, if you take a closer look, you may find that few people actually adhere to these principles.

It has crossed my mind more than once that this book will be considered almost heresy by many people I know. It will quite possibly be considered close-minded, short-sighted and radical, even by my children and their spouses. And that makes me nervous. But it is the truth. It is what we did. It is what God says to do, even if the *way* someone else lives out that message is slightly different from the way we did.

This is my story of how my husband and I raised three incredible children by being solely committed to and dependent on the framework put forth in God's awesome living Word.

> Let the words of my mouth
> and the meditation of my heart
> be acceptable in your sight,
> O Lord, my rock and my redeemer.
>
> Psalm 19:14 ESV

Jonathan's Letter

Wednesday, March 8, 2006

Mom,

I was just thinking about how successful you and Dad have been as parents. Your children turned out pretty good, especially me. But seriously, we all have done well in school and have stayed out of trouble and stayed pretty grounded. I really think you should consider objectively looking back at what you've done as a parent and writing it down, formally. Maybe a book or just a short article depending on the detail you can go into ... the more the better. I would like to know what you did so I can do the same for my children and I'm sure Katherine would have similar desires as she is beginning a family of her own. If you could come up with a thorough enough manuscript I'm sure it would be a fantastic guide for parents everywhere. I'm certain you have some good advice and methods esp. on early childhood education or intellectual stimulation. Certainly, genes play a role too, but I think you got us on the right track. Set your goals high and just do it. Keep up the good work. I love y'all.

Your son,
Jonathan

This unexpected, unsolicited letter arrived in my inbox many years ago. I never imagined I would receive something of such immeasurable value to me—a rare and cherished letter; a tribute that carried serious weight. It was the perfect gift to receive at the end of such a wonderful time in my life. Because it came from one of my children, its effect was deep. Jonathan had no idea just how meaningful this was to me. He was clearly saying that he knew *his* was a childhood that stood out from the rest, that it was notable if not, in many ways, remarkable. And he wanted to know how to duplicate it for his own children. He surely saw it as idyllic. I was amazed. After reading his letter, I thought back over the years since I gave birth to my first child. I had never loved anything as much as being a mother. God had given me three children to love and to be loved by. In one moment, I had gone from being *a girl* to *a mother* and had been handed a new life that was mine to mold and shape for good or bad. It was a completely awesome journey for which no one felt worthy. Though we weren't perfect, my husband and I seemed to be perfectly matched for this task. He and I both wanted the same thing: to raise godly children who had character and grace. It has now been over eight years since I received that letter, and I am just now able to write this little book. It is tough to describe how you raised your children when all you really went by was *love*.

Finally, my keyboard is busy, and I am attempting to put together something that makes sense, something I can pass on to my children that will prepare them to be great parents. *Five* granddaughters have already been born, so I am frantically, in between running to see them, trying hard to complete my book. Paper notes are everywhere, and my scatterbrain head is spinning, but when I finish this, I hope it serves as a real treasure map for anyone embarking on this special journey of becoming parents. I certainly consider my children rare treasures, for which I would pay a king's ransom. And if you give your everything to raising your own children, they will certainly be treasures to you.

I have decided to write this book in the form of a letter to my three children, each of whom I could not love more. Thank you, Jonathan, for giving me a reason to write about the path that Love has led me down.

Letter To My Children

Dear Katherine, Jonathan, and Matthew,

Newborn Margot

You have done something that you will *never*, *ever* fully appreciate. You made me a mother, and gave me the opportunity to fulfill a dream. I have had the great privilege of being *your* mother, and in all honesty, I have always wondered if I was actually such a good mother, or if, in reality, you were each just born *good children*. I know that I was handed an unspeakable blessing each time I walked out of that hospital with a new life in my arms. So, I want to thank you now for the indescribable joy of raising you.

As intent as I was on being a great mother when I was twenty-three, I am just as intent on being a *grand* grandmother now! So Daddy and I will be on your team—on the field, in the (s)wings, and on the sidelines cheering you on. But for now, most of your children and our grandchildren are either very young or still expectations, so you have time to arm yourself with all you will need for this lofty task. This is not a job that you want to do on the fly. And believe me, it *is* a job.

Before I say another word, I want to tell my daughters-in-law and my son-in-law that you should have complete confidence that I am writing this not as instructions for any of you but only in response to Jonathan's request. I will be altogether in your court when you have a different opinion from mine on how to do this or that. And you will! But here I am referring to the nuances of how you accomplish God's plan. You bring your own families' stories with you. All of your traditions and creativity and insight will guide you as you make decisions about raising your children. Whatever your mothers and fathers did on your behalf, they did wonderfully, because you are all wonderful. God has a perfect plan for each of us, but all with the same underlying truths. In that sense, I hope you all will find this compilation of ideas helpful as you each strive to become a parent that is by all measures a treasure to your children.

CHAPTER 1

God *Knew* You Before *You* Were *You*

It is unfathomable to our finite minds, but even before that moment when a miraculous explosion of light signified the second you were conceived, God *knew* you. He had already thought of you, and knew the precise second when you would enter this world, and what mark you would make at a particular time of history. With great intricacy, He fashioned every cell that would become you. You were *His* thought. He planned great things for you, and for your life. He knew what part of that perfect plan you would fulfill, and what part you would not. You are His creation, and His love for you was ever-present and overwhelming before you were created, as revealed by David's psalm.

> For you formed my inward parts;
> you knitted me together in my mother's womb.
> I praise you, *for I am fearfully and wonderfully made.*
> Wonderful are your works;
> my soul knows it very well.
> My frame was not hidden from you,
> when I was being made in secret,
> intricately woven in the depths of the earth.
> Your eyes saw my unformed substance;
> in your book were written, every one of them,
> the days that were formed for me,
> when as yet there was none of them.
>
> Psalm 139:13–16 ESV

Before I formed you in the womb I knew you, and before you were born I consecrated you; I appointed you a prophet to the nations.

Jeremiah 1:5 ESV

Seeing you for the first time, I was in awe of what was before me. I was not afraid or even apprehensive. God had prepared me for that very second when I would meet you. I knew you were perfectly created by someone perfect and that the Creator had a perfect plan for your life. I was to be a part of that plan, and my relationship with the Creator of the universe would be key to successfully raising you.

Consequently, I cannot tell you how important it is for you to nurture your spiritual life. If you do not know Jesus Christ, who made you and made your children, you cannot love Him, and without loving Him, you won't have a relationship with Him, the Father, and the Holy Spirit. *You will be throwing your children to the wind, no matter what you do.*

A deep, abiding relationship with Christ is critical, and that is where you need to start. So prepare now for giving your all to parenting your children. If you haven't already, seek God with your whole heart. Be intentional about cultivating that relationship. Pray with your spouse every day and listen to the Holy Spirit.

For anyone who might be reading this book who does not know Jesus and does not know *how* to know Jesus, it's really so simple. You do not have to change your ways or become sin-free and pure of heart and squeaky clean to be accepted by God. That is what Jesus Christ, God's only Son, did for you when He, who had no sin, died in your place. Yes, while we were all still sinners and totally engrossed in sin, God sent His only Son to pay the penalty for our sins. He loved us that much! Can you imagine sacrificing your only child for someone who is not great and not even good but wretched?

His love is beyond comprehension. If you consider the scope of that love, it will bring you to your knees. And that is where your life begins to change! Acknowledging your own sinfulness, God's love for you, and Jesus's sacrifice for you in His death on the cross takes you across the chasm into a new and abundant life that you will not believe! Suddenly, your eyes will be opened to what God has done through Jesus, and as you accept this high price that has been paid for you, your love for God will change you from the inside out, almost without effort on your part.

There will be no striving to give up those things that enticed you to sin, those things that were so appealing and yet so destructive. You will have a change in your heart that will mitigate all of that so that your turning away will be because of your love for Christ. It will not be difficult, as you might imagine it would be. You will have an unspeakable joy, and the Holy Spirit will begin changing your heart from the inside out.

All you have to do is believe that Jesus, God's Son, died on the cross for your sins. Confess your sins, ask for God's forgiveness, and ask Jesus to be your Lord and Savior. That's it, but that's so much!

> Because, if you confess with your mouth that Jesus is Lord and believe in your heart that God raised him from the dead, you will be saved. For with the heart one believes and is justified, and with the mouth one confesses and is saved.
>
> Romans 10:9,10 ESV

Once you have done this, your excitement will be uncontainable as the Holy Spirit draws you closer and closer to Himself.

> Therefore, if anyone is in Christ, he is
> a new creation.
> The old has passed away; behold, the
> new has come.
>
> 2 Corinthians 5:17 ESV

Since the Bible is Spirit-inspired and contains the very thoughts of God, open it and read it!

> For the word of God is living and active,
> sharper than
> any two-edged sword, piercing to the division of soul
> and of spirit, of joints and of marrow, and discerning
> the thoughts and intentions of the heart.
>
> Hebrews 4:12 ESV

As you grow as a Christian, you will be in awe of how true that single verse is. The Word of God *is* alive! Now find a group of people who are excited about Jesus and study His Word. Get involved and deepen your relationship with the Creator. Your excitement and joy will permeate your life, and those who knew you before you became a Christian will be amazed. And you find out that God loves you so much that when you do sin (because you will), Jesus is your advocate with the Father, and forgiveness is always yours—because of Him!

> So then faith comes from hearing, and hearing
> by the word of God.
>
> Romans 10:17 NKJV

I found out how important my relationship with God really was when my third baby, Matthew, was born and spent two months in the NICU (neonatal intensive care unit). His birth was planned for ten days before his due date, as I was having my third cesarean section. He weighed eight and a half pounds and looked great for the first hour but then began to have difficulty breathing and was moved to the NICU. As soon as we were told he had been moved, we wrote a Bible verse on a big sheet of paper:

> I will praise thee; for I am fearfully and wonderfully made:
> marvellous are thy works; and that my soul knoweth right well.
>
> Psalm 139:14 KJV

The nurses taped it to Matthew's incubator, and we prayed. Initially, the doctors thought Matthew had wet lung or transient tachypnea, a condition that typically resolves itself within a few days. But as Matthew's condition continued to worsen each day, his brilliant doctor, who was head of neonatology, conferred with the other NICU doctors to endeavor to discover the true problem. It was only through much prayer that it was finally revealed to them that Matthew had hypertension around his lungs, or what they then termed persistent fetal circulation. By then, he had been put on a ventilator.

Matthew's condition has caused me to marvel at the complexity and mystery of the human body. Before you are born, your blood rushes past your lungs, not stopping to receive oxygen because you are being sustained by your mother's oxygen. When a baby takes his first breath of air, major changes take place. Blood begins to flow to the lungs, where the blood is then oxygenated. Possibly because of a medication the doctors were giving me for atrial fibrillation, Matthew's circulatory pathways did not make this transition. Consequently, he was getting very little oxygen. And even though he was put on a ventilator with 100 percent oxygen and 100 percent pressure, his oxygen levels were still extremely low. The doctors tried everything they knew to do, all to no avail. They even administered a paralytic drug to prevent him from moving and using the precious little oxygen he was getting. They gave him powerful drugs to dilate his blood vessels, but this did not work either. Doctor Levy came to our hospital room and told us that Matthew's organs were salvageable at that point but that we might have to make some very difficult decisions. We knew what that meant.

Meanwhile, Joe and I were on our knees praying for him. One night Joe met with the elders of the church, and they prayed earnestly for Matthew. Afterwards, he returned to the hospital, and began praying over Matthew and quoting scripture. Each time he looked up, Matthew's oxygen monitor went up! It went from thirty-five to three hundred as Matthew's body opened up right before Joe's eyes! He hollered for the nurse to come take a blood gas, and she responded that she had just taken it—having stuck his heel a few minutes before. He insisted, "Take another one!" Sure enough, Matthew had just been healed in front of his eyes!

Matthew remained in the intensive care section of the NICU for almost two months as they weaned him slowly off of the ventilator. Even after our instant miracle from God, our renowned doctor told us (as well as the insurance company) that Matthew had brain damage. Dr. Levy said that he had suffered "an insult to his brain."

When Dr. Levy told us that Matthew was not acting like a normal baby his age, and that he might never sit up, feed himself, or walk, your daddy told him that we *knew* God would not have brought Matthew that far only to leave him. The fact that we knew Jesus and had faith that He would heal Matthew made all the difference in the world. Our automatic reaction to this crisis was to turn to God. I believe that God heard our fervent prayers (as well as those of so many people we didn't even know), and I believe that is the reason Matthew lived and was unscathed. I doubt Dr. Levy knew quite what to make of that faith, and when Matthew took his first steps at seven months old in front of this brilliant doctor, he literally dropped to the floor in amazement. I believe it changed everything *for him*—even how he treated his future patients. He held on to hope longer. Faith gives you a totally different perspective, and prayer really does change everything.

For years, Dr. Levy would tell us how he used his experience with Matthew to treat other babies. Matthew's doctor, who was head of neonatology, told another neonatologist whom we knew well, "If you believe in divine intervention, this is it!" He said that Matthew's healing was impossible to explain medically and that Matthew was the sickest baby he had ever treated with persistent fetal circulation who had lived, much less been normal. Dr. Levy, as well as the entire NICU staff, knew that they had witnessed the limitless power of the one and only Almighty God.

Let me assure you that when something like this happens, you want to be ready with an established relationship with Jesus Christ, *your only hope.* This type of desperation will drive you to your knees in a very literal sense. Don't wait until you *need* Him to *know* Him! And the truth is you will need Him every day. This story is important because it really underscores the need for a genuine relationship with God before you ever even consider having a baby.

Nico with Her New Purse

When your baby comes, you will *know that you know that you know* that God is real and that He alone could create such a miracle. You will know that He alone could put this deep love in your heart. You will have no doubt of either of these things. But after a few days or maybe a week, you are going to need to know more than that. You are going to need to know yourself and how to control yourself. You will be tired, and you will even wonder what in the world you have done. *This crying baby is so demanding!* That is when it's going to hit you that your time is no longer your own and that you will have to be totally unselfish *for the rest of your life*. And the thought occurs to you—no, it reverberates between your brain and your heart—*I cannot do this!* However, God says you can do this but only with His help, and that's the key.

> I can do all things through Christ who
> strengthens me.
>
> Philippians 4:13 NKJV

To add insult to injury, God really values self-control. And there is the rub. As a parent, you will always have to be the adult, and to do that, you will have to control your temper, put a smile on your face, and take another step forward when you'd love to just lie down and quit. If you make even a small habit of throwing in the towel and not persevering, your child, and ultimately the adult you raise, will reflect your failures. Sad but true. They will unwittingly mimic you and adopt your habits. So have the goal in mind when you start the journey to always stay in control of your *Self*, so that your children will not find you lacking those traits you hope to establish in them.

> Do you not know that in a race all the runners run,
> but only one receives the prize? So run that you may obtain it.
> Every athlete exercises self-control in all things. They do it
> to receive a perishable wreath, but we an imperishable.

So I do not run aimlessly; I do not box as one beating the air.
But I discipline my body and keep it under control,
lest after preaching to others I myself should be disqualified.

1 Corinthians 9:24–27 ESV

For God gave us a spirit not of fear but of power and love and self-control.

2 Timothy 1:7 ESV

Be angry and do not sin; ponder in your own hearts on your beds, and be silent.

Psalm 4:4 ESV

Set a guard over my mouth, Lord; keep watch over the door of my lips.

Psalm 141:3 NIV

Be alert and of sober mind. Your enemy the devil prowls around
like a roaring lion looking for someone to devour.

1 Peter 5:8 NIV

I can do all things through Christ who strengthens me.

Philippians 4:13 NKJV

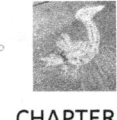

CHAPTER 2

Prayer

Now faith is the substance of things hoped for, the evidence of things not seen.

Hebrews 11:1 KJV

Just as God loved us before we were even born, so you will love your child before he or she is even conceived. And your love will grow as the Holy Spirit prompts you to pray for that baby not yet a reality.

Before they call I will answer; while they are yet speaking I will hear.

Isaiah 65:24 ESV

We know that God hears our prayers and that prayer changes everything. But how should you pray, and what should you say? The Bible says to "pray without ceasing" (1 Thessalonians 5:17 ESV), and that is exactly what I did. It says that "the effective, fervent prayer of a righteous man avails much" (James 5:16 NKJV). When I prayed for my children, especially when I knew I was pregnant, I always prayed for specifics, not generalities. I prayed fervently for God's blessings on my children, but I didn't stop with that. I prayed for their salvation, for them to be healthy and to have godly wisdom. I asked God to make them beautiful on the inside and on the outside. I asked God to make them talented beyond compare. I asked that they have long lives and many Christian friends and that they would love others and be loved by others. Of course, my list went on and on. I prayed that my children would be a blessing to us and that they would always, above all else, be in love with God and walk in His perfect will. I will be forever grateful for your father's great aunt, who was a missionary for 35 years and prayed *every day* for her nieces and nephews. This is extraordinary, and I know that we have all benefitted in extraordinary ways from her devotion and prayer. The thought of her on her knees praying for her family's descendants makes me think about how much our prayers can affect the future in ways we cannot imagine.

I think it is important to mention that when I prayed for something specific, it was specifically *not average*. In other words, if I prayed for my children to be smart, I prayed for them to be brilliant. If I prayed for them to be talented, I prayed for them to be talented musically, artistically, and academically. With great intentionality and drive, and most importantly, faith, I would pray for those things. Not casually or briefly, but as if petitioning. So pray on your knees, and pray in your car, and pray when you are walking by the way. Pray reverently and relentlessly for your children, expecting God to show up in answers and blessings. God puts these desires in your heart and loves to shower you and your children with good things.

> Delight yourself in the Lord,
> and He will give you the desires of your heart.
>
> Psalm 37:4 ESV

Now pray for yourself, because you are going to need it! Ask God to give you wisdom, insight, and grace to teach your children, care for them, and view with the highest regard what God might choose to do with their lives. Pray that you will have the energy, the drive, the commitment, and the determination to live godly before them, challenging them to do the same.

> Ask, and it will be given to you; seek, and ye shall find;
> knock, and it shall be opened unto you.
>
> Matthew 7:7–8 NIV

> O Lord, you have searched me and known me!
> You know when I sit down and when I rise up;
> you discern my thoughts from afar.
> You search out my path and my lying down
> and are acquainted with all my ways.
> Even before a word is on my tongue,
> behold, O Lord, you know it altogether.
> You hem me in, behind and before,
> and lay our hand upon me.
> Such knowledge is too wonderful for me;
> it is high; I cannot attain it.
> Where shall I go from your Spirit?
> Or where shall I flee from your presence?
> If I ascend to heaven, you are there!
> If I make my bed in Sheol, you are there!
> If I take the wings of the morning
> and dwell in the uttermost parts of the sea,
> even there your hand shall lead me,
> and your right hand shall hold me.
> If I say, "Surely the darkness shall cover me,
> and the light about me be night,"
> even the darkness is not dark to you;
> the night is bright as the day,
> for darkness is as light with you.

Psalm 139:1–12 ESV

I have read and reread this chapter on many a morning walk. I have tried to commit it to memory and to understand the depth of its meaning. My human brain struggles with this. I cannot seem to even begin to fathom it. Like David, such knowledge is too wonderful for me. *I cannot attain it*. God knows us so intimately and still loves us so completely. The thought of it boggles my mind and makes me feel lightheaded. This chapter of the Bible will singularly make you stop and be confounded by the majesty of our God, as well as the breadth of His understanding. We serve an awesome God who is able to do unfathomable things to further His kingdom and glorify His name.

> Thy word is a lamp unto my feet,
> and a light unto my path.
>
> Psalm 119:105 KJV

When Katherine and John were expecting our first grandchild, Joe and I went along with them to their first ultrasound. I knew we were going to be able to take a peek inside what, not so long ago, was a secret world that only God could see. Technology has changed our world so dramatically. As the sound waves bounced off of her tiny body, we became witnesses to God's handiwork. The mystery of Caroline actually took my breath away. Just sixteen weeks after conception, she looked to us to be complete. The Creator of the universe was attending to my grandchild in such an intricate, intimate way that it was almost unspeakable. I still cannot fathom any of it, not even the most rudimentary detail. I was privy to the reality of a miracle that I could not begin to grasp. Imagine the beauty and complexity of just the hands, and the perfection of the eyes, that within milliseconds focus and refocus to show us our world in amazing clarity and splendid color. Consider the skin, able to sense touch. Look deeper to find the personality that must be a part of each of us the moment we are conceived, and the reflexes and the emotions. Though all of this complexity was taking place, there she lay, as if in a hammock, sucking her thumb! Just sixteen weeks after conception!

> For my thoughts are not your thoughts, neither are your ways my ways, declares the Lord. For as the heavens are higher than the earth, so are my ways higher than your ways and my thoughts than your thoughts.
>
> Isaiah 55:8–9 ESV

I thought back on those verses in Psalm 139. God's love for us is deep. Can we express this same love to our children? We are made in God's image, but try as we may, our love is deficient when compared to God's love. How, then, can we not want to tell our children of the marvelous love that God has for them? The foundation, it is certain, of all you will do for your children, you must establish early on. Your relationship and subsequently your children's relationships to Christ are the bedrock; they are the cornerstone.

How Deep the Father's Love for Us
Stuart Townend

How deep the Father's love for us
How vast beyond all measure
That He should give His only Son
To make a wretch His treasure

How great the pain of searing loss
The Father turns His face away
As wounds which mar the Chosen One
Bring many sons to glory

Behold the man upon a cross
My sin upon His shoulders
Ashamed, I hear my mocking voice
Call out among the scoffers

It was my sin that held Him there
Until it was accomplished
His dying breath has brought me life
I know that it is finished

I will not boast in anything
No gifts, no power, no wisdom
But I will boast in Jesus Christ
His death and resurrection

Why should I gain from His reward?
I cannot give an answer
But this I know with all my heart
His wounds have paid my ransom

Georgia Greeting Gigi in the Driveway

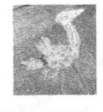

CHAPTER 3

Study Your Child

Every child is born with his or her own personality, but the Bible says, "Train up a child in the way he should go: and when he is old he will not depart from it" (Proverbs 22:6 KJV). There are obviously common tenets that apply to all personalities, but I can tell you now that you can do your dead level best to raise all of your children with the same set of values and in basically the same way, and still, they will all turn out differently.

Some children are compliant and sweet, while others pitch a fit at every turn. It is critical to know, then, at the outset that even if you do everything as right as you possibly can, and you do it with boundless determination, you cannot be responsible *for* your children but only *to* your children. After you do your best, let God be responsible for them! I believe this with all my heart, but I also believe that your best efforts will pay off.

So even when the most difficult child requires all you have, you will give it. It's then you will need to remind yourself that there will be an end to the struggles of parenthood, of childhood and youth. That time will come when you watch them begin life on their own. That "one day" comes so quickly, so be diligent while you can. Be creative and find ways to successfully get your child from point A to point Z—to the adult you know they need to be. For all too soon, you will find yourself staring at the taillights of your youngest child's car as he's leaving your driveway for a distant college dorm, realizing with a mix of grief and relief that the intense phase of parenting does end. Through your tears, you'll be praying that you did a lot of things right, because that will be your assurance that the child you love will make the right decisions and take the right paths. But you'll stand there and wonder if that arrow will fly straight. And you'll wonder if you can bear walking past that empty bedroom and the ripping away from your heart of someone you love so much. The love is something that will take you by surprise. You will ask yourself how God could love you more than you love your child. And how He gave His child for you. It is amazing.

I want you to know that when you walk back through the doorway of that empty-feeling house, you'll wish you could have kept them forever. Toddlers. Innocent. Devoted to you. You will grieve and miss them with something so deep inside you it is almost inexplicable. But the Holy Spirit will keep reminding you that their independence is what you have been preparing them for. God has been preparing your heart, as well, for this moment.

In less than a week, it will suddenly dawn on you how wonderful it is to be free! It occurs to you that you and your spouse can take off for a distant island without consulting anyone or arranging for anybody's care. That's exactly what we did soon after Matthew left for college. There will be no more waiting up for them on weekends or worrying about them until they get home at night, because you will have no way of knowing when they get home. You will no longer be exasperated by unkept bedrooms and messy bathrooms. Laundry will no longer be piled sky-high. There will be no more long grocery lists that include fifty snacks required to keep a teenager going. There will be hot water when you are ready to take a shower. You will embrace this change in your life, because even though raising a child really is the most profound thing and the loveliest thing you will ever have the good pleasure to do, it is hard. It takes time and patience and a lot of love. And boundless energy.

But before you reach that taillight moment, you have the responsibility to create their book—the one they will surely ask you to write one day.

There are no excuses when it comes to parenting. Don't be caught flat-footed. Just as you would do research for an upcoming trip to a foreign land, learn all you can about your new role as Mommy or Daddy. Prepare for the road ahead by reading good Christian books on parenting that always put God first. But rest assured, God enabled even the not so smart to be very effective parents. I have discovered, in fact, that you don't have to be a genius to raise nearly genius, grounded, well-rounded, and talented children. This I know because

I did it! I majored in journalism at the University of Georgia. That was my bent, and I do staunchly believe that there are many kinds of smart. Each of my children tackled subjects that would be considered by most to be much more difficult than journalism. Your majors were risk management, cellular biology, and finance. As young children, I encouraged you to do something when you grew up that would enable you to hang up a shingle and not be at the mercy of an employer. I told you boys to be sure you could make enough money so that your wives could stay home to raise your children. Jonathan and Matthew, you both became doctors—one an interventional radiologist and one an ophthalmologist (specializing in retina surgery). Katherine, I did not encourage you to do this because Daddy and I didn't think you would be happy with the decision. After all, I wanted you to be able to be at home with your children. Going to medical school would have left you in quite a bit of debt that you would have had to work to repay, and I reasoned that it would have put too much strain on motherhood. You were smart enough to do anything at all, and I do hope I steered you right. But in case you are ever tempted to compare your accomplishments to those of your two brothers, just read this unsolicited letter from the owner of the insurance company you worked for in Atlanta when you graduated from college:

Mr. and Mrs. West,

I have been meaning to take a moment and write to you regarding your daughter, Katherine. For some years now I have had the pleasure ... no ... the honor of knowing her. There are few people in the world who you can "take to the bank" ... people that have as strong of values and character that your daughter has. You are to be commended for raising a daughter of such high caliber.
As a father of three, I know raising children is a hard and sometimes arduous task, and we are not usually publicly rewarded as much as we should be. But in the end what we desire are God-centered, mature and disciplined children who share and reflect our values and beliefs. You have achieved no less than a great lady in Katherine.

Katherine has taught me leadership, humility (of which I still fall short of her), character and strength in the years we have worked together. I watch her "servant leadership" and selfless character as she gives SO much to everyone she knows. I cannot begin to tell you what she means not only to me, but especially to our company and all who know her.

I must tell you, she is a great reflection' of your family name and what you stand for. She loves and respects you both more than you will ever know. Be proud. Know that you have raised a fine lady. As I am sure you will one day hear, "Well done, good and faithful servants"!

May God richly bless you and yours in this year!

Warmest regards,
Dale Alexander

No parent could be prouder than Daddy and I both are of each of our children. We are actually astonished. And it has proven my theory that you don't have to be a genius to be a great parent with extra smart children. Sheer determination and abundant love will set your children apart. Side note: your daddy is actually brilliant, so that helped!

Each of our children were very different, and that is why we had to study you closely in order to know what gifts, bents, and personalities God had given you. Only then could we discover what approach to take when disciplining each child. The same tact did not work with Katherine that worked with Matthew or Jonathan.

Katherine was sweet to a fault. For years, I have had to beg her to stand up for herself so she wouldn't get run over by friends. Her nature is to give, give in, and think the best, which of course sounds great. But we found out that when you are too sweet, you are taken advantage of. And that is not good. We found out too that sometimes people are put off by people who come across as too nice, partly because they think it's an act, and partly because they are convicted of their own sin, and partly because they just don't know how to react to it. So we encouraged Katherine to buck up and be a little more formidable. Katherine is still sweeter than anybody I know, and I am always taken aback when I witness the reality of that kindness, and I try to be more like my child.

Jonathan was such an easy child and was very passive. He had a wonderful temperament. He was fun and happy and totally laid back. I don't remember Jonathan ever getting mad about anything. He had an amazingly peaceful and calm spirit. He was usually not difficult in any way, except when he *really* didn't want to do something. As a toddler, he wouldn't be ugly or disrespectful. He would just collapse into a heap on the floor. Literally. I would then have to gather up that dead weight and drag it to the car or to whatever activity he did not want to participate in. But he was innately kind, respectful (if you can say falling on the floor and not cooperating was respectful), and almost always compliant.

I believe God was building up to our third child, Matthew! We immediately knew that Matthew was special, coming into the world with a bang. Within an hour of birth, he turned our world upside down as he was ushered into the neonatal intensive care unit, where he stayed for two months. This was a life-altering experience for our whole family, in amazingly good ways.

I surely should have known right then that Matthew was going to be a handful! It quickly became evident that he had a very strong will, which the doctors acknowledged was one of the main reasons he lived. However, once he began to thrive, that strong will took center stage. He was never still, and he loved to climb on anything and everything. This alone is enough to test a parent's resolve as well as his or her sanity. When he was around four years old, we were at a Little League baseball game, and I turned my head for just a second (for I was seriously a hawk watching my children). I suddenly heard parents exclaiming that a child was at the top of the backstop. They were all frantically screaming, "Whose child is that?" I didn't even have to turn around. I knew it was my child—my Matthew!

Matthew was an adorable toddler and so entertaining that he gave our family an extra helping of sheer fun. But his boundless energy was more difficult to manage, and I found that his strong will and high energy combined to form a challenge that the other two children had not presented. Throughout his childhood, Matthew threw down the gauntlet more than the others, and I had to use a totally different approach with Matthew, hoping to carefully steer him away from becoming an all-out rebel. I tried not to be confrontational with Matthew and continually tried to find the easy pathways where he was compliant. It was clear from the beginning that he was the standout child, and our methods of discipline had to be creative. He didn't mind spankings. In fact, nothing hurt Matthew, and very little persuaded him to change what he was doing. Time-outs did not hold the promise of changing a behavior. One time, when Joe was spanking him, Matthew looked at him and said, "Are you through?" Joe responded, "Well, I thought I was, but I guess I'm not!" So he required diligence, fervent prayer, and late-night discussions on how to handle our strong-willed child.

We knew that his tenacity would serve him well as an adult if channeled properly, but we just had to get him to adulthood *with him still on our side.* We wanted to be sure we didn't break his wonderful spirit, while at the same time we were trying to preserve our own. Matthew was an amazing child, with more personality than you could shake a stick at. He was the one who was boldest about his faith and confronted his three-year-old friends about their salvation, asking one befuddled toddler if he was a Christian. The child just said, "I think so." He had no idea what Matthew was talking about. But Matthew did.

Although Matthew generally did want to do what was right (he even won an award for always doing the right thing), he was extremely smart and busy, and that threw him into another category that required extreme attention. We prayed and prayed and prayed some more. We had to use finely crafted and extensively thought-through psychology in a big way to outsmart Matthew—reverse psychology, behavior modification, etcetera, etcetera, etcetera. We knew we had one precious, strong-willed child that we had to keep on the right path, and we believe that it was through God's help that we were able to do that. I became an expert in the use of psychology.

Amazingly, and by God's grace, Matthew was never a behavior problem throughout his entire childhood and youth. He was fun, funny, and delightful and had a contagious personality that just lit up our lives. But I focus on him because his temperament kept us looking for different ways to keep him focused on the right things. He is the example of why you can't just treat your children all the same, or give up when the going is tough. A situation like that can go south quickly, with resentment and disrespect bubbling up like a bad storm—that is, if you let it. But joy is the other side of that coin, if you go to the trouble to turn that coin over.

So this is my point. You have to find the right answers when it comes to raising each of your children right, and you cannot waver or give in to the temptation to just let it slide or give up on getting the desired results. *Even when it is an extreme challenge requiring everything you've got.* Yes, there are definitely times when discipline requires a little bristling on your part, but remember, if you want to preserve relationships, you sometimes have to choose to smile when you feel like gnashing your teeth. You must choose to keep your mouth closed when you are exasperated beyond measure and find something to praise a child for when all you can see is red. If you do this, the momentary flares of your temper will temper and eventually turn to joy as you see that child become all you hoped he would be. And on top of that, your child will learn to be patient and kind to you too.

I studied my children from the day they were born. I saw on that first day what *might* be. That is, I saw what might be if I put my all into raising you, and what might be if I didn't. The wonderment of it! A person; a living soul. All God's but all yours. God has given you the opportunity to be His hands, His heart, and His love to shape another human's life. But believe me, it is much harder than you think to put your all into anything, especially raising children. When you are tired, and when you have given your all *all* day, it is tempting to give up, give in, and walk away. After all, this is not a class where grades will be awarded, or you will receive the immediate gratification of a pat on the back for your great performance. If you are not committed, you will forget the opportunity God has afforded you, and you will say yes when you should say no, because it's easier to take the path of least resistance. You will look away and pretend not to notice when something they are doing is wrong, detrimental, or dangerous with far-reaching consequences. So you have to be determined to stay in the game, win the battles, and lead them triumphantly. You've got to be smart and keep your edge, because if you don't, they will outsmart you. Giving it your all will mean the difference between a long life of blessing and a lifelong curse.

You and your spouse have an opportunity, before your baby looks at you for the first time, to talk about how you want to raise your child. (You may not have time afterward!) Take that time to discuss in detail how you will discipline your child. Come to an agreement on how major issues will be handled. Most importantly, agree to always present a united front. If you don't, you will have already lost the battle, whatever it may be. Every time. Hands down. Disagreeing on the method or degree of punishment in front of a child is not wise. Don't call your spouse down when in this situation. Do not! Children will sense the division (even as babies), and they will not respect you or your decision. Back up your spouse unless his or her behavior is outside of God's biblical instructions for raising a child—or what he or she is doing is seriously harmful in some way. Don't criticize your spouse in front of your child. That just serves to undermine the whole discipline process and leaves the door open for the child to find fault in, distrust, and disrespect the parent. *That is the last thing you want.*

One thing you need to do is take a look at how God sees your family. When we first got married and started our family, I was a little taken aback by my soulmate's priorities. He declared in no uncertain terms that in his life, God came first, then me, then the children. He told you the same thing as you got older, and this put into clear perspective who was going to rank where with him. When considering the fact that God designed the family, this all makes sense. The man's first obligation is to nurture his relationship with God, to listen to Him, and to try to do His will. Then, his next priority is to nurture his relationship with his wife. Together, they are to train the children and keep the family together. The husband's concern is to help his wife and children grow spiritually in the Lord, which he cannot do if he himself is not in close relationship with God. So as he tries to submit to God in these areas for our benefit, the Bible says this:

> Wives, submit to your own husbands, as to the Lord.
>
> For the husband is the head of the wife even as Christ is the head of the church, his body, and is himself its Savior. Now as the church submits to Christ, so also wives should submit in everything to their husbands.

Husbands, love your wives, as Christ loved the church and gave himself up for her, that he might sanctify her, having cleansed her by the washing of water with the word, so that he might present the church to himself in splendor, without spot or wrinkle or any such thing, that she might be holy and without blemish. In the same way husbands should love their wives as their own bodies. He who loves his wife loves himself. For no one ever hated his own flesh, but nourishes and cherishes it, just as Christ does the church, because we are members of his body. Therefore a man shall leave his father and mother and hold fast to his wife, and the two shall become one flesh. This mystery is profound, and I am saying that it refers to Christ and the church. However, let each one of you love his wife as himself, and let the wife see that she respects her husband.

Ephesians 5:22–33 ESV

A woman needs love, fundamentally, and a man needs respect. So if things are going to function as God designed, you will pay close attention to those needs and those ideals of marriage. And as much as we'd all like to be in charge, someone has to be the Indian, and someone has to be the chief. This is true in businesses and in organizations and in families. You will ultimately find that this is the only arrangement that really works. The Bible may seem offensive to you (if you are a woman), because God talks about us being the weaker vessel. We are all sensitive to any such reference and rebel against it, as our culture has made that a negative. But clearly, God's intent is to differentiate between the man and woman's roles. They are simply different, and frankly, I don't understand why any woman would not want to be protected and loved by a man. Anyway, the husband and wife are to complement each other.

Though it seems the man has been bestowed a great honor by being made the stronger vessel, in reality, he has actually been handed a heavy responsibility. It is not easy to be the one who makes that final decision for the family when, at times, much is at stake. If he makes a mistake, the weight is on him. He alone will have to bear the burden of having made a poor decision. And besides, he has to answer to someone too. His authority is God.

The man may have the final word, but he should never ignore his wife's opinions. In important matters, your father almost always considered carefully my input, acknowledging the fact that God might be speaking to him through me. After he heard me out, he had to weigh the pros and cons and prayerfully make that final call. I was glad it was him and not me. There was protection there. I usually felt a big *Whew!* that I was not the one in charge (and I am hardheaded and strong-willed). I think the reason the man is called to be the leader is that God equipped him to make decisions based more on pure logic than on feelings. I'm not saying that I couldn't be logical, but I always seemed to have more feelings, whether empathy, compassion, or sympathy, that I had to deal with. Even though I know that my sensitivity and feelings are just perfect for nurturing a child or a relationship, they sometimes cloud my ability to see the pure logistics of any given matter. And sometimes that is just what's required to make a sound decision. On the other hand, my feelings were sometimes very good gauges of what we should do, so Daddy's responsibility to consider my advice was not taken lightly.

Since the father is usually the leader, he is the one who has the job of setting the tone of the home. This makes a huge difference in the sublimity, the functionality, and the happiness quotient of the family. As I write this, I am still not sure why the father sets the tone, but I believe this is generally true.

> Fathers, do not provoke your children to anger, but bring them up
> in the discipline and instruction of the Lord.
>
> Ephesians 6:4 ESV

Of course, the mother's disposition is of critical importance, and she should do her best to be her best when her husband comes home, presenting a peaceful home and a happy sanctuary for him (hard to do when children are running about, tearing the house apart!). But for some reason, when the father walks through the door at the end of the day, his mood solidifies the mood of the family, which then affects dinner and play and sleep—for better or for worse. Right then, a busy, stressful day becomes tranquil and restored with love, or goes off the rails in piles of disaster. Thankfully, your daddy almost always came home from work happy. He never brought the troubles and weight of work home with him. This was a great accomplishment! It was another form of protection for his family and a burden that he was saddled with. I didn't have to suffer through the trials and tribulations that he dealt with while out in the world. (I think statistics bear this out. A woman's life expectancy has fallen in recent years. Perhaps it's because women have begun to take on the role of breadwinner with all that the title entails. If you are working and mothering, I know God will give you what you need. But by all accounts, you will be hit with more stress from the outside world.)

I'm not saying that your father never talked to me about problems, but when he arrived home in the evening, he set the tone for the family's time together, and I have to say it was overwhelmingly good. Depending on your nature, this might be something that takes considerable effort to pull off. However, love is an act of the will. And this is probably the number one tenet your father and I tried to live by: *You always have to put your best foot forward, even when you feel you can hardly move that foot. There are no days off with this job.* (Please don't misunderstand me. You will fail, just as we did at times—bad attitudes, tempers that flare.) However, imagine if your daddy regularly came home in a huff; the rest of the evening would be tense and unfulfilling. What could be dinner with distinction because you are shooting for the stars might turn into dinner with disdain and even damage. So setting the tone for the family is an important priority. It speaks of self-control, grace, love, and especially the joy of the Lord. It also screams commitment—that is, commitment to do the right thing with love. But make it genuine.

Couple this with another critical tenet: the most important thing you and your spouse can do for your children is to *love each other.* This one thing gives them security, and that gives them a foundation for everything in their world. Confidence, contentment, peace, and happiness. So one wonderful thing Daddy did that announced to the children that he loved me was he made me feel beautiful. I know you remember this: your daddy always called me "Beautiful." That is just what he called me, and he still does, even now. He always tells me how beautiful I am (and believe it or not, I've fallen for it). Upon leaving a party, he always tells me that I was the prettiest one there. Just yesterday, we were getting ready for the day, and I looked down to find him on one knee, telling me how beautiful I am. Talk about a confidence builder! Talk about falling in love again! Talk about respect for a great guy! Those small but frequently spoken reassurances and affirmations have helped to build my confidence, convey his love, and solidify our relationship. It makes me feel cherished and adored. Sons, you would be very wise not to underestimate a woman's need for affirmation, both spoken and demonstrated. And children love to hear their parents talking to each other in love.

Even now, the love of my parents for each other is a constant witness to me. They are ninety and ninety-three years old. My father's face lights up so visibly when he sees my mother; it is amazing. He will say, "There's that pretty lady!" He is taken with her beauty, even at ninety-three, and it's quite obvious that the sight of her almost takes his breath away. The women who care for them are moved tremendously by this love that has only grown stronger and stronger over the sixty-nine years since they said their wedding vows. They say, "I want to find a love like Franke and George!" I am so thankful for all that love has meant in my life. The strength of it is there because over a lifetime they committed themselves to it. Love is truly an act of the will. But as you live that love out, it really does form an unbreakable bond, held together by shared hardship and happiness, stress and joy, heartbreak and triumph. But the key is you have to stick with it.

Now, girls, don't underestimate a man's need to be respected. It means the world to him, and giving him that respect brings nothing short of harmony, peace, and contentment to the family. It's God's design. Children feel it if it's there, and they know it if it's not. Men, in my mind, are not such complicated creatures compared to women with all of their different feelings. The one thing that sets it all straight for a man is respect.

I'd like to add that it's interesting that a man tends to command respect by virtue of his size, masculinity, and strength. It is a God-given thing that we all recognize. The respect that children naturally have for their father must be the reason that they so often are influenced and impacted by his personality, mannerisms, and character. I've always been in awe of this fact, since fathers are usually with their children less than mothers. The father's words and actions are taken to heart by the child and are mimicked, it seems to me, much more than the mother's. So watch out, fathers! Your leadership is important because someone is almost always following you.

In this lead-and-follow relationship of husband and wife, the one who follows is just as important as the one who leads and sometimes has the harder job. Following is an art, just as leading is, and requires grace and submission and love. These traits can only be had if both leader and follower first allow Christ to take over, and *He* will love and respect *through you.*

There is one other piece of advice I'd like to pass along to you. Your daddy insisted that we never put ourselves in a compromising position. In other words, we didn't go anywhere alone with someone of the opposite sex or otherwise place ourselves in situations that could lead to compromise. Of course, we would not eat alone with someone of the opposite sex, even in a public place, since even this could lead to something more intimate. It was a strict philosophy that we both agreed to abide by in order to protect our marriage. Evangelist Billy Graham and his staff made a decision in 1948 that while traveling around the country preaching the Gospel, they would never be alone with a woman who was not their wife. Billy Graham reportedly would not ride in the car alone with his secretary or, for that matter, any woman other than his wife. It's now known as the Billy Graham Rule and is timeless in its wisdom. Take careful steps when you venture out away from your spouse and stick by this rule. Even your children will one day thank you for your faithfulness.

CHAPTER 4

How Your Children Will View You

Your true character has to be beyond reproach, and that, your daddy taught me, begins with honesty. There is no room for hypocrisy. However, honesty is like a foreign language to most people today. You may not even bat an eye when someone tells an untruth to you, even when you *know* it's an untruth, because the truly honest person is such a novelty these days. It is so rare to run into an honest person that I think I've only known a few in my lifetime. I think that's why I've always been so amazed and disarmed by your daddy's honesty. And convicted. I've never had to wonder what he was thinking, and I've never had to be afraid that he was doing something behind my back. I could always trust him to tell me the truth. I have known few other people who really tell the total truth all the time. Little white lies are so common.

In the South, I was taught by society to avoid saying things that were in any way hurtful. Refinement dictates tactfulness in all situations. If someone got their hair cut and it looked hideous, you would say you loved it, or at least think of something nice to say. You certainly wouldn't say what you thought, because that would be mean. I love the softness of southerners and how they try to avoid harsh and abrasive language. In fact, southerners often can identify northerners right off the bat by their directness and lack of sugarcoating. We would rather make everything okay, and make everyone feel good. A northerner's candor is perceived as offensive, harsh, and unfeeling. When we hear it, we southerners are thinking, *That was not sweet! Where's the sugar?*

So I think love and sensitivity are the intent of this understood but unspoken rule of always being sweet and courteous in our speech. Though I am not condoning saying things that are not true, I do think you should be loving in your speech and not just brutal in your honesty. I would not negate the importance of the southerner's *shugah coating* bad news either, but again, I'm not suggesting dishonesty. If it is evident to your children that you sometimes fib or twist the truth for your convenience or to save your own hide, you will have damaged your character, and that damage may be irreparable. However, there is a way to say most anything that will be truthful, but will cushion the truth or the blow.

My own father and his siblings have a rare respect for their father, and when I asked my father to explain why, the primary reason given was that he was always honest, and you always knew where you stood with him. Your father is the same way. He's a straight shooter, and if he tells you something, you can take it to the bank. You know he's going to be honest with you. And that just seems to be the one virtue that begets all the others. And it is a rarely found virtue.

Character. I talked to my children often about the significance of having a good name and what that meant. I tried to spotlight the importance of integrity a great deal, because I knew that without it, they would be lost. Children are constantly asking for limits, including limits on behavior. They want to know how far they can go and where the boundaries are. They are learning what is safe and acceptable, but also what it means to have character. There are boundaries for adults too, and if you are a Christian, those boundaries are defined and governed by love. Your character is defined by those boundaries, and this ultimately involves love. So, for instance, because of love (because you love God and other people, desiring the best for them), you are driven to keep moral boundaries. You are determined to be moral, trustworthy, loyal, honorable, and self-sacrificing. Because this is what God loves. He wants you to love others. This is important for your children to learn.

A good name is to be chosen rather than great riches, and favor is better than silver or gold.

Proverbs 22:1 ESV

Keep your focus on this subject, and the dividends will be great. Your children will be solid and will not be tossed about in the wind. They will value God's name, their own good name, and that will dictate many decisions they make in their lifetimes.

So that we may no longer be children, tossed to and fro by the waves and carried about by every wind of doctrine, by human cunning, by craftiness in deceitful schemes.

Ephesians 4:14 ESV

Have I not commanded you? Be strong and courageous. Do not be afraid; do not be discouraged, for the Lord your God will be with you wherever you go.

Joshua 1:9 NIV

A perfect child in the eyes of the world is not your aim. Rest assured you will not have that. Mine were not perfect. Jonathan and Matthew were typical boys who, when they got older, occasionally had to be sent outside to just have it out. And I've recently heard stories about a Jeep that Katherine drove into a ditch with friends one night. No one is perfect. Amazingly, however, God sees the Christian as wholly righteous—perfect *through faith alone* in what His Son accomplished on the cross. When He looks at us, he sees not what we used to be, but He sees Jesus. So your aim is for them to know the One who *is* perfect, and to know that through their faith in Him, they are perfect in the eyes of God.

Humility will be theirs because they will know that they did not earn righteousness through anything they did but through faith alone and thereby grace alone. This will be important for so many reasons as they walk through their lives. They will know that the righteousness given them by the grace of a loving God is everlasting and will never be taken from them. It is a gift. They did not earn it and cannot un-earn it.

When they fail in life, it will be so important for them to know that they are instantly forgiven. And they need to know that if they put the burden of paying for that sin on themselves, they cannot pay the debt, and they would be effectively saying that Jesus's sacrifice was not enough, thereby negating what He did on the cross.

Children need to know that they have been bought at a great price, and through that, they are forgiven for sins they have committed, are committing, and will commit in the future.

There is such freedom in knowing there can be no condemnation. This is important because if your children ever find themselves guilty of something, and the devil is using it to lead them to depression or destruction, you want them to know that God has already forgiven them and that not accepting that work that He did through Jesus would be like saying the pain He suffered was worthless. Trying to redo what Jesus already did is insulting.

Love comes from this knowledge and permeates life, so that love rules the day. Your children will be more apt to want to do what's right and what's pleasing to the God who loves them so unconditionally.

Selah Swinging in the Park

CHAPTER 5

Your Voice, Your Countenance, Your Home, Your Goal

Scientists have documented that a baby recognizes and prefers its mother's voice while in the womb. According to a study done at the Pacific Lutheran University in Tacoma, Washington, your baby will be actively listening to your voice during the last ten weeks of pregnancy. He will respond to your singing and talking. So even before you meet, your baby is getting to know you. Surely, the very first moment your babies open their eyes, they are searching for information about this world. Don't keep them wondering. Immediately answer those searching eyes. "Hey, precious! I am your mama, and this is your daddy. We love you so much and are so glad God gave you to us to love!" Assurance that you are there, that you love them, and that you are going to be there to care for, comfort, and teach them is part of the information they will be seeking. This is the beginning of a lifelong relationship and joy inexpressible for both you and your baby!

Beginning with the very first days of your baby's life, you should walk them around the house, pointing out objects and repeating their names three or four times. I remember the first time I saw someone doing this (my older sister), it occurred to me that this seemingly silly act was key—no, critical, really. I had not even considered doing something as simple as this. And yet this was profound. It was opening up the baby's world, providing a springboard for learning the next, more complicated thing. You are stimulating their brain early and getting a huge head start on increasing their awareness and intellect. Even at this early age, you are broadening your baby's horizons by associating names with objects. Call your baby by name and tell them who you are. Touch their toes, nose, ears, eyes, mouth, and hands and name each one. Count their toes, sing to them, and recite nursery rhymes. Use each ordinary experience to teach new things and encourage them to think, introducing math, other languages, and anything else that would expand their thinking. Over the next few months, when you walk through the grocery store, make sure your baby knows what they are seeing. Above all else, bring God, the Creator, into the conversation to help your child develop a relationship with Him. It is never too early to point babies toward a love for the One who created them.

While you are strolling, talk about the creation and who created it. Express *your wonder* over what you are seeing. Your excitement will be contagious. Not only will your baby be getting a head start toward learning language as well as other valuable information about their environment (the red apple, the bright light, four bananas), your precious little one will be learning to love the awesome God who gave him or her breath. Be intentional about doing this. Don't spend your child's childhood racing through the neighborhood behind a jogging stroller. Take time to stroll with your child and to talk about things that matter.

Clara (5), Georgia (3), and Caroline (7)

Charles Swindoll wrote a book called *Home, Where Life Makes Up Its Mind*. I've always loved this title, because it holds so much truth in it and because of the wonder it evoked in me knowing that my child will decide who he or she will be under our roof and under our direction. Think of it. Your children's character will be formed primarily in your home, with you, before they ever really take a step out into the world. There, in your home. With you. This is key. They will develop an understanding of God's view of them and their world at home with you, and this will be reflected in countless decisions they will make in their lives.

Because of this very important premise, I wanted to present to my children, first, the best that there was in this world. I wanted to be sure that when they encountered something less than God's best, they would recognize it and not like it. By comparison, it would pale, and they would have a good comparison. I always tried to paint the rosiest picture possible of myself and of the world. I acquainted them with the best that I had, first. My best smile, my happiest disposition, my most positive responses. I think this sounds like what any normal parent would do. Ho hum. But it wasn't at all. It was different. Through the years, I have witnessed the difference, and even though it doesn't sound like it, this way *was* radical. Listen to yourself and your responses. Are they always, or *almost* without exception, positive and happy?

I wanted my children to experience the joy that only comes from knowing the love of Christ and the abundant life He offers. I wanted them to have that as a backdrop with which to judge everything else—that is, the world and all of its alluring temptations. I knew that if they had seen what was right, they would be better able to discern when something was wrong. An understatement would be to say I spent my children's childhoods smiling, laughing, and communicating happiness, love, and uplifting thoughts. This was deliberate and consistent. This seems like a given and seems so simple as not to be worth mentioning. But hear what I'm saying. It was foundational and profoundly important in the outcome.

I worked at this, though it never seemed like work, because I was (almost all of the time) happy. But even when I was not happy, I tried with great determination never to waver from this. I put aside a bad mood or a bad attitude. I kept a happy face with a disposition to match. When I addressed my children, I made it inviting and exciting and fun whenever I could. I know that some people are just happier about mothering, and I was one of those people.

So this could be quite difficult and unnatural for some people. I have to be honest and tell you that most of the time I really did feel joyful with my children. Still, if that's not the case with you, try to do it anyway. So often when you smile, that smile elicits a good mood from anyone who sees it. The dividends you receive from your commitment to this single act will be incredible.

Of course, I had failures, and at times had to discipline you or be stern or talk about something unpleasant. But I focused on the good, and I established a pattern. I kept a happy countenance and insisted that you did so as well. If things were going downhill, and one of you had a bad attitude with a frowning face, I would tell you in a *lighthearted way* to put a smile on your face (not as a harsh command). Approaching children with a cheerful countenance and with an expectation of that happiness returning will usually produce the desired results. It works most of the time. Love begets love. I think this was key in my own upbringing. For the most part, my parents were happy and jovial, and consequently, I loved them and loved being around them. I saw an example today of what not to do. I was at a car wash, and a mother and her child were there. The child asked his mother, in a nice voice, if he could have something, and she reacted by saying, simply, "I'm leaving you here." I hear this type of thing often, and I just cringe. That mother is setting the stage for a disrespectful teenager, and she can expect to hear the same type of response and tone of voice from her child when he becomes a teenager.

So, aside from when a disciplinary action is required, make sure that when you address your child, your countenance is happy. This seems so simple, but it is so important. You end up having a more positive and optimistic view of the world, the day, and the children. It makes sense, then, to make sure your child puts on a happy face. A smile just changes attitudes and outlooks. If the lighthearted reminder didn't work when one of my young children seemed out of sorts, I would smile and say, "Someone got up on the wrong side of the bed! Let's go get back in the bed and get out on the other side. Then you'll feel better." And they would do just that. Literally. It really worked!

Think about what you are doing, use self-discipline yourself, and make sure you display the characteristics you are demanding of them. Look for them to behave with as much decorum as you would expect of yourself. It will take time to achieve this decorum in your children, but surprisingly, when they are trained from the beginning to behave courteously, for instance, they will generally do just that. If you consistently have a pleasant countenance and happy smile, they will too. The key to what I am saying here is that you should expect good behavior. Don't focus on the negative and don't look for bad behavior. Praise them for good behavior and don't dwell on anything less. Make sure that you, yourself, don't deliver a sourpuss attitude to them or allow your words to reflect an unattractive or cranky mood. Otherwise, they will quickly adopt the same, and it will be almost impossible to put back in what has already gotten out of the box.

I knew a couple who encouraged their child to express his anger. They told him it was okay for him to be mad at Mama and Daddy and that he should tell them with his words when he was angry and why. Well, that just fed the fit! It encouraged the bad behavior. Instead, when I had a child who was pitching a fit, I would tell him, without any fanfare, to go to his room. I explained that if he wanted to pitch a fit in his room, he was welcome to do it, but it would not happen in front of everyone else. Then I would whisk him off quickly and without discussion, and he would have a fit without an audience. Not much fun! That quickly took care of the desire to have a fit, since it got him nowhere and no attention. Your grandmother, my mother, Mankme, taught me this technique; I think she had to use it on her redhead (me) a few times!

Being available, and even more to the point, being present, means even more this day and time, when the temptation is to spend every waking moment *looking at your phone*. Emails, texts, games, photos, and just generally searching for more and more information have invaded and almost taken over our lives. And as I said before, your children are going to mimic your behavior. So watch out. If you cannot put your phone down to give them undivided attention, it's going to be awful hard to tell them to talk to you, or even look at you, when it means denying the appeal of their phone. *Your undivided attention is one of the most important things you will ever give your child.* If you are intentional in this one area, you will be amazed at the affect it has on your child.

Never discipline a child when you are mad, or incensed, or ready to scream. And believe me, you will be all of the above. Count to ten, walk outside, and wait a while to discipline.

Give yourself time to cool off before you act, so that the discipline is controlled and not an attack. If you need to spank, always do it with control. I think that the psychiatrists who tell us not to spank have gotten beatings mixed up with spankings, the former being out-of-control anger and the latter being loving chastisement. There is a major difference. When you spank your child, always do it with complete control. Explain why you are doing it, and love the child afterward. Keep in mind that all of the advice that I am giving you is tempered with the fact that I loved my children, and I demonstrated that fact with a warmth that went along with any discipline. "Sweetie, I love you too much to allow you to behave this way. It would not be good for you." After a spanking or time-out, I always gave them a hug and a kiss and told them how much I loved them. I made sure they knew that the discipline was coming from someone who loved them and wanted the best for them and from them. I also made sure, once again, that they understood why they had been disciplined. Afterward, I always, and immediately, brought them back into the fold.

Of course, if the child is in danger because of disobedience (such as about to run in front of a car), grab them up *immediately* and administer punishment. That quick intervention and shocking (though still controlled) response will get their attention, teach them a valuable lesson, and may save them from a tragic accident. I have been dismayed to learn that many young parents feel unable to discipline their children in public for fear of retribution. They are justly afraid that someone will see them and call authorities and that their children will be taken from them. This is the equivalent of tying their hands behind their backs and rendering them totally ineffective parents. Instead, they have to watch without recourse or authority as their children behave like wild animals and dance taunting circles around them. They have to pass up teachable moments, and the child quickly learns that, particularly when they are in the company of others, they can get away with murder. It is a bad fix we have put these young parents in. And they are perplexed as to what to do about it.

When my children were young, a visit to a store or to a restaurant became a learning opportunity, so it was an important outing where they learned how to behave in public. Inevitably, one of the children would go for broke, and rather than letting the discipline play out in front of an audience, embarrassing the child, I would take them out to the car, administer the punishment (a little spanking), and take them back into the store. After the spanking, I would talk to them and make sure they understood what was expected, and that if it happened again, I would take them back out to the car. If the first removal did not have the desired effect, I would follow through with my warning, and take them out again. Yes, it was difficult, especially when I had other children in tow, but necessary to get my point across. However, in this new era of "let the children rule," you have to worry about someone watching your actions even in your own car, as they may mistake your love for mistreatment of the child. It's created a terrible situation based on a foolhardy concept. I love children and would never promote harming a child in any way. I think parents are actually exacting way more harm by assuming the child will refrain from undesirable activities when there is virtually no consequence for misbehavior.

My generation laughs about the fact that parents today are afraid to discipline their children; that they are instructed not to spank them. They note that when they, themselves, misbehaved, they got whippings, and they always add that it didn't hurt them. They are incredulous that children speak to their parents the way they do today, with so little respect. It seems that refraining from spanking has resulted in a great lack of that respect. Proverbs 13:24 NIV actually says, 'Whoever spares the rod, hates their children, but the one who loves their children is careful to discipline them.' I again want to make it clear that *I am in no way* advocating harsh treatment or beating your child. Quite the opposite. But anyone who has known children who were left to their own devices and not disciplined knows that that parenting route produces children with out-of-control behavior, families in chaos, and families with major problems. Once you have gone down that road a bit, it is very difficult to turn back or repair the damage done. However, I reiterate, be in complete control or do not spank.

I do not remember ever receiving a spanking from my father. He administered discipline in a different way, a way that I found more hurtful than a mere spanking. My father is hysterically funny and fun to be around, but he is 6'1", a big-boned and rather big man. His stature was imposing to a child, and all he had to do was look at you with displeasure, and you did exactly what he wanted you to do. That sounds rather good, but those angry looks last longer than a spanking. They can be interpreted as disgust, disdain and even dislike. I think it is a dangerous way to discipline, unless, after the desired result is achieved, love is conscientiously reinstated, and the child is consoled to know that he or she is treasured and loved. With all anger abated, the relationship needs to be clearly restored and confirmed. I would rather have had a quick little spank than a look from my daddy that in my mind felt like condemnation. A spanking is over in an instant. A look can last a lifetime. You want to shape your child's will, but *you don't want to break his or her spirit.*

Be sure that spankings are reserved for serious infractions. If you are constantly spanking, the spankings will lose their effectiveness, and you will ultimately be viewed as a mean-spirited tyrant. There are many other ways to handle bad behavior. Diversion is a great tool and valuable tactic. Whenever possible, when a child was misbehaving, I would divert their attention by bringing up something more pleasant, more interesting, and more positive. Usually they would drop what they were doing and turn their attention to something else, and we would not have to have a knock-down-drag-out fight over something insignificant. I would also try to anticipate undesirable behavior whenever I could and head it off at the pass with the quick (and somewhat startling) sound, "Uh-uh!" (meaning, "No!"). If they did it again, I would issue the same demand (not a warning to be taken as a dare). "Uh-uh!" When said sternly with conviction and expectation, and with a look that showed I meant business, the behavior would stop. You have to say it quickly, before the words get out of your child's mouth or before he has a chance to take the undesirable action. You can't hesitate. The speed and abruptness with which you say it provides a little bit of shock and awe. Don't overuse this tactic, however, or it will become ineffective.

Asking them a question about an unrelated topic would often turn their attention to a more favorable activity. Most of the time, I would be able to stop an undesirable behavior simply by changing the subject. When you're able to do this, you forego the fight, and you don't reinforce a bad habit by giving it your attention. When they are subsequently engaged in a better activity, you can take that opportunity to praise them, which in turn makes them want to repeat that behavior. Although there are obviously times when it will be necessary to point out a child's misbehavior, I think one of the worst things you can do is label the bad behavior and repeatedly refer to it.

As you surely noticed, your father and I never used profanity. This may seem unworthy of mention, but it made a world of difference in our world. When you're raising children, you shoot for the stars. Therefore, the standards you set for yourself should be as high as the heavens. It would have bothered me tremendously if I had tried to accomplish the difficult task of raising you while my husband was cussing at me or you and using crass language with you. One of the things the Holy Spirit did for us when your father and I became Christians was to take away any desire that we might have had to use bad language. He replaced it with a greater desire to love and please Him. That's the way God works. He died for us while we were yet sinners, and He accepts us just as we are. He transforms us from the inside out. If you call on the Holy Spirit to renew your mind in Christ Jesus, He will. Period. Amen. And remember, children learn what they live. So be sure to teach them the way they should go by living it yourself!

The Bible says to control your tongue, and I believe that my children were greatly affected by the fact that your daddy and I were able to do that with the help of the Holy Spirit. And I want you boys to remember this: if you control your tongue, you will be respected by your wife and children. You wouldn't believe how many verses in the Bible talk about controlling your tongue. It's worth taking a look, because of the importance God has placed on this one admonition. Here are just a few verses on the subject of controlling your tongue; there are many.

> Let no corrupting talk come out of your mouths, but only such as is good
> for building up, as fits the occasion, that it may give grace to those who hear.
>
> Ephesians 4:29 ESV

> If anyone thinks he is religious and does not bridle his tongue but deceives
> his heart, this person's religion is worthless.
>
> James 1:26 ESV

Whoever restrains his words has knowledge, and he who has a cool spirit is a man of understanding. Even a fool who keeps silent is considered wise; when he closes his lips, he is deemed intelligent.

Proverbs 17:27–28 ESV

A soft answer turns away wrath, but a harsh word stirs up anger.

Proverbs 15:1 ESV

Your daddy always backed me up. When I was disciplining you, Daddy would make sure you minded me. He would reinforce my authority and make sure you listened and obeyed me. He transferred his authority to me, which is very important if you want your children to mind. I did the same for him, and we absolutely refused to tolerate disrespect from the children, no matter who it was directed toward. Even when I did not totally agree with a tactic used by your father, or when he would have handled something a little differently than I did, we still presented a united front by supporting the other wholeheartedly.

Be godly, of course. But don't forget to be *fun*. In fact, be the most fun person your child knows. Be the most winsome, the silliest, and most fun-loving person ever. Be ready to laugh—that is, have a good belly laugh—whenever the moment presents itself. Laughter should be right nearby any conversation, just waiting for an opportunity to come out. I'm not suggesting that you should be an embarrassing parent who sounds like a laughing hyena, who doesn't know when to be serious and composed. But I mean you should be lighthearted and look for happy moments with your children. Enjoy your children and the time you spend with them. Make it fun and joyful, always pointing your children toward the Light.

I love winsomeness. I even love the word *winsome*. It's a hard word to define, because no other words seem to do it justice. If someone has a winsome personality, you know it. You're attracted to it and persuaded by it. A winsome person has a childlike charm and innocence. Take every opportunity to have a good time with your children and to be winsome in their eyes, because that alone will go a great distance in winning them over and keeping them on your team.

The world will be serious enough, and home should be a refuge and a place of joy. Therefore, laugh a lot, because when you laugh, you remedy many things. And when you laugh, you're lovable.

<blockquote>

A merry heart doeth good like a medicine.

Proverbs 17:22 KJV

</blockquote>

There are other benefits of this as well. I believe it helps children learn not to take their circumstances too seriously. It helps to put into perspective the temporal problems we all face. I think that sheer laughter might even help a child scoff off the blues and help deter depression. Admittedly, I know nothing about clinical depression, but I think it is possible to crowd out the blues with laughter, especially if it is coupled with a mission to help someone else. Turning your attention to someone besides yourself is a good remedy for the temptation to dwell on your own perceived problems. Whenever my children seemed to be dwelling on bad thoughts (which wasn't often), I tried to steer them away from those thoughts with happy thoughts and laughter, not allowing them to focus on those things. I was sure that if they continued to enjoy that line of thinking, those thoughts would ultimately fester.

I tried to turn their attention to happier things, interesting activities, important tasks, or meaningful ways to help others. It seems unreasonable for me to suggest that this is a cure for depression, but I actually believe that skillfully and intentionally using diversion to take that child to a better place, thereby nipping the blues in the bud before ever being allowed to take hold, may be critical. If your children see you laugh a lot, and if you laugh with them, you will probably be more likely to have a happy home with happy children. And I really pulled out all the stops on this! I would redirect my child's thinking to a discussion of something of some importance, or we would go shopping for something new or plan an exciting trip. Usually, however, it was only a matter of focusing on a new subject. But I didn't make the focus *focusing or not focusing on the subject.* I did not say, "Let's focus on something else,' because then we both just focused on it more, and it became a thorn in the flesh, a much bigger problem than it should have been. Instead, I tried, under the radar, to simply redirect their focus. Wallowing in the mire can be dangerous. I firmly and wholeheartedly believe in the effectiveness of prayer, but I actually think that spending a lot of time praying about something that should otherwise be a fleeting problem will cultivate more problems and issues. It's focusing on the thing you don't want to focus on.

Thankfully, laughter seems to have always been a prominent characteristic of our family. We tend to laugh through things, even when the situation is not funny. I remember when our family had a particularly bad year. In one year, my sister was diagnosed at thirty-two with breast cancer, my other sister was diagnosed with thyroid cancer, my grandmother was diagnosed with lung cancer, I was hospitalized with atrial fibrillation when I was four months pregnant, and our third child was at death's door in the NICU for two months. After my sister's thyroid operation, I remember going into her hospital room and laughing, halfway exclaiming and halfway asking the question, "What are you doing?" Even with her throat slit and stitched, she laughed and said, "I know! This is ridiculous!" The situation had just gotten so serious it was comical. Recognize the value of laughing to keep from crying. It helps. When my grandmother (who was such a special and beloved person) was dying that same year, I heard my mother and her sister laughing about the things their mother was saying (due to the pain medications she was being given). It really helped me not to feel so dire about that situation. Again, laughing helps to put the temporal in perspective. I am not suggesting that you should make light of something heartbreaking, but when appropriate (and sometimes when it's not!), you should help your children learn to laugh through life's trials. They will be much more likely to find the light of God's presence in the storms.

Having a persistence that can outlast your child's persistence, or for that matter, another parent's, will catapult you into a superior parenting category. That is, you will be able to stay the course when everyone else is throwing in the towel. You will still be in the game when others are giving up and giving in and losing their children. Persistence, as defined by my Google dictionary, means 'firm or obstinate continuance in a course of action in spite of difficulty or opposition.' Learn to be obstinate when you need to be. You will have to hold out with conviction and hold on with sheer determination.

So even if you have sufficient persistence, you will still need unforgiving determination. Unwavering determination and *persistent* persistence! I knew that God had given me a child that He loved and that He had a special plan for. It was my singular mission to do everything I could do to make sure my children became all God created them to be. I knew that in my own weakness, I needed God's direction and strength. And I knew that only God could provide that determination that would be required. I wanted nothing to be left undone, and therefore, with painstaking perseverance, persistence, and determination, I worked toward my goal. I kept everything under my watchful eye and was in control of most everything concerning my children. Extreme? Radical? Yes. Extremely radical and even, to many, ridiculous. A lot of well-meaning parents would think this might be a reason to send me to the looney bin, and I know that just because it worked for me, it does not mean it will work for everybody. Maybe this was just the leading that I felt from the Lord. Because it did work for me. The goal encompassed having children who loved the Lord and who were grounded in the Word, who were well adjusted and who did not go down paths of destruction with alcohol, drugs, and tobacco. I do not mean to say you need a barbed wire fence around your children, but I don't believe, either, that you let them roam where they will.

I made sure I knew what was going on and that I kept you headed in the absolute right direction. I've decided I'm not ashamed to say that I orchestrated a lot of things, while making it seem like I didn't. I tried to say yes to everything I could possibly say yes to. But I said no to anything that wasn't in your very best interest. Not appearing to be controlling was of utmost importance, and a nonchalant attitude was essential in some instances. You have to be creative, winsome, and fun to pull this off. On the other hand, there are times when it is healthy for children to make a mistake they can learn from. As a parent, you will know when that is appropriate, but it won't be when it is going to cause irreparable harm to the child, or when you are just too lazy to do what you need to do, or because you will be embarrassed by your peers. So often, what appears to be a little innocent diversion from the right path might actually turn out to be a long journey down a bottomless pit. So be careful. Your daddy tells a story about a day when he and his identical twin, Bob, were about six years old, and they were furiously digging a hole in their backyard. Your daddy remembers, "Mama was watching us from the kitchen window and saw that we had a shovel and a baseball bat. She came outside and asked us what in the world we were doing, and we said, 'Mama, we're diggin' a hole to where the devil lives, and when he sticks his head out, we're gonna pop him on the head with this baseball bat!'" Your daddy was pretty wise. Pop the devil as soon as he sticks his head out!

I'm so far from perfect, and even though well intentioned, I faltered and failed. But the point is that I set out to be steadfast, and I was determined to do just that. To be effective, you will have to call on Jesus, for He is everything good, and you will want the light of His presence to illuminate your way and surround your family. Jonathan, I know that it is because of the light of His presence in our family's life that you came to see your childhood as having been extraordinary.

Oliver, our first grandson!

CHAPTER 6

Tell Your Children Who They Are

So much of who your children turn out to be depends on who you tell them they are. I faithfully embraced this idea. I really studied my children to discover their strengths and their bents, and I told them I loved those things about them. I tried to encourage the talents I saw and tried to present every opportunity for them to grow in the direction in which I saw God had gifted them.

Not only was I careful about who I told my children they were, but I was also careful about who others told them they were. Because of this, I never criticized them or made fun of them, especially in front of others. I didn't poke fun at them or laugh about their failings or their physical features. If another adult made reference to a characteristic I didn't want my child to be labeled with, I would downplay what was said or ignore it. I wouldn't go along with it. Instead, I made a point to recognize the good things I saw in them and say, "You are a very good writer or artist or dancer or chef or mathematician or scientist." I affirmed them whenever possible and made sure I pointed out the gifts God had given them, not their flaws. I told them over and over how good they were, how kind they were, and how talented they were. I believed they were 'fearfully and wonderfully made,' as the Bible says, and I looked for that miracle in my children.

Your daddy would always remind me, "The world will tear them down, and it is our job to build them up." This is so true, and we tried hard to do just that.

Children do not benefit in any way from public humiliation or sarcasm. Even when my child was not nearby, I refrained from talking about any of his or her negative traits, as I was convinced that my friends and my children's teachers would be more inclined to look for those areas of weakness in my child if I told them they were there. I did not want them to expect something negative from my child. I wanted them to look for the best and expect to find it. If I did discuss my child's behavior with a trusted friend, it was in order to gain some insight into how to handle it from someone who would give me wise, godly counsel.

In the same way, I encouraged my children to love each other *by talking about how much they loved each other*. If you do this from the beginning, I believe you will see them become more and more loving toward one another, more protective of one another, and more likely to look for the good in one another.

Self-deprecation can be funny, but never treat your children as an extension of yourself in this regard. In other words, don't criticize, poke fun, or condemn them to get a laugh. A lot of parents laugh and joke about their children to enhance comradery in their friend group. It makes sense, since it makes everyone feel more comfortable if the playing field is level. Being real just helps everyone feel accepted and acceptable. Let's face it: no one wants to hear another parent talk about how perfect their children are. But when the temptation arises to share your children's flaws, be careful. Honestly, when I hear parents giving other parents a laugh at the expense of their child, I cringe. I still hold fast to the same premise that whatever you tell them they are, they most likely will become.

Never (ever, ever, ever!) tell a child they are *bad* or *worthless*. I hate to hear a parent label their child with a negative label. I would never say, even in jest, that my child was bad. As I said before, I rarely discussed bad behavior with another adult (and certainly not in the child's presence). I did not want them to see themselves as bad, because I knew that they would, in turn, give me what I was expecting—bad behavior.

When Matthew started kindergarten, his pediatrician advised us to inform the teacher of the medical history surrounding his birth and the possibility that he might have developmental issues. Daddy and I decided that we did not want his teacher to be looking for problems, so we did not tell her. Instead, we were on our knees praying that Matthew was perfect in every way, that he was not only smart, but brilliant. Knowing Matthew's activity level, we also prayed without ceasing that he would be able to sit in the classroom without incident. We enticed him to do his best by holding out positive rewards for a good day in school. God answered those prayers, and we never had even one negative report from a teacher. All reports were glowing, and Matthew was as smart as a whip. So, focus on the good in each child. Don't brag, but never point out their weaknesses.

Now that you have built up your children's images of themselves to the point that they think they're invincible, it's time to temper their perception of themselves. If you are studying your child, you'll know just when this dose of corrective action is needed. You'll know that if you do not act, that child will march out of your house believing they are too wonderful for words in the eyes of all the world. Their self-confidence, if way overblown, will inevitably lead to conceit and arrogance. How, then, can you handle the delicate job of instilling humility?

You certainly would never take back anything you said, suggesting that you had been disingenuous. But you will have to make sure they understand who they are in Christ and who others are in the eyes of Christ. Remind your child that we have all fallen short of the glory of God. We have *all* sinned. We all need a savior, the Savior Jesus Christ, because all of our hearts are evil. By one man's (Adam) sin, we all became sinners, and by one man's sacrifice (Jesus), we are forgiven. God is Love, and He loved each of us (in our sinfulness) so much that he sacrificed His Son, Jesus, on a cross, so that we could be with Him in heaven. We owe Him everything, and Jesus commands us in Matthew 22:36 (ESV) to "love the Lord your God with all your heart and with all your soul and with all your mind. This is the great and first commandment. And a second is like it: You shall love your neighbor as yourself." An understanding of God's authority over you and His view of you produces humility. There has to be that healthy fear of God. We are far from perfect, and God loves us anyway. He sent His precious Son to die for us, and this is humbling. His love for us is extraordinary, and the Bible says that "we are God's masterpiece" (Ephesians 2:10 NLT), but we still need the Artist's touch! It's hard to be haughty in the face of this reality.

It's fun, amazing, and downright awesome to help your children see the handiwork of God in nature, in the science of the human body, and even in mathematics. His hand can be seen in, of course, everything. You will be fascinated yourself when you look for and acknowledge Christ's handiwork when teaching your children about the world they live in.

He, and He alone, created everything.

> In the beginning was the Word, and the Word was with God, and the Word was God. He was in the beginning with God. All things were made through Him, and without him was not any thing made that was made. In him was life, and the life was the light of men.
>
> John 1:1–4 ESV

God created the universe, so every story you tell your children can be related to the glory, majesty, might, and amazing grace of their heavenly Father. You really cannot talk about the seasons, the planets, the wind, the marsh, or the rainbow without the opportunity to bring the Creator into the discussion. What He has done is so incredible that even having the limited view that I have, I am astounded and filled with wide-eyed wonder when I consider it. It is microscopic and immense. It is gentle and scary. In all forms, it is stunning and inconceivable to our finite minds. And believe it or not, we are the crowning glory of it all.

Every subject you can think of has Christ the Creator at the center of it. Your children were born longing to know their Creator, so tell them about Him. Don't reserve the spiritual for Sundays. Make sure that God is on center stage every day. The earlier you start communicating this, the earlier they will love their Creator. They will be in awe *as you are also in awe* of the awesomeness of the Almighty.

Discovering the Creator in your math or science lesson is nothing short of jaw-dropping. It is fascinating and mysterious and mind-boggling. Every subject has lesson after lesson about God and His magnificence. And that makes learning tremendously joyful and will render the one learning nearly speechless with humility.

Just take a superficial look at the human eye. Look at all it can do. It focuses and refocuses *instantly* on objects at different distances. The eye can see the tiny flame of a candle ten miles away. It keeps itself lubricated, and it expresses sadness with tears. It is a window to the soul. God, and God alone, could have created this wonder. Consider the hand. Its unbelievable abilities are staggering. Tell your children about the heart and the kidneys that cleanse their blood. Tell them how intricate our bodies are and how, like little soldiers, our white blood cells stand at the ready to attack any foreign or unwanted agent. Then tell them about the voice that spoke everything into existence.

I have never understood the atheist who thinks that all of this just came into being by accident. Fred Hoyle, a British astronomer, who formulated the theory of stellar nucleosynthesis, said this in 1983: "A junkyard contains all the bits and pieces of a Boeing 747, dismembered and in disarray. A whirlwind happens to blow through the yard. What is the chance that after its passage a fully assembled 747, ready to fly, will be found standing there? So small as to be negligible, even if a tornado were to blow through enough junkyards to fill the whole universe." Lee Strobel, atheist turned believer, said, "An intelligent entity has quite literally spelled out His existence through the four chemical letters in the genetic code. It's almost as if the Creator autographed every cell." When you explore these wondrous parts of creation with your children, you open those beautiful eyes and their hearts to so much.

There is a book that I highly recommend you read to your children. It's called *In the Likeness of God*. It was written by a famous hand surgeon, Dr. Paul Brand, and Philip Yancey, a best-selling Christian author. It will send your head spinning with revelations about the human body and its likeness to God and its comparisons to the church (the body of Christ).

In the past few years, when wondering how I could know God more intimately, I realized that my knowing God is inextricably tied to my witness of and my wondering over His creation. When I feel God is distant, or when I feel I am lacking in my love and devotion to God, I can walk outside and immediately feel closer, just being in the midst of His creation. A smile comes over my face, my faith deepens, my heart quickens, and I hover in disbelief over what my whole being recognizes as the majesty of God. I know He is there, and I suddenly know more of who He is, just by being in the midst of what He has created.

> For since the creation of the world God's invisible qualities—
> his eternal power and divine nature—
> have been clearly seen, being understood from what has been made,

so that people are without excuse.

Romans 1:20 NIV

God's handiwork speaks to me. There is just no denying the divine when you consider the intricacies of what has been made. It is a divine footprint. During the triumphal entry of Jesus into Jerusalem the Bible says the following:

The whole multitude of his disciples began to rejoice and praise God with a loud voice for all the mighty works that they had seen, saying,
"Blessed is the King who comes in the name of the Lord! Peace in heaven and glory in the highest!" And some of the pharisees in the crowd said to him,
"Teacher, rebuke your disciples." He answered, "I tell you, if these were silent, the very stones would cry out."

Luke 19:38–40 ESV

Even the stones know their creator.

I encourage you to listen to the late D. James Kennedy's sermon that he gave August 1, 1990, at a Creation Conference in Pittsburg. He cites several highly respected scientists who acknowledge the incredible odds of even one cell appearing *by chance* throughout all of the history of the universe are so extreme as to be *impossible*. And think, then, of this: engineers at Washington University have estimated that there are around 100,000,000,000 (a hundred trillion) atoms in one typical human cell. And interestingly, the number of cells in a human body is approximately the same as the number of atoms in one cell! There are so many fantastic facts such as these when you delve into science that studying it cannot be in any way dull. And it can only lead you to the Creator Himself.

CHAPTER 7

The Critical Foundation

One of the most successful things I did to help my children prepare for learning and get ahead of the game is that I took every opportunity to lay foundations that they could then build on. Even though I was not the most intelligent or well-read person in the world, I was able to expose them to a myriad of experiences, information, and different trains of thought that would teach them foundational things. This automatically put them in a position to learn more. They were able to build on the information they already had when they were being taught a particular subject in a formal setting. In many instances, this put them a step ahead of their peers. Since they already knew the basics and were familiar with so many subjects, this gave them great advantage. They heard more than their classmates and were able to absorb more of the information presented. They already knew and understood much of what was being taught, so they were looking for the next step, the more complex information, the answers to more complicated questions. The details. The nuances. They were curious to open the next door. They were, in many cases, able to build premise upon premise much faster than others.

This approach has, without a doubt, been a good one, but in telling you this, I want to make sure that you have thought through a few things. First of all, you want to be sure that you do not sabotage your children's happiness and well-being by making them walking encyclopedias. Of course, you want your children to excel academically, but you don't want them to be bookworms who have no other interests and are not well rounded. These types of people will almost always become strange and ostracized. I sometimes fear that status with children in this present generation because everyone is so fixed on their children being not only brilliant but tops in everything. I cannot get over how things have changed in my lifetime in that regard. It used to be that if a girl was a student at certain academically challenging universities, you could almost count on that same girl being unattractive and socially awkward. The same may or may not have been true of their male counterparts. This doesn't sound like a good thing, but what I am saying is that they couldn't be all things to everybody. They were brilliantly intelligent but never quite learned how to be attractive in a social situation. But today, things have changed dramatically. Boy have they learned to do both! Young people are being accepted to the most difficult learning institutions in the country, they look like models, and they are outstanding in every sport they play. It seems like so much to ask of them, and I think it's no wonder that they sometimes end up finding relief where they shouldn't. It's something to consider, and the best thing to do is make sure your children are grounded in the Word, have a clear understanding of God's overwhelming Love that looks at their heart, and that they have a firm understanding of where they stand with you in terms of acceptance of who they are and not who this world may want them to be.

There are several stories that your children need to hear more than a few times during their childhood. The first, of course, is the story of our Savior. There are so many ways to tell this fascinating story. Read to your children often and let it often be about God. Be deliberate, talking to them about the things of God not just when you are putting them to bed but when you are riding in the car, when you are walking by the way, when your family is enjoying conversation at dinner. When something needs to be brought to God in prayer, don't hesitate to take that moment to pray. Let them hear you pray, expecting God to answer that prayer.

> You shall therefore lay up these words of mine in your heart and in your soul; and you shall bind them as a sign on your hand, and they shall be as frontlets between your eyes. You shall teach them to your children, talking of them when you are sitting in your house, and when you are walking by the way, and when you lie down, and when you rise.
>
> Deuteronomy 11:18–19 ESV

The second story you should tell your children is the story of how you both met. Joe and I told this story to our children many times, and they loved it. Joe often tells it still, to grandchildren and acquaintances, so I will record it here for grandchildren to come.

I was at the University of Georgia finishing up my last quarter in college, and as I walked past the student union one day, I noticed a group of people trying to win converts to their religion, a branch of Hinduism called Hare Krishna. They looked deeply devoted to something mysterious, something I did not understand. This type of thing is particularly interesting to people around that age, I believe, because they are trying to find spiritual meaning, and these people seem to have a secret that no one else possesses. It easily draws them in, because they are longing to fill a God-shaped vacuum that every human created in the image of God has. I went home that night and began to pray about my spiritual condition, asking God to reveal Himself to me. Thank goodness I realized that I needed to understand my own faith before I considered another. I had grown up in the Methodist Church, and my family attended Sunday school and church almost every Sunday. Still, I had never really heard a sermon on salvation or one on how to be saved. The message I got from my years of attending church was that we were all nice people, and we would therefore all go to heaven. Unfortunately, nothing could be further from the truth. A relationship with Jesus and an acceptance of His sacrifice on the cross and forgiveness of my sins was what I needed. I guess I realized something was missing, so I began to pray for someone to help me understand the path to God.

Joe was already a Christian, and four years older than I. He was living and working in Columbus, Georgia, where we both had grown up but had never met. One night he attended a revival and heard the true story of a missionary who was on the mission field pleading for God to give him a much-needed bicycle. He was mad at God because the bicycle he had been praying for had never come. As he prayed, he heard God say, "Son, you have not told me what kind of bicycle you want. Do you want a blue bicycle, a red bicycle, or a yellow bicycle? Do you want it to have a basket on the front? Do you want a ten-speed or twelve-speed? Tell me exactly what you want." So he got very specific with God and told him everything he needed on that bicycle. The very next morning, the exact bicycle he had described to God showed up at his mission. Mysteriously, it had been shipped months before. This was a true story, and that missionary went on to be the pastor of a megachurch with many thousands of members. So Joe went home that night and made a very specific list of what he wanted in a wife. He began his list by saying he wanted someone who was a Christian, then someone who would be a good wife and mother to his children. He proceeded to list other things, and the last thing on the list was, "And, Lord, You know how much I love redheads!" That was Wednesday night, and on Sunday morning, I walked into his Sunday school class. I had red hair down to my waist. He was so shocked that all he could think was, *God, you have got to be kidding!*

Joe was a mature Christian at the time, and was on fire for the Lord. As I got to know him, I knew I wanted what he had. Christ living through him was so attractive, and God's love was so evident in him that I began to ask Joe questions about his faith. His excitement about Jesus was contagious, and I recognized quickly that what I had been praying for and longing for was the saving grace that Joe had experienced. With the guidance of my new friend, I gave my life to Christ and asked Him to be my Lord and Savior. My prayers and Joe's prayers had been answered by the Lord who sees, and loves, and provides. It is an awesome, true story of how God moves in our lives and how prayer changes everything.

I'll never forget how shocked I was at the end of our first date. Joe walked me to my door, he asked me if he could *say a prayer*. Whoa! I assure you, that was a first for me! This marked our dating life from then on out, and kept our relationship in God's will. Becoming a Christian changes your life. A year or so after we started dating, when Joe asked me to marry him, he stopped me from answering right away, saying, "Before you answer, I want you to think about this. This is for life. If you are not ready to commit to that, I want you to say no." He said I opened my eyes wide, looked at him, and exclaimed, "For life? I've never thought about it like that before!" He responded to my innocence and immaturity with an absolute certainty that sounded almost scary to me. He said, "I will always be with you. Nothing you can do will make me leave you. You'll be stuck with me!" I have always been beyond grateful for his question, because it made me think about the vow I was consenting to take. Joe's unwavering commitment to me that day was something I have thought about many, many times through the years. It gave me a security that I will always and forever be thankful for. I knew that Joe would always be by my side. I would never have to worry about him being unfaithful. And as I've looked around this old world, I've realized what a rare treasure God has given me.

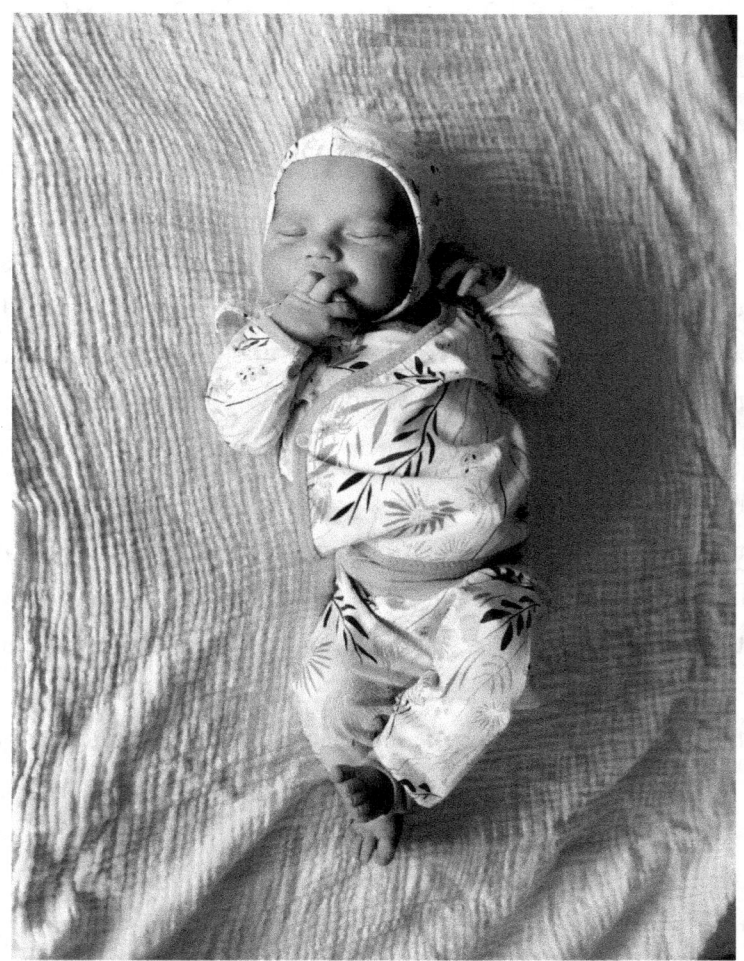

Zadie, Number Six Granddaughter!

CHAPTER 8

Hide the Word in their Hearts

Sing songs about Jesus and to Jesus with your children before they can understand a word. When they are in the cradle, in the crib, in your arms. Sing fun songs that incorporate Bible verses. Singing the words makes them more memorable, and this will help them hide the Word of God in their hearts. Then, when they need them, the Holy Spirit will bring those very verses back to their remembrance. They will learn so much from singing scripture. They will learn to love Jesus as they learn who He is, and they will learn Bible stories, gaining great wisdom from them. It's so much fun. No effort required.

There are many wonderful songs that simply are scripture verses put to music, and there are many others that rhyme, are fun to sing, and help teach the Bible stories. But there are songs that need to be sung too, for the simple reason that they permeate love. Though the words may say nothing about love, love is conveyed. My grandmother, Mammy (Clara Alderman Foy Roberts), and my mother, Mankme (Franke Foy Roberts Adams), were so full of life and so much fun. They always sang to the babies. Here are some old songs, rhymes, and blessings that have become traditions in our family. Many of these songs were sung to *my mother and grandmother* as babies. I sang these songs and recited the rhymes and blessings to *my children*, and I now take much pleasure in doing the same for *my grandchildren:*

Hush, Little Baby, Adapted
Mother Goose

Hush, little baby, don't say a word,
Mama's gonna buy you a Mockingbird.
And if that Mockingbird don't sing
Mama's gonna buy you a diamond ring.
And if that diamond ring turns brass
Mama's gonna buy you a looking glass.
And if that looking glass don't shine
Mama's gonna love you all the time.

Bye Yo Baby Buntin'
A Eufaula, Alabama, interpretation of the original

Bye yo baby buntin'
Daddy's gone a huntin'
To catch a little rabbit skin
To wrap his baby buntin' in.
(Repeat! Again and again!)

The Old Gray Mare

The old gray mare,
She ain't what she used to be,
Ain't what she used to be,
Ain't what she used to be.
The old gray mare,
She ain't what she used to be,
Many long years ago.

Many long years, ago,
Many long years, ago,
The old gray mare,
She ain't what she used to be
Many long years ago.

Go Tell Aunt Tabby

Go tell Aunt Tabby,
Go tell Aunt Tabby,
Go tell Aunt Tabby,
The old gray goose is dead.
She died last Friday,
Died last Friday,
She died last Friday,
To make a feather bed.

Rock-a-Bye Baby

Rock-a-bye baby
In the tree tops,
When the wind blows,
The cradle will rock.
When the bough breaks,
The cradle will fall,
And down will come baby,
Cradle and all.

Tea Rosie

I don't know the origin of this little two-word song or what the meaning of it might be, but again, Mama would always sing it to our babies. She would alternate touching her thumbs to her index and third fingers as she sang, 'Tea Rosie, Tea Rosie!' in front of the baby. She would, at the same time, turn her hands back and forth, which I guess amused the baby. It seemed so sweet for some reason, and the babies did appear to stop and watch the hand movements and listen to the repetitious sounds.

Tea Rosie, Tea Rosie.
Sing these two little words again and again while making hand gestures for the baby.

I've Got That Joy, Joy, Joy
George William Cooke

I've got that joy, joy, joy, joy down in my heart!
Where? Down in my heart! Where? Down in my heart!
I've got that joy, joy, joy, joy down in my heart,
Down in my heart to stay!
I've got that peace that passes understanding down in my heart!
Where? Down in my heart! Where? Down in my heart!
I've got that peace that passes understanding
Down in my heart, down in my heart to stay.

Jesus Loves Me

Jesus Loves Me, This I know
For the Bible Tells Me So

Little Ones to Him Belong,
They are weak but He is Strong.
Yes, Jesus Loves Me,
Yes, Jesus Loves Me.
Yes, Jesus Loves Me,
For the Bible Tells Me So.
Anna Bartlett Warner

Arise and Shine

When you wake up in the morning, sing this!

Arise and Shine,
And give God the Glory, Glory.
Rise, and Shine,
And give God the glory, glory.
Rise and Shine, and,
Give God the glory, glory
Children, of the Lord!

My Own Verses to the Tune of 'Arise and Shine'

Katherine woke up early this morning, morning!
Katherine woke up early this morning, morning!
Katherine woke up early, early, early!
Children of the Lord!
Jonathan (or Matthew) woke up early this morning, morning!
Jonathan (or Matthew) woke up early this morning, morning!
Jonathan (or Matthew) woke up early, early, early!
Children of the Lord!

I Love You!
I made up the following song, which I sang often to my children. My grandchildren now love, love, love hearing me sing about them! I would continue verses with each child's name and change the italicized adjectives as I felt led and as the words fit the melody.

I love Matthew!
I love Matthew!
I love Matthew!
I love him, yes I do!
He is so *handsome*,
He is so *smart*,
He is so *wonderful*,
I love him with my heart!

I Love You! (II)
I was astounded at how delighted my grandchildren were when I sang these next two little made-up songs to them. They kept saying, "Gigi, now sing it to *me*!" They loved to hear me sing about *them*, describing *them*. It was amazing.

I love you, Jonathan! Oh yes I do!
I don't love anyone like I love you!
When I'm not with you,
I'm blue!
Oh, Jonathan, I love you!

Daisy, Daisy, Give Me Your Answer True
Title and words altered slightly from original

Daisy, Daisy, give me your answer true!
I'm half crazy, over my love for you!

It won't be a stylish marriage,
I can't afford a carriage.
But you'll look sweet, upon the seat,
Of a bicycle built for two!

Swing Low, Sweet Chariot
Francesco Mocchi
Words altered slightly from original

Swing low, sweet chariot,
Coming for to carry me home.
Swing low, sweet chariot,
Coming for to carry me home.
I looked out over the Jordan,
And what did I see
Coming for to carry me home?
A band full of angels coming after me,
Coming for to carry me home.
Swing low, sweet chariot,
Coming for to carry me home.
Swing low, sweet chariot,
Coming for to carry me home.

If You Don't Like My Peaches

If you don't like-a my peaches,
Honey don't you shake my tree!
'Cause I'm just a Georgia freestone,
and nothing clings to me.

You ain't the only omen on my track,
I can make a livin' ballin' the jack.
So if you don't like-a my peaches,
honey don't you shake my tree!

I Left

A silly but fun little recitation we often say while *marching* along with the children

I left, I left, I left my wife and forty-nine children
Alone in the kitchen in starving condition
With nothing to eat but gingerbread.
I left, I left.
(Repeat)

Moravian Blessing

This is a blessing Mammy learned in her travels and our family adopted it, often saying it together while holding hands before dinner.

Come, Lord Jesus, our guest to be,
And bless these gifts bestowed by Thee!
Bless our loved ones, everywhere,
And keep them in Thy loving care.
Jesus's name we pray. Amen

God Our Father

A child's blessing set to music, that often is sung so innocently by our grandchildren when we are eating at a restaurant

God our Father, God our Father,

We thank you, we thank you,
For our many blessings, for our many blessings.
Amen, Amen.

Lord, Make Us Thankful

My father, George Mortimer Adams, Jr., *always* recited this *very quick* blessing!

Lord, make us thankful
For these and all our many blessings.
In Christ's name we pray.
Amen.

Thank You for the World So Sweet

A child's dinner blessing that I dearly love

Thank You for the world, so sweet!
Thank You for the food we eat!
Thank You for the birds that sing!
Thank You God for everything!

God is Great

A child's dinner blessing that I often said as a child

God is great,
God is good.
Let us thank Him for our food.
By His hands, we all are fed.
Thank You Lord for daily bread.
Amen.

Now I Lay Me Down to Sleep
A child's bedtime prayer that I said as a child before going to sleep

Now I lay me down to sleep,
I pray the Lord,
My soul to keep.
If I should die before I wake,
I pray the Lord, my soul to take.
Amen.

Bless the Lord
A Bible verse that has been set to music

Bless the Lord, O my soul, and all that is within me, bless his holy name!
Psalm 103:1 KJV

I Will Sing of the Mercies of the Lord
Scripture set to music

I will sing of the mercies of the Lord forever,
I will sing, I will sing;
I will sing of the mercies of the Lord forever;
I will sing of the mercies of the Lord!
With my mouth, will I make known
Thy faithfulness, Thy faithfulness,
With my mouth will I make known
Thy faithfulness to all generations.
I will sing of the mercies of the Lord forever,
I will sing, I will sing'

I will sing of the mercies of the Lord forever;
I will sing of the mercies of the Lord!
Psalm 89:1 KJV

Morning Has Broken
Eleanor Farjeon,

This beautiful song, sung by Cat Stevens, is one of my favorites!

Morning has broken like the first morning;
Blackbird has spoken like the first bird
Praise for the singing! Praise for the morning!
Praise for them springing fresh from the Word
Sweet the rain's new fall, sunlit from heaven;
Like the first dewfall on the first grass
Praise for the sweetness of the wet garden;
Sprung in completeness where his feet pass.

Amazing Grace
John Newton

Amazing Grace how sweet the sound,
That saved a wretch like me.
I once was lost, but now I'm found,
Was blind, but now I see.
When we've been there ten thousand years,
Bright shining as the sun,
We've no less days to sing God's praise,
Than when we first begun.

His Name Is Wonderful
Audrey Mieir

His name is Wonderful, His name is Wonderful,
His name is Wonderful, Jesus my Lord.
He's the great shepherd, the rock of all ages,
Almighty God is He.
Bow down before Him; Love and adore Him.
His name is Wonderful, Jesus my Lord.

Joyful, Joyful We Adore Thee
Henry van Dyke Jr.

Joyful, Joyful, we adore Thee,
God of glory, Lord of love;
Hearts unfold like flow'rs before Thee,
Op'ning to the sun above.
Melt the clouds of sin and sadness;
Drive the dark of doubt away;
Giver of immortal gladness,
Fill us with the light of day!
All Thy works with joy surround Thee,
Earth and heav'n reflect Thy rays,
Stars and angels sing around Thee,
Center of unbroken praise.
Field and forest, vale and mountain,
Flowery meadow, flashing sea,
Singing bird and flowing fountain
Call us to rejoice in Thee.

Thou art giving and forgiving,
Ever blessing, ever blest,
Wellspring of the joy of living,
Ocean depth of happy rest!
Thou our Father, Christ our Brother,
All who live in love are thine:
Teach us how to love each other,
Lift us to the joy divine.
Mortals, join the happy chorus,
Which the morning stars began;
Father love is reigning o'er us,
Brother love binds man to man.
Ever singing, march we onward,
Victors in the midst of strife,
Joyful music leads us Sunward
In the triumph song of life.

I Love You, Lord (Song)
Laurie Brendemuehl

I Love You, Lord
And I lift my voice
To worship You
Oh, my soul rejoice!
Take joy my King
In what You hear
Let it be a sweet, sweet sound
In Your ear!

In Everything Give Thanks
Scripture set to music

In everything give thanks,
For this is the will of God;
In everything give thanks,
For this is the will of God;
In everything give thanks,
For this is the will of God,
In Christ Jesus concerning you!
1 Thessalonians 5:18 KJV

Seek Ye First the Kingdom of God
Scripture set to music

Seek ye first the kingdom of God
And His righteousness;
And all these things shall be added unto you
Hallelu, Hallelujah!
Ask, and it shall be given unto you,
Seek, and ye shall find.
Knock, and the door shall be opened unto you
Hallelu, Hallelujah!
Man shall not live by bread alone,
But by every word,
That proceeds from the mouth of God
Hallelu, Hallelujah!
Matthew 6:33 KJV

Spirit Song

John Wimber

Oh, let the Son of God enfold you
With his Spirit and his love;
Let him fill your heart and satisfy your soul.
O let him have the things that hold you,
And his Spirit like a dove,
Will descend upon your life and make you whole.
Jesus, O Jesus, come and fill your lambs.
Jesus, O Jesus, come and fill your lambs.

In Christ Alone

Stuart Townend

This is one of my very favorite songs, which has more beautiful verses.

In Christ alone my hope is found
He is my light, my strength, my song
This cornerstone, this solid ground,
Firm through the fiercest drought and storm.
What heights of love, what depths of peace,
When fears are stilled, when strivings cease!
My comforter, my all in all
Here in the love of Christ I stand.

One of the best things you can do for your young children is to help them learn Bible verses. Hiding those words in their hearts means that when they need that wisdom, the Holy Spirit can bring it to their remembrance. That will be crucial for their success in walking consistently in the will of God. And besides, they will be so proud, while at the same time gaining great knowledge and profound wisdom. Let them recite the verses to grandparents and other family members. In my grandmother's (Mammy's) family, the children had to recite a verse before eating dinner. But Mammy and her first cousin, Florence Strang, were such sights and such cut-ups, that they would try to say the shortest verses they could think of. Laughing, I'm sure, Clara (Mammy) recited her verse, "Jesus wept" (John 11:35 ESV).

> Let the word of Christ dwell in you richly,
> teaching and admonishing one another in all wisdom,
> singing psalms and hymns and spiritual songs,
> with thankfulness in your hearts to God.
> Colossians 3:16 ESV

I want you to know that I am not proposing that you drive your children to the brink of insanity quoting scripture all day, or that you qualify for a medal for being the biggest geek or the most prudent prude on earth. I'm not advising you to talk so much about the spiritual that you are no earthly good. No! Use your good sense! Have more fun with your children than any other parent on the planet. But soak them in the Word and make it real to them. If you are truly sold out for Jesus, you are truly fanatical about Him, and the way you live your life is radical! Remember, they will likely not get this wisdom and devotion to God anywhere else in this old world. Our world, in general, has turned its back on God. When we look around, it appears that the world does not need God. But we, who know Jesus as our Savior, know this is far from the truth. The world is blinded, and you don't want to take a chance on your children being blinded too.

So help your children learn the word and retain it because they will surely need that information and affirmation and confirmation. There are many different methods and games you can use to help them memorize and understand the Word. Just start early, and it will be a natural and necessarily integral part of their lives.

Hide the Word in your own hearts and pass them on to your children. The Holy Spirit will use these God-given words to comfort and lead both you and your children all of your lives.

When you can't think what to do or where to turn or how to handle a situation, the Holy Spirit will bring theses verses to your remembrance.

For the Word of God is quick, and powerful, and sharper than any twoedged sword, piercing even to the dividing asunder of soul and spirit, and of the joints and marrow, and is a discerner of the thoughts and intents of the heart.
Hebrews 4:12 KJV

In the beginning was the Word, and the Word was with God,
and the Word was God.
John 1:1 ESV

For God so loved the world, that he gave his only Son, that whoever believes in him should not perish but have eternal life.
John 3:16 ESV

For all have sinned and fall short of the glory of God.
Romans 3:23 NKJV

And as it is appointed for men to die once, but after this the judgment.
Hebrews 9:27 NKJV

For the wages of sin is death, but the gift of God is eternal life in Christ Jesus our Lord.
Romans 6:23 NKJV

But God demonstrates His own love toward us, in that while we were still sinners, Christ died for us.
Romans 5:8 NKJV

All we like sheep have gone astray; we have turned, every one, to his own way, and the Lord has laid on Him the iniquity of us all.
Isaiah 53:6 NKJV

For by grace you have been saved through faith, and that not of yourselves; it is a gift of God, not of works, lest anyone should boast.
Ephesians 2:8, 9 NKJV

A new commandment I give to you, that you love one another; as I have loved you, that you also love one another. By this all will know that you are My disciples, if you have love for one another.
John 13:34, 35

I have been crucified with Christ. It is no longer I who live, but Christ who lives in me. And the life I now live in the flesh I live by faith in the Son of God, who loved me and gave himself for me.
Galatians 2:20 ESV

Therefore, if anyone is in Christ, he is a new creation. The old has passed away; behold, the new has come.
2 Corinthians 5:17 ESV

Rejoice in the Lord always: and again I say, Rejoice.
Philippians 4:4 KJV

Finally, brothers, whatever is true, whatever is honorable, whatever is just, whatever is pure, whatever is lovely, whatever is commendable, if there is any excellence, if there is anything worthy of praise, think about these things.
Philippians 4:8 ESV

But do not let immorality or any impurity or greed even be named
among you, as is proper among saints.
Ephesians 5:3 NASB

…but they who wait upon the Lord shall renew their strength; they shall mount up with wings like eagles; they shall run and not be weary; they shall walk and not faint.
Isaiah 40:31 ESV

In every thing give thanks: for this is the will of God in Christ Jesus concerning you.
I Thessalonians 5:18 KJV

You will keep him in perfect peace, whose mind is stayed on You, because he trusts in You.
Isaiah 26:3 NKJV

And my God shall supply all your need according to His riches in glory by Christ Jesus.
Philippians 4:19 NKJV

Search me, O God, and know my heart: try me, and know my thoughts: And see if there be any wicked way in me, and lead me in the way everlasting.
Psalm 139: 23-24 KJV

Be strong and courageous. Do not be afraid of them; for the Lord your God, He is the One who goes with you. He will not leave you nor forsake you.
Deuteronomy 31:6 NKJV

Let not your hearts be troubled. Believe in God; believe also in me. In my Father's house are many rooms. If it were not so, would I have told you that I go to prepare a place for you? And if I go and prepare a place for you, I will come again and take you to myself, that where I am you may be also.
John 14:1-3 ESV

God is not a man, that He should lie, nor a son of man, that He should repent. Has He said, and will He not do it? Or has He spoken, and will He not make it good?
Numbers 23:19 NKJV

And do not be conformed to this world, but be transformed by the renewing of your mind, that you may prove what is that good and acceptable and perfect will of God.
Romans 12:2 NKJV

But seek first the kingdom of God and his righteousness, and all these things will be added to you.
Matthew 6:33 ESV

Behold, I stand at the door and knock. If anyone hears My voice and opens the door, I will come in to him and dine with him, and he with Me.
Revelation 3:20 NKJV

I can do all things through Christ who strengthens me.
Philippians 4:13 NKJV

Peace I leave with you; my peace I give to you. Not as the world gives do I give to you. Let not your hearts be troubled, neither let them be afraid.
John 14: 27 ESV

Jesus said to him, "I am the way, and the truth, and the life. No one comes to the Father, except through me."
John 14:6 ESV

For by him were all things created, that are in heaven, and that are in earth, visible and invisible, whether they be thrones, or dominions, or principalities, or powers: all things

were created by him, and for him: And he is before all things, and by him all things consist.
Colossians 1:16-20 KJV

All scripture *is* given by inspiration of God, and *is* profitable for doctrine, for reproof, for correction, for instruction in righteousness, that the man of God may be complete, thoroughly equipped for every good work.
2 Timothy 3:16-17 NKJV

Love is patient and kind; love does not envy or boast; it is not arrogant or rude. It does not insist on its own way; it is not irritable or resentful; it does not rejoice at wrongdoing, but rejoices with the truth. Love bears all things, believes all things, hopes all things, endures all things.
I Corinthians 13:4-7 ESV

But God chose what is foolish in the world to shame the wise; God chose what is weak in the world to shame the strong;
I Corinthians 1:27 ESV

Claiming to be wise, they became fools, and exchanged the glory of the immortal God for images resembling mortal man and birds and animals and creeping things. Therefore God gave them up in the lusts of their hearts to impurity, to the dishonoring of their bodies among themselves, because they exchanged the truth about God for a lie and worshiped and served the creature rather than the Creator, who is blessed forever! Amen!
Romans 1:22-25 ESV

Heal me, O Lord, and I shall be healed; save me, and I shall be saved, for you are my praise.
Jeremiah 17:14 ESV

And Jesus went about all Galilee, teaching in their synagogues, preaching the gospel of the kingdom, and healing all kinds of sickness and all kinds of disease among the people. Then His fame went throughout all Syria; and they brought to Him all sick people who where afflicted with various diseases and torments, and those who were demon-possessed, epileptics, and paralytics; and He healed them.
Matthew 4:23-24 NKJV

Confess your faults one to another, that ye may be healed. The effectual fervent prayer of a righteous man availeth much.
James 5:16 KJV

But this I say: He who sows sparingly will also reap sparingly, and he who sows bountifully will also reap bountifully. So let each one give as he purposes in his heart, not grudgingly or of necessity; for God loves a cheerful giver.
II Corinthians 9:6,7 NKJV

The thief comes only to steal, kill, and destroy. I come that they may have life, and have it abundantly.
John 10:10 ESV

For even the Son of Man did not come to be served, but to serve, and to give His life a ransom for many.
Mark 10:4 NKJV

Greater love hath no man than this, that a man lay down his life for his friends.
John 15:13 KJV

CHAPTER 9

No Formal Speeches Necessary

Don't insist your children listen to regularly delivered formal speeches. Just casually talk to them, and whenever appropriate (and not bothersome), add some godly insight. Teach them why you love God. Your goal is not to start a rebellion and drive them away but to excite them. There should be joy, joy, joy in your communication of God's love. If they are not interested, you need to adjust your method of delivery. Make it fun and fascinating. If you sense they are tiring of the message, back off a bit but don't forget it. Don't be like a pestering gnat that the child feels compelled to swat away. Let them digest the words and do not come across as demanding that they accept it, but rather come across as having belief in something that is a given, a fact, and a wonderful secret that you know they want to hear. But be genuine, be real, and be timely.

One thing I will tell you is of utmost importance: *start these conversations when they are babies.* Don't wait until they've already found an alternate pathway (or they've realized they know everything!) to start trying to convince them that you are right and they are wrong. When they witness, from the very beginning of life, how important your walk with Jesus is, they will accept it and adopt it also. When you make going to Sunday school and church, along with having a quiet time and studying the Bible, a priority, your children will likely follow suit. There is always a chance they will veer away from it for a moment in time, but as the Bible points out, if you raise them up in the way they should go, they will return to it. You're not raising a robot, so they will surely question beliefs as they grow up, but we are responsible, as Christians, for teaching them about the Creator.

> Train up a child in the way he should go:
> and when he is old, he will not depart from it.
> Proverbs 22:6 KJV

It is safe to say you should anchor your life and your children's lives by following the advice of this verse:

> But seek first the kingdom of God and His righteousness,
> and all these things will be added to you.
> Matthew 6:33 ESV

As they see you do this, they will fall in love with Christ too, and no formal speeches will be necessary.

I want to tell you how important a father's spiritual leadership is in the family. I found it to be all important in ours. Joe knew the Bible, and he knew the Lord, and he made sure his family understood and followed God's ways. His willingness to take on that role was everything for us. If we had not had his leadership, I can only imagine that we would have done considerable wandering through the weeds. It was critical in my estimation. His leadership coupled with his clear-cut, black and white honesty made me face truths that I would have otherwise liked to keep in that blurry zone of maybes. You know what I'm talking about: the biblical truths that are easily rationalized and paraphrased and minimized to fit your own agenda. With Joe, it was black and white. It was clarity and conviction and understanding that helped us so much to truly know God.

As a father, your job is to protect the physical, mental, and emotional well-being of your child. However, don't be confused by what I am saying. I'm definitely not telling you to be weird. You don't want your children to end up with phobias because you are so spiritually minded that you never come down to earth, or because you (or other adults) are discussing the underworld within your children's scope of hearing. Not everyone will agree with me on this, but I just don't think young children are prepared to deal with adult topics such as Satan and demonic activities. I believe it would be quite easy to put something of this nature in their little minds and have it spin out of control into some major psychological problem. Children are very perceptive, and elsewhere I have written that you should tell them stories like they are adults who understand what you are saying. At the same time, you should tailor the extent of the details and subject matter to fit their young ears. The Bible even says the following:

> Give no opportunity to the devil.
> Ephesians 4:27 ESV

> Be sober-minded; be watchful. Your adversary the devil prowls around like a roaring lion, seeking someone to devour.
> 1 Peter 5:8 ESV

This means don't give him any prominence, or attention, or a foothold; don't open any doors to him. I personally interpret that to mean don't even talk about him—that is, unless you are doing a Bible study or have some academic reason to discuss him. I say don't give place to the devil.

If you don't think that's radical enough, listen to this. Your father was adamant about not having anything in our home that opened the door to Satanic influence. No decorative figurine representative of Buddha or some other idol, for instance. We did not have books whose contents included profanity or took the Lord's name in vain. At that time, there was no streaming of movies and videos, but we were careful not to have DVD movies in the house that were ungodly. We didn't watch television programs that were inappropriate for our children because invariably they were inappropriate for us as well. We weren't weird, y'all, but we were *sold out* Christians, and as such, we guarded our home against the enemy.

> We do not wrestle against flesh and blood, but against the rulers, against the authorities, against the cosmic powers over this present darkness, against the spiritual forces of evil in the heavenly places. Therefore take up the whole armor of God, that you may be able to withstand in the evil day, and having done all, to stand firm.
> Ephesians 6:12–13 ESV

There is one thing that has impressed me as I've read through the Bible, and that is that there *is* a spiritual realm that most of us ignore. Warfare is taking place around us, and there are souls in the balance. And because of this, we were radical.

So, daddies, teach them the wisdom of your convictions and make sure they know that the decisions you make are always based on the Bible. It is amazing that no matter what your circumstances, the Bible will address them. Regardless of the question, the answer can be found in the Bible. Teach them to have spiritual discernment. Acknowledge your need for God's help in your helplessness. You are not perfect; neither are they.

Nico at the Playground

The ultimate goal is to lead your child to Christ. You want to make sure he or she understands the free grace God has extended to us and that there is a decision to be made. You want to be so attractive in your love for Christ that your children want what you have.

You are your children's first witnesses to faith in Christ. You will be the first ones to live out your faith in front of your children. So be faithful! Be genuine, and be tireless, and when you fall short (because you will), own up to it by asking their forgiveness. And be conscientious about this if you're never conscientious about another thing in your life. At this, you just can't afford to fail. This is much easier than it sounds because all you really have to do is love Jesus. Ask for His help, His power, His wisdom. It will never happen through your own strength, so there should be no striving. His Love will be sufficient, and the Holy Spirit will lead you. As you pray and seek God's face, He will direct your paths.

Make Jesus personal and very real to your children by telling your children your own testimony. Tell them how God changed your life and what He means to you now. This will be fascinating to them. Children love stories, and my grandchildren just love to hear tales of when I was young and when their parents were young. So take the opportunity to tell them your most amazing story of the transformation of your life. Tell them *with exuberance* how you invited Jesus into your heart, when you did it, what happened when He came in, and how He now abides there. Tell your children who was instrumental in leading you to Him. Tell them about the day He saved you.

Give them age-appropriate information about your life before you were saved and how it changed when you met Jesus. In my opinion (for what that's worth), it is unadvisable to offer your children specifics concerning regretful things you did before becoming a Christian. I just believe that this opens the door for them to do the same things, maybe to a greater degree, with consequences that would be even more serious or damaging. You've learned important lessons, so steer them away from making the same mistakes. Suffice it to say to them that you were not on the right road. You cared only about yourself and did not know the Creator. Now that you do, He has given you an exciting and abundant life beyond all description.

If you tell them all of your mistakes, assuming they will see the error of your ways because of the negative consequences they produced for you, you may find out that the reality is that most children (especially teenagers) will be looking for any excuse to do what they want to do. So, in their view, if you did it, got away with it, were forgiven for it, and *lived*, they should be able to do it too. They may even do it to a greater degree than you did, and that is probably a dangerous situation that you don't want.

Explain to them how much God loves them and how He wants to live in their hearts too. This is a story you can tell and retell. After all, it's an exciting story of redemption and freedom and love. Make sure they know how to pray for salvation and what salvation means—forgiveness of their sins and eternity in heaven with God. Joe and I made a point to tell our children the story of how we met each other and how we met Jesus. The stories are intertwined, and the children loved to hear them. My children each became Christians when they were three years old. I really believe they each knew what they were doing, and, of course, that commitment and love increased as they gained a deeper understanding of what the decision meant and who Jesus is. But I believe, even now, that their salvation took place at that young age. So don't pass up opportunities to lead them to Christ. Once they have given their hearts to God, they will be set apart as the Bible says they will be.

> Do not be conformed to this world,
> but be transformed by the renewal of your mind,
> that by testing you may discern
> what is the will of God,
> what is good and acceptable and perfect.
>
> Romans 12:2 ESV

Help your children learn as much as they can about the God they have given their hearts to. As they learn to discern the truth, they will be able to make decisions in their everyday lives based on God's Word. This is critical. One thing I found very helpful was a series of children's books that told Bible stories in poems. Each book featured a different character in the Bible and told his or her story. With each book, your child will learn more about ways of God. The name of this series is Arch Books. The books are simple yet informative, and they are illustrated to catch a child's eye. When I was about to read one of these books to my children, I would stimulate your interest by telling you we were going to read about a hero in the Bible. I would make a big deal out of it, and if I was excited, you all would be excited too! We would read the stories over and over again, adding new ones all along. There are surely many new books with even better content and illustration, but these are simple enough and teach them a lot. There are also many wonderful teaching tools online that will capture their attention so well it's amazing. Do your research to find these excellent resources, but the Arch Books are still good!

Reading the Bible will do even more than introduce them to their heavenly Father. It will advance your child's education in the fields of literature and history in a magnanimous way. Reading this one sacred book is considered by many to be one of the most critical paths to a broader education. Poet Laureate Andrew Motion believes all children should be taught the Bible from their earliest years. He asserts that without extensive knowledge of the Bible, an adult has little chance of understanding the works of John Milton, T. S. Eliot, Keats, Tennyson, and the like. So reading the Bible seems to be important for many reasons. It is the inspired Word of God, so no wonder!

> All scripture is given by inspiration of God,
> and is profitable for doctrine, for reproof, for correction,
> for instruction in righteousness …
>
> 2 Timothy 3:16 KJV

CHAPTER 10

Priorities

Your father announced something to me early in our marriage that didn't quite fit into my 'queen bee' storyline. He talked about the order of his priorities, and I was not first! He would say, "My priorities are God first, then you (me), then the children, then everything else." At first, my selfish nature rebelled, and my sense of importance was damaged. I had to think about that and process its meaning and significance. I was not first in his lineup of what was important. But after I considered this concept and understood it, I appreciated it. I am so glad that I am married to a man who puts God first, a man who loves God unwaveringly and puts nothing and no one before Him.

What a difference this has made in our marriage. The implications are great, and it has strengthened my faith, trust, and confidence in my husband and who he is. I know who he will be and how he will act in any important situation based on his relationship to Jesus. This was important for me to know and for my children to know. He would tell them that they were just passing through and that he and I would be together long after they were out of our house. So, after God, I was his priority. They understood the implications. And even now, they know, that they know, that they know that they can trust him to be faithful first to God, then to me, then to them. It's a good and necessary and biblical hierarchy of the family.

I can't tell you how fortunate I have always felt that I married a man who knew the Word, and loved the Word, and kept the Word.

CHAPTER 11

Wisdom, Words, and Ways

Even though I always tried to script my message for young ears, I did talk to you as I would have an adult, like a good friend with whom I could reason and expect to understand. I'm not talking about when I was disciplining you but when I was discussing significant matters with you that I knew you needed to understand from an adult's perspective. As silly as this sounds, I believe this is one of the big reasons none of you ever started smoking, doing drugs, and drinking (I don't think!) when your peers did. I would talk to you casually, not preaching but casually, as if to a friend. I suppose I used psychology, and a lot of it, if you get right down to it, because I would carefully craft my approach and what I said. I just used every and all opportunities to talk about the things I wanted to impress on you, but I would try to come at it naturally, as if it just came up because of something we heard or saw. I tried not to come on too strong or threatening. At the same time, I used strong sentiments, relating stories of friends and acquaintances that illustrated the ways you could mess up your life and have huge regrets. I tried to make it clear how the friend should have avoided the devastating conclusion to their story. Most of the time, I would use a backdoor approach, saying something like, "Did you hear about …" not specifically directing my comments to my children but talking about the poor decisions made.

    I would use people you knew, if I could, to tell a story about the hazardous effects of drinking, smoking, chewing tobacco, doing drugs, illicit sex, and other harmful things. I would deliberately try not to be confrontational, but I would warn you by saying things like, "Don't ever start smoking, because if you do, it's almost impossible to stop. I am so glad Daddy and I never started smoking. It gives you bad breath, and it will turn your lungs black!" Especially when children are very young (even two or three years old), they will be impressed by this and agree wholeheartedly with your logic. At that point, you have brought them successfully over to your side, and they will probably stay there as you continue to help them think through the dangers of those activities.

In discussing these subjects, I was very low-key. I talked to my children like I was talking to a friend, so as not to sound like I was preaching or trying to drive them to distraction by beating a dead horse. I trod carefully when I spoke. But you do have to speak. They will not get it if their parents don't talk to them, and talk to them, and talk to them. I wanted my children to hear my opinion and agree with it, almost without needing to consider another point of view, because on these issues, there really wasn't a worthy opposing view. With the world as it is today, a parent needs to pull out all the stops to make sure their child doesn't go down one of these deceptively attractive paths. You want to keep that child on your team and on the right path.

As I said, one of the most effective ways to get across a point is to use the example of people your children (especially tweens and teens) know who have experienced the consequences of clearly destructive behavior. For instance, a friend of one of my children had an uncle who chewed tobacco (we did not know the uncle). He ended up with mouth cancer as a result and had to have his tongue cut out! Well, that story was pretty convincing! But the idea is to be instructional without them really realizing it. Tell the story. Talk about the bad consequences with dismay in your voice. Sound the warning without necessarily directly warning them. Do it early and do it often. Let them hear about most of these things (except sex, of course) as toddlers and gradually add more details as they get older. Talk to them about making wise decisions. For instance, you might say, "That is so sad! That's what's so scary about these people who chew tobacco and smoke. It's not worth it!" You're just trying to make them think. You are giving them the tools they will need to be wise.

Remind them that their bodies are temples of the Holy Spirit and that they need to honor and protect their bodies. Their bodies operate best when they are given the proper nourishment and treatment. Talk about God's design for them. And again, talk about not having regrets. Start talking early, early, early, early, when you are pretty sure they have very little concept of what you are talking about. Before they understand what smoking is, or drugs are, or what divorce is. You'll be surprised how perceptive they are. But more than that, this is when they are receptive and not defensive. Continue to bring it up frequently throughout their childhood. Make your opinions known and make them count toward your child's well-being. This means you will have to be tuned in and not preoccupied with friends, social events, volunteerism, or work. I think it is very possible to even be too involved at church or spend too much time doing wonderful things for others, leaving no time for what's important at home. I think this is why having one person at home, preferably the mother, is so important. There is beginning to be a realization, and a wake-up moment has come, that has caused a lot of talk about how important it is to have the mother at home the first three years. However, I believe the children need Mama a lot longer and maybe even more as they head into the teen years. Still, if this is not your plan, you will figure out how to make it work. I have no doubt. But tread carefully with a lot of thought.

I think one of the biggest mistakes parents make is to be confrontational in the instruction. I don't know if this makes sense to you, but I see it often, when a parent thinks he or she is laying down the law, but they are sort of laying out a challenge instead. It provokes the child to anger and rebellion, and it isn't productive.

> Fathers, do not provoke your children to anger,
> but bring them up with the discipline and instruction of the Lord.
>
> Ephesians 6:4 ESV

There are definitely times when you have to lay down the law, but if you are deliberate and have these conversations when they are very young, you will have hopefully won them over to your point of view, and confrontations will be few. There is a fine line between keeping the child on your team and driving them away. And this is very important: studying and knowing your child and their temperament is imperative so that you will be able to craft your instruction to get the best payoff.

Whatever you do, don't leave these topics unaddressed until the teen years. You certainly don't want to just belabor the topics, but jump on them early, finding inoffensive, creative ways to talk about them. If you wait, there *will* be a confrontation, and it probably won't yield any effectiveness.

Encourage your children to use words that are positive and uplifting and thoughtful. There are a few words or expressions that my parents insisted my siblings and I not say. And now, as a consequence, I do not like them either. My parents did not allow us to say the words *hate*, *stink*, or even *kid* when referring to children (because a kid is a baby goat). These were the less offensive words that were off-limits in my family, so you can imagine some of the other words that are very commonly used by the general public that were highly frowned upon by my parents. We were instructed to replace these words with words that sounded less harsh and mean. "I dislike this. I don't like this or that. That smells bad. I don't like the way that smells." I can think of several words and phrases that they considered 'not nice' and offensive that cause me now some degree of pain when I hear them. They are not 'cuss' words or profanity, yet they still sound base and unpleasant and ugly. And they are commonly used in our society today without the least little bit of shame. I cannot list them here without feeling uncomfortable, as they sound so coarse and uncouth to me. We were not allowed to shout out that two-word phrase to make someone hush. Instead, we said, "Please, be quiet!" My parents thought these words were mean-spirited and degrading. It is true that when I hear these words, I cringe a little, because it makes the person speaking them sound crude, insensitive, unpolished, and unrefined. Even unintelligent. Choosing these words may also indicate to others the limits of your vocabulary. You will have to give this some thought to figure out which words I might be referring to. I just can't bring myself to write them!

I know that you don't like hearing this, and in your eyes, I'm totally outdated and out of the mainstream of what is considered the acceptable norm. All of my children have a more extensive vocabulary than I. In your considerable erudition, this is low on the totem pole of what is and isn't important. I get it, but now that the cat is out of the bag, let me say this in my defense. It's my contention that there must be a gateway to cultural decline and demoralization, which, if not checked, would ultimately lead to the collapse of civilized society. I apologize for sounding like a crackpot, but I honestly believe that the careless use of language might be the grease that first makes us lose our footing and sends us sliding. Now hear me out.

Everything is clearly more casual these days—our dress, our speech, our manners. But I think that in some ways we've also made society a little less beautiful, less interesting, and less compelling. We no longer have the time or the compunction to send a lovely handwritten note with carefully chosen words; our language and our writing is abbreviated in texts and emails. We are less thoughtful. Our thank-you notes are often now just three or four-word texts that say, quite clearly, "You and your kindness are not worth the effort and the time it will take for me to write you a nice note or pick up the phone and tell you how much I appreciate you." So maybe the cultural trend is also less kind.

Think about some of the expressions used by young people today, and ask yourself if they are really things you'd like to hear your child say. So many words that used to be considered taboo or uncouth or embarrassing are just commonplace speech now. The more you hear them, the less your senses react. But I tell you truth: the very second those words slip out of someone's mouth, they sound wrong to me. And I hope they always do. To me, if nothing else, they are just not very ladylike and gentlemanlike. When a person is dignified, polished, and refined, you recognize it immediately. They are composed, and they command the respect of others. Their language will just seem more elegant and tasteful. Would you consider going into a job interview or into the home of someone you were courting and using even one of those words I listed (or the words I didn't list)? I think not. Simply put, if you want to be well thought of, you will give thought to your words and messages in order to elevate the thoughts of others.

By way of ending this wasted argument, let me ask you to consider consistently choosing words that uplift and inspire. No one wants to hear words that refer degradingly to body parts or unpleasant bodily functions. Don't be afraid to demand that you and your children reach for higher ground. Higher ground will always be the safer place to be, because if the harsh words are acceptable at all in your family as your children are growing up, they will be acceptable words for them to direct toward you when they are teenagers. It's amusing to me to note how politically correct people have become, fearing they will offend someone, yet they care so little about the delicate and easily influenced ears (and eyes) of their children.

I thought that I remembered hearing this quote somewhere in literature, but I can't seem to find it anywhere now, so I think I may have made it up. I do love it, and it's something I think about often, especially when I frequently miss this mark!

Never pass up an opportunity to be beautiful.

Maybe it's silly, but I think that by dressing up your language just a bit, you are making the world a little more beautiful! I think you'll find that one day your children will thank you for being careful when choosing the words you have spoken to them.

Things that used to be considered too indecent to even mention to a close friend are now openly discussed on TV during the dinner hour among perfect strangers. Believe it or not, things like divorce used to be whispered about in hushed and shameful tones. Now, even TV ads are happily indiscreet. Even during children's programming, you may be subjected to anything. Erectile dysfunction. Constipation. Incontinence. Nothing is off limits and certainly nothing is sacred or private anymore. Sadly, the barn door has been left open, and the horses are out of their stalls. Those now wild horses are running roughshod over the daisies, and predictably, we can't seem to get hold of the reins.

As it turns out, unbecoming words are not the bottom of the degradation barrel. They are just the beginning of a downward spiral. Our young children are inconceivably and casually sending nude photographs to each other and sexting. The violence, profanity, adultery, and extramarital sex that we have become all too accustomed to in movies is now prevalent in video games aimed at children. Our young boys and men, especially, are getting an eyeful and an earful. Our children are being propagandized into thinking they should defend every form of perversion. There is a defensiveness about homosexuality that is so constant in our news and entertainment that is beyond the pale. We are to accept it all as normal, and we are to do this with abandon. No one is willing to express intolerance for any type of perverted behavior lest they, themselves, are held to account. Perversion is now definitely politically *in*correct to condemn. What, for generations, was considered by everyone to be wrong and harmful to society is now right. What was right is now wrong. But what does the Bible say, since that is all that matters, if you're are truly a follower of Jesus Christ?

And this is the judgment: the light has come into the world,
and people loved the darkness rather than the light because their works were evil.
For everyone who does wicked things hates the light and does not come to the light, lest his works should be exposed. But whoever does what is true comes to the light,
so that it may be clearly seen that his works have been carried out in God.

John 3:19–21 ESV

Woe to those who call evil good and good evil, who put darkness for light
and light for darkness, who put bitter for sweet and sweet for bitter!

Isaiah 5:20 ESV

For from within, out of the heart of man, come evil thoughts,
sexual immorality, theft, murder, adultery, coveting,
wickedness, deceit, sensuality, envy, slander, pride, foolishness.
All these evil things come from within, and they defile a person.

Mark 7:21–23 ESV

For you may be sure of this,
that everyone who is sexually immoral or impure,
or who is covetous (that is, an idolater),
has no inheritance in the kingdom of Christ and God.

Ephesians 5:5 ESV

And although what's happening today is bad enough, it's just a hop, skip, and a jump from there to the normalization of polygamy, incest, sex with children, and euthanizing those people we consider a drain on society. There is no limit to how low we can go. If we are going to stop the slide, we are going to have to insist once again that our movies and our games meet standards of past generations when the family unit was considered important enough to protect and held sacred. We're going to have to work at inspiring ourselves, our children, and others to do better, to try harder, and to raise the bar. And that just might have to start with our words.

Pay close attention to the matter of holding your family together, and in so doing, use your words to show your children how to treat a spouse. Never, ever speak harsh words to each other in the presence of your children's listening ears. Do not allow yourself to argue in front of them. They won't understand, and it isn't fair to let them be party to your problems. My grandmother, Mammy, gave me some valuable advice. She said that when she and my grandfather (Clarence Archibald Roberts), 'Pa,' had a disagreement, my grandfather would say, "Clara, let's talk about this later, when we've both had time to cool off." If you follow this admonition, it is much more likely that you will be able to control what comes out of your mouth, and you won't say things you don't mean. Agree to wait awhile to talk, or at least take some time to count to ten. Remember that even as an adult (and especially as a parent), you don't want to litter the lives of those you love with words you will later regret. It's clearly not good to go to sleep mad, but make every effort not to have the discussion when you know your blood is near the boiling point.

> Be angry and do not sin;
> do not let the sun go down on your anger.
>
> Ephesians 4:26 ESV

Just as hearing cruel words from someone you love can be devastating to a relationship, withholding words that could easily resolve a problem can be just as harmful. If you walk away from a disagreement, failing to address a problem, you are denying that person something precious, and that can actually be a form of punishment. Your indifference or refusal to come to the bargaining table then becomes a formidable weapon. When you said your vows, you committed to love your spouse for the rest of your life. How could you then refuse to give them the peace that only you can give? You will surely reap the rewards of that decision. Instead, you have to make sure that you give them the satisfaction of clearing the air.

Sometimes it is better to say nothing at all. When the issue is not that important, let it go. Don't harp on every possible injustice and relish every opportunity to argue about silly things. Life is just too short. Try hard to do just the opposite. Let marginally important offences and misunderstandings go. Think about whether it makes sense to cultivate good memories or bad. Remember that *you* have things too that your spouse has to put up with. No one is perfect, and part of the wonder of marriage is that you learn many virtues in the living out of that bond. So don't be touchy or overly sensitive or dramatic. The Bible says not to be easily offended. Focus on helping each other be the best you can be.

> Not to be quickly shaken in mind or alarmed,
> either by a spirit or a spoken word.
>
> 2 Thessalonians 2:2 ESV

An arguing, nitpicking couple repels everyone they come in contact with, including their children. But love attracts everyone. A friend of mine died the other day, and just a few days before she left this earth, she gave her only son the greatest piece of wisdom she possessed. She told him to love his wife and told his wife to love and care for her beloved son. She said only this:

Just love each other. It's just that simple, and that's all there is to it!

Remind yourself often of the *words* in your vows and the commitment you made, because if you stick by what you said, it will make all the difference in the world to you, your spouse, your children, and actually, to generations to come. It's your responsibility, not your spouse's.

Another grand piece of advice I received from my grandmother when I was old enough to contemplate marrying my sweetheart was that both partners give 110 percent to the marriage. The woman does, and the man does. No less will suffice. And be the first to forgive and to ask for forgiveness.

I want to mention a word that your daddy and I decided to erase from our vocabulary the day we got married. That word is '*divorce*.' We agreed to pretend it was not in our vocabulary, and we have always adhered to that decision. It is a wise thing to do. When you are mad, it is easy to start throwing around threats and saying things you don't mean. But once you say divorce, you begin to get more and more comfortable with the word, then the idea, and before you know it, it becomes an acceptable reality. So the best remedy is to never say it. Not once. No threats.

I think your marriage should be filled with days and moments of trying to find ways to win your spouse's love all over again. If we all did this and treated each other as though we were still courting each other, we would have much more fun, significantly more laughter and a gracious plenty more love.

I heard someone say that the secret to forbearance is respect and trust, meaning that one is more willing to forbear someone else's faults and missteps when they respect and trust that person. We all have unattractive behavior from time to time, and we all need our spouse's forbearance. The person who said this about forbearance had, herself, experienced this. She had a husband who played tennis at dawn. And every single day, after his match, he came home and prepared a tray of muffins and juice for her and delivered it to her in bed. This is a small but significant act of love, and in return, he received respect, trust, and forbearance! Try your version of this love thing, because I'm sure it works every time. My grandmother, Mammy, once told me, "Love begets love." She was so right. When you love your spouse demonstratively, your spouse will love you back. And on top of this, one of the most effective things you can do to raise a secure and happy child is to love each other. Be willing to forgive your spouse first, even when it is not your fault. Be ready to give 110 percent. You'll be amazed at how this one act will affect the person you love—and yourself.

Mammy loved people, and one day she told me something I'll never forget:

Always look for the good in people, because you're going to see the bad anyway. You can find something you love in every person.

    This little piece of wisdom applies to your spouse and your children as well as other people. I knew a couple who decided they would each make a list of words that described what they didn't like about each other. So they gave it some thought and came up with all of the things that bothered them or made them mad about the person they had vowed to love forever. Needless to say, their marriage quickly ended in divorce. So focus on those things that you love and adore about your spouse and your children. Focus on the blessing that they are and the gifts God gave them that you are fortunate enough to enjoy. Put those things into words and use those words frequently. Observe and reaffirm all of your children and your spouse with genuine praise for the positive traits you recognize in them and do this as often as the opportunity arises. Teach your children Mammy's saying, and they will marvel at the different types of people that God has made and be more likely to exhibit unconditional love. They will look for the good, the talents, and the beauty of those they meet and the one they fall in love with.

    There have been times when my red hair has gotten the best of me and I've gotten mad at your father for something. It dawned on me some years after we got married that when this happened, it helped immensely for me to reflect on what I love about him and the many things he has done to show me his love for me. I think about all of the kind words he has said to me, and I then have to smile. It reminds me that he is a genuinely good person and he loves me. Just remembering how he loves me changes my attitude. Like my friend said, just love each other. This is pivotal and will mean everything to your child for years and years to come. Parents that loved each other through the storms is pivotal. It changes so many things and avoids so many pitfalls and calamities. That's why God's instructions to love and respect each other are so important. If followed, you and your relationship are protected.

    Before they become teenagers, you will have to address some topics that aren't so fun to address. The *way* you handle this is crucial. And *you* need to handle it. Don't leave it up to someone else. It is up to you to gather your courage and talk to your child about *the act of marriage.* Mothers, take your daughters, and, fathers, take your sons, at the appropriate age, on a trip or whatever you think will afford the best opportunity to talk candidly with them about the biology of this act. You want to catch them before someone else does. There is something important about taking on this task yourself and not leaving it up to a book or a friend. Because when you talk to them, you have taken away the wall of secrecy and unveiled a mystery. It's with you, and you are their guide. Not someone else. Then they will know they can approach you, if they need to, to get your opinion. And that is what you want.

You are able to tell them that this is a God-given expression of love between two married people and explain God's design in a way that the world never would. The thrill of doing something grown-up that Mama and Daddy don't know about is eliminated.

I think we told our children when they were entering the fourth grade. Looking back, I'm not sure they were ready for the discussion! When I told Katherine, she exclaimed, "I've never seen y'all do that! I want to see you do that!" I'm sure that reaction speaks to the innocence that we had preserved by not having cable TV and not allowing you to attend PG movies. We chose the timing based on what we heard was going on in the schools. We wanted to tell them before friends started talking about it and make sure they understood how a baby is conceived and when a baby can be conceived. Since this information is certainly more important when they are a bit older, it will be appropriate then to give them a book that clearly gives the facts of conception. Even though you want this to be clinical and factual, be sure that the talk is guided by the principles in the Bible. They should know that it is God's opinion of sex and marriage that counts. It's not your opinion that matters. As they are approaching middle school, have something to hand them that includes all the many Bible verses that address the issue of God's blessing on the institution of marriage and His warnings against fornication and adultery. You may also want to give them something tangible to remind them that the act of marriage is to be saved for marriage. We gave Katherine a sterling silver "key to her heart" necklace and explained the meaning. This is also a good time to talk to them about laying the foundation for a good life by making wise decisions. They should consider the best order for life's big moments, such as getting an undergraduate education first, then a college degree, then marriage, and then having children.

Spell out the biology clearly. Leave no what-ifs unaddressed. At some point, while they are speeding toward becoming a teen, make sure you tell them how quickly conception happens, when it happens in a woman's cycle, and how very soon the embryo has a beating heart and becomes a living soul. Talk about abortion and the sanctity of life. Otherwise, today, the media, the schools, and their friends will tell them how easy it is to have an abortion if they should "get caught." This is such a critical issue and one that many disagree on. In my opinion, at the moment of conception, God has created a living soul.

When your children are a little older, speak openly about God's best, and make it clear that God's best is not living with someone outside of marriage. Make sure they understand, when you feel they can understand, that living with someone outside of the marriage covenant is unacceptable to God and is certainly not an option for us as Christians. Let them know that you would be astounded by it. If you have a great relationship with them, you should be able to broach the subject without having them become rebellious or defensive. Remember, you want them on your side. You can sort of joke about it to keep from sounding like you are lording it over your teenager or grown child, but at the same time, be sure they know that you *seriously* would not put up with that. Tell them that even if they were twenty-five years old, you would be extremely upset and that it would not go pleasantly. Then explain why you feel the way you do. I think I told mine all of this and mentioned in a joking tone that they would have no inheritance. I'm pretty certain they knew I meant it. So many people gloss over this issue. They may say they don't agree with living together before marriage, but they don't really go to the trouble to explain why or express the depth of their feelings. They shrug their shoulders and say that their child is too old and that they can't say anything. They do this because the easy thing to do is to just pretend you have no control. Yes, if you wait until they are in college to discuss it, you probably don't. But you can't wait. Period. As soon as you know that they understand the subject and are old enough to talk to about such matters, find a nonthreatening way to bring it up. For instance, someone you know is doing it. Come to think of it, that may be one subject that I didn't try to take the threat out of. I made sure they knew how I felt about it by saying it in no uncertain terms. The reason this works is because of the foundation you have laid through the years. They know your love, they love God, and they know you have their very best at heart.

So now, begin when they are young to teach the basics and gradually add more information and guidance. Ultimately, you want them to think about how a moment of persuasion and pleasure can lead to a lifetime of regrets, disappointments, and grief for them and their children. Then, when you have said everything you know to say, read them the priceless letter that my sister wrote to me when I was in the seventh grade, and have a little laugh! Just make sure your child realizes it's actually the truth. Timeless wisdom. Claire's letter is recorded here, just as she wrote it:

October 4, 1968

I was so glad to get your letter. I am glad you wrote me and asked me the questions you did. I'm going to answer all of your questions and I'm not going to tell anybody what you asked me, and if you are smart you will take my advice. Georgia, you know I'm all for fun, don't you. I think that's fine, but sex in any form is not to be taken lightly. I mean kissing or anything. This is one of my favorite subjects and one I feel very strongly about. You may think it's the thing to do to kiss boys because the other girls do, but let me assure you it is not. Georgia I just can't emphasize this enough! Mama made me believe it and I hope I can impress it upon you. Billy Tucker and I went together for 1½ years when I was in the 7th and 8th grade. When we first started going together (Jan. 1st—middle of 7th grade year) for 6 months I wouldn't even let him hold my hand. He didn't kiss me until 8th grade. Georgia, I just can't tell you how much it means to the boy you love that you are a nice girl. You have to be a nice girl to gain the respect of those you associate with. You can never expect to receive the honor ... .(Illegible) or win class officer or anything else without the respect of your friends. I know you think one little kiss is no big deal. Well, you are wrong. Every single kiss you give is precious and should mean something. Georgia, kissing itself is not fun. It's not fun or meaningful unless you love who you are kissing. Sometimes when you are older or maybe even now you are going to be in the position where you have to say no to a boy. Believe me when a girl can say no to a boy he can respect her for it. On the other hand a girl who can't say no is considered a make out or her kisses don't mean anything! How much do you think a boy will value a kiss that anybody can get? He won't think too much of it. A kiss should make someone feel special. Georgia please take my advice on kissing! I know it's hard to believe that one kiss could mean that much, but when the one you love says Georgia who all have you kissed, you are going to feel pretty bad if you are free with your kisses … … .and I would give the world if I had never kissed one boy other than Bobby. You have the perfect opportunity to start out pure and innocent. Don't be a fool and mess that up. I think Kim does the same thing I do and always have. Believe me Georgia because I have been in situations where a good night kiss might be acceptable. But I hope you are smart enough to know that if a boy attempts to do anything other than kiss you that you will slap his ever loving face off! I trust that you have that much sense. Something is very much lacking in your moral standards if you are even considering ever letting any boy do anything besides kiss you! A boy may date cheap girls but he will never marry one! You better remember that! Please be good! And if you have any doubts about anything write me and ask me, O.K.? You and I are growing up in a fast generation (especially you). A lot of girls are bad, but they are wrong. Boys always respect and love nice girls. You can ask Bobby. Georgia be able to tell the boy you love you are everything he wants you to be. This boy may be cute but so are you! You can get lots of boys with your great personality. Have friends that are boys until you meet the right boy for a boyfriend. You don't have to go steady with every boy that asks you. Play the field and … .boys will like you because you are good and nice and fun to talk to and go places with, not just because you are a make out. Take my advice Georgia because I love and miss you. Write me! Be sweet.

Love ya-
Claire

PS Georgia: be able to walk down the aisle in a white dress! I've been aiming at that goal for years and it seems like I may make it very soon!
This letter is full of good advice. I advise you to read it about 4 times to understand it, look up words you don't know. Then I advise that you take this advice and live a good life not only for yourself, but for your family and God. It won't be easy, but if you want this bad enough you can do it!

Claire's letter was very effective! Apparently, I got confused, however, and thought she said to slap any boy who tried to kiss me, because that's exactly what I did! In the seventh grade, I went to a prom party (that's what we called it) at a friend's house. At this party, the signal was given for boyfriends and girlfriends to walk out into the garden or along some shadowy path through the wooded, empty lot next door (don't ask me what misguided adult came up with this idea!). It was orchestrated by the parents, and I remember my sister having a prom at our house in Eufaula, Alabama. It must have been the fashionable thing to do. No matter how fashionable, I found it rather comical that Mama would ring a bell, then resort to banging on a pan with a spoon to beckon the couples back to the house when the promenade was over.

Anyway, off my boyfriend and I walked, hand in hand, into what seemed like the woods to me. We were both very nervous, and when this poor boy got up his nerve to try to kiss me, I slapped him right across the face! I had remembered the essence of the letter and did exactly what I thought it said! My boyfriend promptly broke up with me that night, but that was okay, because I started going steady with someone else the next day. So I've always considered Claire's advice to be wise advice. That letter gave me the courage to do what I thought was right. And she's right; giving a young man the privilege of holding your sweet hand is huge. Don't skip that special step.

Margot Learning to sit on her own!

    Be sure you are available to talk to your children whenever they want to tell you something. Keep that line of communication completely open. It seems that the social mores are changing fast, and the loose behavior that has been taking place on college campuses is finding its way to high school campuses. So be aware of what is happening. When Katherine was in high school, she would come home from school, and we would sit at the kitchen table with a snack and talk about everything that had happened during the day. I learned more than I ever wanted to know. Another great opportunity to find out what's going on in their worlds is at night when you are lying down with them to say their prayers. They just seem to open up at this precious time. We would say prayers, and I would lie there for what seemed like an hour just listening to them talk about whatever was on their mind, and then move to another child's room and do the same thing. I loved that time with them, and I continued to do this until they were ten or twelve (at least!). It was a great way to end the day.

Be intentional about having the set goal of eating two meals a day with your children. Breakfast and dinner are so important to bring a family together and to keep them close. While holding hands, God is acknowledged, and blessings are asked, and everyone is reminded that they belong to other people who love them. They belong to a family and are an important part of that group. It's a time when family members can share and bear their burdens and celebrate one another's triumphs in a way that no one outside of the family can really do. Take advantage of that opportunity. And also give some thought to the wisdom of signing up for too many activities. It is so tempting to make sure they are exposed to every opportunity and that they are skilled in every area, whether it is academics, art, music, or sports. But as Katherine and I acknowledged the other day, you may be sabotaging their health. They are exercising, but you are so busy running around shuttling them here, there, and yonder you are left with little energy and no time for cooking when supper rolls around. Way too often, you are then faced with handing them fast food, which is really bad for their little bodies. It appears to me that America has an epidemic of fat children, and this means a future of diabetes and other serious health problems. Make sure you preserve their health. Crock pots are helpful in this department. If you must go out to eat, choose from the menu carefully.

Princess Selah at Disney World

CHAPTER 12

Teenagers

Now we are entering another arena. Goodness gracious! How in heaven's name do you get your children through the treacherous teenage years? There are so many incredibly attractive lures and deceptive traps along the way. My children's pediatrician had a print on the waiting room wall that was a colorful painting of many fly-fishing lures. Each lure was beautiful but had a menacing hook that represented one of the temptations your child will face along the path of life. It was enlightening, and I wish I had taken a picture of it, for it was an effective alert for parents. The scariest thing is your children will plow through those minefields with hardly a sideways glance because they are convinced that they are invincible and will live forever. God has put you here to stand in the gap, and you have got to be up to the task and up to speed on all of the possible dangers on their path. You have got to be on your toes.

Incredibly, we had no real trouble with our children during those years. The classic rebellions and "I hate you!" moments just didn't really happen, thank the good Lord. I think there was a reason. We had done our due diligence. We had laid the foundation of wisdom, good judgment, discernment, and grace—all of which was adorned with love. And we had prepared them for the lures to come. They understood the lies behind them.

Even if you have prepared them, this is the time to be totally tuned in to what your children are doing, who they are with, and where they are. Think of toddlers just learning to walk. They require constant supervision. You cannot take your eyes off of children this age for a second, because in one split second they could fall against a sharp object and wind up with a permanent scar or something much worse. Well, teenagers are sort of like toddlers, just in a bigger, more complicated arena. They are learning to take their first steps out into the world, so you, as their parent, cannot afford to turn a blind eye or leave outcomes to chance. The goal is to get them through these years without regrets and without permanent damage. The goal is also to do this *without appearing to be doing this.*

So now is the time to discuss the road ahead with all of its temptations and lures. Talk to them like adults, providing them with frank information. Without saying, "No drugs, no sex, no drinking!" just talk about the consequences of doing these things and look into their eyes to convey your will and your hope that they will not get involved in these life-wrecking activities. You want to impress them with the absolute truth of what you are warning them about and the gravity of your strong feelings. Still, this is to be a conversation and not a sermon or a demand. Remember, this conversation began when they were tiny little things on a very simple level. They are already familiar with the dangers and your views on those dangers, and now they need to make up their minds (hopefully recommitting their previously formed convictions) about how they will behave before they are in the middle of a situation in which a bad decision could yield life-altering compromise. It's time now to make sure they have given considerable thought to what they want their futures to be and what they want their own character to be. Having a close relationship with Jesus is the key, because with a head and heart knowledge of Jesus, the foundation of their character is already established. And you can be sure that Gigi and Joe Daddy have been praying for years that your children would invite Jesus into their hearts early and have an intimate relationship with Him from their childhood.

You make known to me the path of life;
in your presence there is fullness of joy; at your right hand are pleasures forevermore.

Psalm 16:11 ESV

Though you have not seen him, you love him. Though you do not now see him, you believe in him and rejoice with joy that is inexpressible and filled with glory. 1 Peter 1:8 ESV

It's amazing to me how important the parents' decisions are in these years. Choosing a school is not just choosing their academic curriculum. You are choosing a life path that can include everything from how deep their relationship with God grows, to whether or not they have Christian friends who are kind and supportive, to who they marry, to what profession they choose, to what experiences they have, to what connections they have when they are looking for employment. It's hard to believe that all of that hinges on where you send them to school. So, of course, you will just have to pray for God's divine guidance and even intervention in the matter. Pray that your children will always be in His perfect will.

I imagine that by the time your children reach middle school, alcohol, drugs, cigarettes, and even sex will be things they will have to contend with. It's more critical than ever that they be equipped to make wise decisions about what's right and what's wrong, what's safe and what's not. To make these decisions, they will need the facts.

Let's start with alcohol. They should know that when you have never had alcohol, even a small amount can and will make you sick and will (at least to some extent) make you lose control of your body and your inhibitions. My mother, in her effort to discourage me from drinking, would say, "You have to know your limits." And she cautioned that even a little bit of alcohol may make you do things you wouldn't ordinarily do. She wanted to deter me by making it sound a little scary, which she did. At the same time, I advise you to be sure that your child knows what to expect should they try the alcohol even after all of your warnings. Don't ever intimate that you expect them to give in to the temptation to try alcohol (which would be underage drinking and illegal), but during your conversations, equip them with what they need to know should they find themselves in that situation. You want them to know what happens to a person when they are drinking, so that they are prepared to react with as much sobriety of thinking as is possible. In my opinion, if they know that they will not be thinking clearly after having a drink, they will be more apt to recognize a foolish thought and think better of any foolish decisions.

My mother is very trusting, and she never worries about anything. Though she loves us all dearly, we joke about how Mama could get word that one of us had died, and she would just say, "Oh really? That's terrible," but go on her merry little way. She was blessed from birth with this unbelievable ability to let anything negative roll right off of her like water off a duck's back. How I wish I had more of this quality. It has been great to have a mother who doesn't wine or complain, and who smiles and laughs when walking through trials. She also loves people and was always engaged in social activities with friends. She went to the coffee shop in our small town of Eufaula, Alabama, with friends twice a day when I was growing up. At eighty, she was going to the country club gym to walk on the treadmill twice a day. She is a very active person! She was a wonderful mother, but she never dwelled on any possible bad thing that might happen. (I don't know what happened to me. My children call me Head of Homeland Security). She expected us all to behave, and she expected everything to always turn out fine. I think she took after her mother, who told our neighbor (who was also our preacher's wife) that she just needed to trust Jesus. So this sounds good, right? To an extent it is. She's right about having faith, but in truth, I think she lacked the drive to make sure her children were on the straight and narrow. None of us got into trouble, but I do think there may have been a little too much trust in her teenaged children's capacity to make wise decisions. Or at least their will to do so. Again, you can't turn a blind eye to the snares that will be lurking on your child's path. You need to come alongside them in a big way.

So when it comes to alcohol, I would go further than Mama did. Though she talked to me, I don't think it was enough. During high school, I came home from a date with my boyfriend, and we were a few minutes late. My mother expected us to be home on time, and she would be waiting up for us. If we sat in the car in the driveway for a few minutes, Mama would flash the porch lights to let us know the date was over. That night, I came in, and Mama was pretty mad (which she rarely was). I'll never forget her telling me I smelled like a brewery. This was such an uncommon way for her to talk to me, and I could tell she was disgusted. I had probably had one beer. As I said before, I never drank much. One beer was enough for me to feel tipsy. Of course, I never should have been drinking at all. At that time, the legal drinking age was eighteen, but I was still underage. With trepidation, I went to my room and sat down on the bed. Mama had followed me into my room and I'm sure was about to read me the riot act when, thank heavens, something in the backyard caught my eye as I looked out of my window. Daddy had put a light in the doghouse to keep the dog warm, and the doghouse was on fire! In my tipsy state, all I could think to say was, "Is the doghouse supposed to be on fire?" Mama tore out of my room hollering for Daddy, and screaming, "Call the fire department!" I was literally saved by the fire engine bell! Mama never said another word about my escapades. Although I never did it again, I don't think her lack of attention to the issue was wise. I don't think my mother was persistent enough. In my opinion, she probably left too much to chance and too much unsaid.

During high school, my sister was a passenger in a car full of friends (as I recall, they were not even drinking), and the driver decided to take off on a straightaway going way too fast. They were unable to stop at the dead end and wound up running into a tree. The driver was partially scalped. It was a sheer miracle that no one else was more seriously hurt than they were, but they all left the scene covered in blood. The poor judgment of a driver with limited experience caused this accident, and you can only imagine what would have happened had alcohol been involved. Teens are just not as likely to make the same decisions that an adult would, and your children need to know that. You need to talk to them about that. If that child makes a wise decision based on information you have taken the time to give them, it might mean the difference between life and death. So take the time to talk.

As an aside, my mother actually did take the time to give me some valuable advice about things to watch for when driving that I have carried with me into adulthood. I think of them often. Her advice is worth passing on to your children. When passing a car parallel parked on the street, look under the car as you approach it to watch for children walking into your path. When you are driving on a highway, particularly a two-lane highway, scan the shoulder of the road to evaluate where you would be able to go if someone or something came into your lane. In other words, have a plan. My father always warned us to never, ever swerve for an animal. It could cost you your life. He also cautioned us repeatedly about the danger of running off the shoulder and how calamitous it would be to jerk the car back onto the road. He said take your foot off the accelerator and gently and slowly ease back onto the road. If you are driving over ice or pooled water, take your foot off of the accelerator and coast through. If you are sliding, turn the wheel into the slide. Make sure your children hear and understand these things, because even when they are behaving, their judgment will not be that of an experienced adult driver.

Speeding, driving erratically, and taking chances that you wouldn't ordinarily take are all typical behaviors when one has been drinking. Don't be afraid to warn them of the possibility that an innocent person could be killed and that this could ruin their life. Even if they were not driving and were just a passenger in such an accident, they would never get over being a party to it. A split second of foolishness is all it takes. Tell them the true story about the time I was a teenager driving through my neighborhood with my good friend, Clara. Freewheeling and cutting up (we were not even drinking), we approached a stop sign and screamed, "Let's run the stop sign!" Well, we almost did run it, but thank goodness something told me to stop, and a second later, a car came barreling through that intersection. I'll never forget that. It was a real lesson not to do dumb things in the name of fun. You hope your children will be wise enough to stop short of doing something like this because they hear again your cautionary words, by virtue of the prompting of the Holy Spirit. Pray for your children, that they have the courage and wisdom to just stay away from drinking at all. When my children were on the road, I always prayed that God would surround their car with a zillion of His angels and that those angels would be the strongest, the most astute, and that they would keep my child safe and not let that child hurt anyone else. I would pray that my child would be wise and alert and careful.

And be not drunk with wine, wherein is excess; but be filled with the Spirit.

Ephesians 5:18 KJV

Drunkenness is a great excuse for behaving badly. It provides cover for mindlessness, and while drinking, even a little, you are much more likely to be persuaded to do something you never would have considered doing were you completely sober. So arm your children with this fact: if you are even a little tipsy, you will suddenly think the most irrational things make perfect sense—whether driving or compromising your morals.

Continue to tell them stories you've told them before about people who ended up either dead, addicted, pregnant, or in jail because of alcohol. Or maybe they just marred their own precious character in the eyes of all who knew them. I know people who had bad reputations in high school, and without fail, those reputations followed them into adulthood.

> A good name is more desirable than great riches;
> to be esteemed is better than silver or gold.
>
> Proverbs 22:1 NIV

Now you need to let them know that drinking too much alcohol can kill you. Alcohol poisoning is one thing you must discuss. Make sure your children are aware of the absolute danger of going along with anyone encouraging them to drink a lot of alcohol. Tell them stories, when appropriate, about college students who, during a hazing, drank too much and it killed them. Specify how much might be too much. Make it understandable and make it real.

Alcoholism occurs quickly for some people, so beware. It seems one can inherit the tendency to become an alcoholic or to have an addictive nature. According to my mother, we have relatives in our background who were alcoholics. They lived too long ago for me to have known them, but my mother knew them and would stress this fact to me as a road sign of caution. And it's worth noting, too, for you and your children, that it's important not to let yourself start the bad habit of having a drink every night. It can very quickly turn into two drinks a night and soon a bottle or two. Even if you are able to function fine during the day, you would definitely be damaging your bodies, asking for diseases that come from abusing the temple of the Holy Spirit.

> Or do you not know that your body is a temple of the Holy Spirit within you,
> whom you have from God? You are not your own,
> for you were bought with a price. So glorify God in your body.
>
> 1 Corinthians 6:19–20 ESV

My mother and father did drink in moderation socially. At Christmas and other holidays, when our extended family gathered, there was always beer, wine, and cocktails for the adults. I think that when a child sees this and the ensuing merriment (no one in my family ever got drunk, but everyone got fun), it gives license, intrigue, and desire to the children observing the scene. Your daddy used to always say, "What you do in moderation, your child will likely do in excess." Be careful. I look back and am thankful for my mother's cautions and for the fact that more than one glass, and sometimes just a few sips, made me sick!

An interesting story to share with your children when they are old enough to understand is the story of your great-grandfather, George Mortimer Adams Sr., who was a teetotaler. He lived to be ninety-seven years old. One day he was visiting his young married son (my father, George Jr.) and happened to open the refrigerator. In it he saw some beer, and he asked his son, with all sincerity, if he was one of those "liquor-heads"! Funny tales keep your stories interesting so that the seriousness of the instruction seems incidental. In this case, make them see what a great person their great-great-grandfather was and associate that with his ability and commitment to abstain from alcohol and other destructive vices.

We called him Grandpa, and he was a very interesting person. He was only about 5'7" and probably never weighed more than 145 or 155 pounds in his entire life. He was lean and tough and intentional. Self-disciplined, he never had a drop of alcohol, and he carefully watched what he ate. While at his farm, Twin Springs Plantation, he would stop working long enough to grab a can of sardines along with some soda crackers and a Diet Coke from his little country store, and that would often be his lunch.

Even though he was not a big man, his four boys (who were much taller than he was; one was 6'7") and one daughter had uncommon respect, love, and affection for their father. He saw to it that they minded him and respected his authority, as difficult as that is to imagine these days, since society now demands adults subjugate themselves to their children. The story goes that if his boys misbehaved, my grandfather (on at least one occasion) used a razor strap to spank them. You probably have never heard of a razor strap, but that's flexible strip of leather, canvas, or other soft material that is used to sharpen a straight razor. My daddy said that if he and his siblings were fussing and no one admitted to being the source of the argument, they all got a spanking (so as to ensure fairness), and no one got to enjoy whatever it was that was being fussed over. This tactic ended many arguments before they got started.

Now I don't know how often he had to resort to a razor strap, but when he had to discipline them, they knew he meant business. It sounded like he was never out of control, but instead, he calmly made his will known and made sure his instruction was followed. Even so, I am not suggesting you use a razor strap or any such thing, but I am suggesting that you make sure the child does what you ask him or her to do. Win the argument!

On the other hand, when his children had, in obedience, done something they were told to do, he would often reward them by telling them to go to a certain place on the property where they would then find something he had left for them—a note and maybe a little money. He showed his love for them by making sure they did as they were told, making sure they knew they could trust him, and making sure they knew they could rely on his love and care for them. His children all adored him and had an incredible respect for him that came from knowing he was straight as an arrow and could be counted on to love them justly. He was a teetotaler, and he accomplished a lot with his sober life. So take a sober look at how you will approach drinking while your children are young, and think about how that one decision will affect the next generation and even the next. Be an example to them. Express your relief to them that you never started smoking or doing drugs. Be a window into adulthood. Make them think about their future and what it will be like if they go down the wrong road.

Growing up, my siblings and I were fortunate to walk down some beautiful sandy roads at my father's homestead and at Twin Springs Plantation. Those roads now remind me that roads are important—the ones we choose to take and the ones we turn away from. We all need to examine the roads and the crossroads that we come to in this life and take care in our choosing. The straight and narrow road may not at first glance look as appealing, but it leads to abundant life. So don't be fooled, and don't let your children be fooled. Remind your children that the straight path is part of their heritage, and although not always the easiest, it is always the most esteemed in the end. God says to enter by the narrow gate, and that broad is the way that leads to destruction.

You can be a teetotaler and still have great fun. You can take part in God's idea of the abundant life, which guarantees you are going to have a good time. My grandfather had two farms—one in Columbus, Georgia, and one in Twin Springs, Alabama. He drove or flew his airplane to the farm in Twin Springs every day. He had a blacksmith shop and a woodworking shop at his home, and he was very skilled at his hobbies of blacksmithing and furniture building. He was industrious, and he was fun! He built a water ski slalom course in Little Barbour Creek on Lake Eufaula and began slalom skiing at the age of seventy. He had tennis courts built "on the place" behind his home on Hamilton Road in Columbus, Georgia, and his children became extremely good tennis players. One played on Georgia Tech's tennis team, one on Auburn's team, and one on The University of Georgia's team.

He was sporty and had a ball driving his two beautiful red sports cars (that I loved). One was an Austin Heely, and the other one an MG. One of Daddy's fondest memories was going to the Indianapolis 500 with his father. The other was flying with him. He was an eccentric man, and he was not without fault, but he built an exciting, honorable, and wholesome life for his family by taking the path not often traveled—the straight and narrow path. A person has to make a conscious decision to take that road and then commit himself to it. I have told you this story because this man had a vision, took the right road, and lived by his principles. And he impressed me. I think his story can impress your children and encourage them to live their lives more soberly.

I have beat a dead horse talking about alcohol, and I'm not finished yet. I am convinced that one of the best things your father and I ever did was not drink alcohol during our children's formative years. While you were growing up, we were teetotalers. We didn't drink a drop for three reasons. First and foremost, we had no need for it. We were on fire for the Lord Jesus and already on a spiritual high from our love for God and the revelation of His love for us. Second, we were driven by a determination not to cause you to go down the wrong path. And third, we did not want to cause someone else to stumble in their faith if they saw us drinking.

In the interest of full disclosure, there was actually a fourth reason we did not drink, and that is because I didn't like it, and if I drank much at all, I had a stomach ache or would throw up. But the first three reasons were reason enough.

One night, we were at a big party at the country club, where a friend, who was a born-again Christian, was having a glass of wine. Someone came up to her and said, "You're a Christian! I didn't think you drank!" Since this person did not understand, she most likely concluded that my friend was a hypocrite and not a sincere Christian. Even worse, she may have been confused by what she saw and used it as a justification for drunkenness herself.

We have known people who were big drinkers and seemed to be invited to all of the parties because they were fun and cute and were considered the life of any gathering. So they were heavily invested in time away from their children enjoying every social event. In the same category were people who traveled frequently abroad and to beautiful islands, either without their children or with babysitters in tow. There is absolutely nothing wrong with traveling and occasionally leaving your children with sitters, but I would caution you not to make this a frequent occurrence. They need you at home, and just because you can afford to do those things doesn't mean you should. The lifestyle that this initiates and fosters is just not healthy for obvious reasons, yet the children will quickly pick up on how much "fun" this is and determine to follow suit, especially if they feel left out or left behind. So if you can be a teetotaler and be home during these years, do it. It will pay off big time. You will definitely find that you are not invited to as many parties or events, but I've always considered that to be God's divine protection. Do you have the faith to be set apart and to believe that this is God's best? There is no doubt that the decision to distance ourselves in this way cost us friends, but it wasn't a hard decision; we just lived out what we loved.

We now enjoy, very much, a glass of wine or a little beer with friends over dinner, but with grandchildren present, we will be careful not to have even that in front of them. It's not that we think one beer or one glass of wine would be detrimental or a sin; it's just that we are convicted about our responsibility to lead our children's children down paths of righteousness, and we know this could be a stumbling block for them. Teenage drinking can be deadly. And that's a sobering thought.

Alcohol may be a major problem, but illicit drugs almost always cause a crisis. It is frighteningly common to hear of parents who have lost children to either alcohol or drugs, and this is astounding to me. It continues to hit close to home as we hear all too frequently of high school and college-age children who have lost their lives to alcohol poisoning or drug overdoses. Children full of promise gone forever. Drugs entice people from all walks of life, promising to make them feel better about themselves and make them feel less pain. What a lie from the chief of all liars. No one is spared exposure to these alluring lies, not even your children. So you better make sure they are prepared and willing to run the other way.

The dangers of dabbling with drugs and alcohol seem to elude even the most educated, sophisticated young people. To them, it is incomprehensible that anything really bad could happen. When they are young, they think everything and anything is safe. I don't know why that is, but it's true. That is, unless you tell them, and tell them, and tell them that it is not safe. Even into their early twenties, they don't seem to care that they are playing with fire. Sadly, many of our precious children are finding out too late that the fire is real and really out of control, and they are getting burned.

Outstanding schools in our area are now finding it necessary to begin drug testing their students. Drugs have become such a serious reality among so many students that a school very well known for its superior education is referred to tongue in cheek as The Pharmacy. Clearly, this school is not alone. There are many factors responsible for this situation that may be out of a parent's control, but I want to point out one thing that I think you can do to apply some positive influence and initiate some control. Don't give them any more money than you know they absolutely have to have. And be sure you know what they are doing with it. Now that's going to take some work on your part, but you have to do it. Don't give in to the temptation to shower your children with money so that they can keep up with the popular crowd. Make your children earn their spending money, and make sure they tithe with it first (give 10 percent to the church or to a Christian organization that ministers to your child). Encourage them to save some of the money. Don't allow the amount of money they earn each week to exceed what is reasonable for someone their age to need. Make sure you are aware of how that money is being spent, and do this by being interested, not by invading their privacy or being overbearing. Be a wise and caring parent, considering the requests of your child. Keeping their spending money at a minimum is smart, and their momentary discomfort and anguish (if they convey such) will buy you a lifetime of happiness and gratefulness. But don't deny them a little extra money when they want to participate in something fun that you know will be good for them. I am a big believer in rewards for achievement and good behavior, so I am not at all opposed to giving your child a special gift for a job well done. In fact, I encourage you to find ways to build good will between you and your child by planning trips together, purchasing something educational, working together on building projects, or just bringing home a surprise that you know he or she will love. Remember, you want them to love you, and you want to keep them on your team. This takes vigilance, thoughtfulness, and unrelenting determination to find paths that lead to a great relationship with your child.

In this last paragraph about alcohol and drugs and smoking, let me just say one more time: talk to your children, from toddlers to tweens to teens. While driving in the car, say very casually, "Oh, do you know what I heard today?" Then tell them a story that will make them think twice about getting involved with drugs. Add some facts to shore up your argument, but say it as if you are just pondering it yourself. "Some drugs, like meth, are so addictive that if you try them *just once*, you are hooked! Isn't that horrible? These people have ruined their lives, and they traded their future for a few minutes of pleasure. It's so sad! Don't ever let anyone talk you into trying it even once." You never want to be annoying, so try to limit the story and cut it off before you hear, "Oh, Mama! I've heard this a hundred times!" Just before they reach that moment, change the subject completely to something fun that totally takes their mind to a different place. Then, it will not seem like you are batting them over the head constantly with cautions and admonitions. If you do this when they are little, they will gain an appreciation for what you are saying while they can still hear!

You have a huge opportunity to influence their thinking before they are thinking—and before they are being influenced by friends. It's like setting Jell-O. When you pour jell into a mold and it sets, it should come out in the shape of the mold. That's what you are doing with your children. You are molding their character and shaping their future.

Sex is another difficult subject you will have to tackle, so hold on to your hat. Intimacy is no longer intimate. It is plastered all over the television, the movie screen, and the internet for all to see. Producers have put seduction, adultery, and perversion front and center in so many movies and TV shows that most children are bombarded with it from a very young age. After seeing it glorified in film after film, in advertisements, and on billboards, why in the world wouldn't your children believe that adults have given immorality their stamp of approval? And that is exactly what you are going to have to combat. So how in the world do you, as a parent, protect your child and preserve their innocence? I truly believe that the movies that are not good for children are generally not good for anyone. Daddy and I have always protected ourselves from temptation to compromise our convictions by not going to R-rated movies and by turning off the television when we know a scene is going south. If, in a movie, the character takes the Lord's name in vain, that movie is over. This demonstrates your love for God. In the same vain, we did not allow our teenagers to listen to ungodly music. Once, Joe happened to drive one of our children's cars, and as he cranked the engine, the CD player began to crank out music that was totally inappropriate for a Christian (or for anyone, for that matter). He listened to hear profanities peppered throughout the music, and he promptly called for the child. Before the child's eyes, Joe proceeded to break in half the CD and to tell that child he had better not ever have music playing in his car like that again. Take a stand when you need to take a stand. Don't give in to the temptation to let it go so that you don't have to ruffle feathers. If you choose your battles wisely, your children will know that when something like this happens, it is because you care about them.

Nico Building a Sandcastle with Her Daddy

The Code of Practices for Television Broadcasters, or the Television Code, was adopted by the National Association of Broadcasters on December 6, 1951. During closing credits, a Seal of Good Practice would be displayed, indicating adherence to this code. This seal would be displayed on most United States television programs fro m 1952 through the early 1980s.

To our desensitized eyes, ears, and hearts, it seems unreasonable, silly, and altogether unbelievable that The Television Code *prohibited* the following, among other things:

- profanity
- the negative portrayal of family life
- irreverence for God and religion
- illicit sex
- drunkenness and addiction
- presentation of cruelty
- detailed techniques of crime
- the use of horror for its own sake
- the negative portrayal of law enforcement officials

Incredibly, the Code of Practices went so far as to regulate how performers should dress and move to be within the bounds of decency. All news reporting was to be "factual, fair and without bias." Broadcasters were expected to make time for religious broadcasting and were discouraged from charging those religious bodies for access.

In other words, they attempted to protect people in the interest of the common good. Their goal was to preserve relationships and society's moral compass. After it was suspended, it became clear over the years that the Code of Practices had, indeed, helped to keep our society out of the gutter and individuals striving to become better people.

Think of it. Those who were responsible for programming content to be disseminated to the public adhered to this code because of a corporate concern for how that programming would ultimately affect the citizens of our country and our society in general. Imagine how different our TV programs are today, as we have thrown out that concern along with the boundaries of decency. The code became less and less a consideration through the years, while at the same time, we collectively decided to eliminate God from the public lives of our countrymen. The boundaries are so blurred that now no one knows where the boundaries are, nor do most people concern themselves with it. We've given up on being moral and have let immorality take over our television sets and so, too, our private lives. There is no high standard that we aspire to, and it seems that immorality, perversion, criminality, cruelty, and horror have taken center stage. Liberal-minded, enlightened folks have forfeited love for God for compassion for those who want to do what they want to do, even when it clearly flies in the face of a holy God. We need to take a long look at where this has taken our society. Our children deserve to be inspired to be better, and they should not be subjected to a constant barrage of indecency. If we have good sense, and if we love God, we will insist that these boundaries are brought back to bare. As Christians, we no longer have to live by rules. We live by love. But true love does not condone those things that God hates.

The code was suspended in 1983. Now they are self-regulating. But do you see much regulating? I don't. Turn on your TV and watch as garbage truck after garbage truck dumps trash into your living room and into the hearts of those who live there. No one is even astounded or offended anymore. We are all so used to it and have learned to laugh with the offenders. We are desensitized to the ways of God. I found this in my Bible reading today, and boy did it ring a bell:

> Thus says the Lord: Stand by the roads, and look, and ask for the ancient paths, where the good way is; and walk in it, and find rest for your souls. But they said, "We will not walk in it."
>
> Jeremiah 6:16 ESV

We need to be inspired to be better than we are, especially when society has taken such a big step farther away from God with the readily accessible pornography that exists on everyone's phones, iPads, and computers today. It is so disgusting that I can hardly speak of it. Fifty years ago, America's citizens would have rioted in the streets over such a thing as this. My children, you have your work cut out for you as you try to navigate these waters with your child. Do your homework. Be equipped. Know how to secure their phones and computers, and by all means, don't let them have a computer in their rooms. If they are in the family room with the family while on a computer, they will not be looking at the wrong things. Cell phones are going to be much more difficult, along with whatever new device is on the horizon. But it's up to you to figure out what to do to make sure they are not surfing inappropriate material. We didn't allow our children to have a television in their rooms for the same reason. But now it has gotten oh so much more serious. If you ever question how serious it is, just read about it in the Bible. When God's people drifted into this type of sin, He was extremely clear on how He felt about it, and He handed down the sentence and the punishment. He was dead serious about immorality, and I suggest you read about it. You need to know, boys and girls, that when God says something is wrong, it is all too serious, and you best not close your eyes to it. And you better not let your children close their eyes to God's way, becoming insensitive to it. God loves us, but He is holy and just. If you have a real relationship with Him, you won't practice sin, because you won't want to grieve Him. If it were me, I'd keep cell phone use close enough that I could monitor it without seeming to be intrusive. I would not let them sit in their rooms with a phone at night, and that might mean putting those phones in a place in your room at eight or nine so there's no question about where they are. Of course, explain to your child your convictions about limiting phone use and the dangers associated with easy access to the internet. As a family, discuss the need to do all you can to protect the innocence and godliness of each member and to please God. At some point, they will have the freedom to choose what they will look at, explore, and search for on the internet. But for now, you just don't want to take a chance on them searching for something as innocent as "the White House" and finding something horrible that will never be erased from their memory. Make sure they are prepared for things like this because even in your presence, it is going to happen. Have a mantra such as "Cell quell," indicating a quick response to getting off of a site. Try to make it lighthearted while still getting the critical message across. And don't be afraid to set a high bar with technology either. Don't let it be a god or an idol, which it could easily be. Express this concern to your children and make appropriate decisions based on the fact that you cannot let the phone control you. You control it. No phone use at dinnertime, in restaurants, or at other times when the family is trying to be together without interruption. Make the call on cell phones and make sure you manage them, not the other way around. Telephones and technology can be idols. Don't bow down to them. Texting falls in the same realm, and boy do we all have to watch this temptation. Your children will follow your lead. If you sneak a text here and there while driving, they will too. And it could cost them their lives or someone else's. Be careful. And if you spend time preoccupied with your phone reading (no matter how informative it might be and how much you think you are bettering yourself for the sake of the ones you love) while you are also spending time with your children, they will soon learn to do the same with you. And you will never have their undivided attention again once they reach the age of accountability. You will have indoctrinated them and ordained the practice. So think twice before you pick up that phone.

In the Old Testament, the chosen people of Israel had decided to go their own way, and they sashayed down the road of immorality until they found themselves sacrificing their own children to foreign deities as part of their worship. They had married people from other idolatrous cultures (that God had forbade them to do), and they had been "enlightened" to the ways of these idolaters. Let me tell you something. We are on a similar path. Some of the vilest things are going on in our dear homeland, and it's hard to believe that the most depraved forms of perversion and immorality are within inches of most of us twenty-four hours a day. Our cell phones, iPads, and computers unlock worlds we would otherwise never have imagined could exist. Watch out!

Aside from the perils and pitfalls associated with technology, we Americans have found other reasons to abandon our morals. As the example from the Old Testament, we too have embraced the morals of godless cultures. We have raced to diversify our country, unwilling to examine the effects of that diversifying. The influx of cultures that do not know or love the one true God opened our minds to the possibility of adopting the immorality and standards of these other cultures. We did this of our own accord. There is no one to blame but ourselves. We have fallen all over each other trying to put diversity on a pedestal, as if it were our religion, and with that has come an exchange of ideas ushering in new standards and morally abject codes of behavior. Our Christian heritage, standards, ideals, and morals have been all but thrown in the garbage heap. We have gladly turned our backs on the one true God and opted to fawn over any foreign ideas, their deities or lack thereof. Doing this has made us feel more sophisticated and enlightened.

So now here we are. Enlightened. And we've no anchor and no moral compass. My children were born in the 1980s, and sadly, their generation is hardly surprised by anything. Profanity, fornication, perverted sex, and pornography are all now commonly embraced and glorified by the millennial culture. Extreme desensitization is taking place right under our noses. Although the introduction of other cultural ideas and religions has played a part, it is just as much an outcome of our own turning away. Our decision to allow filth in every avenue of the entertainment industry. Music, movies, TV, video gaming, social media. It's appalling to me that adults have so carelessly orchestrated this barrage of immorality and perversion to be dumped on our youth. But they did, and they do, with a vengeance.

At a glance, one would think that there is no moral code at all anymore. Sex outside of marriage is now perfectly acceptable to many, many Americans, as is living together before you are married. The things that society has considered perversions for thousands of years are now being paraded out into the marketplace and promoted with great fervor as *normal*. It's clear to me that when we took God out of the schools and out of our public lives, we opened the flood gates for the devil to rush in. The same thing happened with our entertainment. And rush he did.

> Furthermore, just as they did not think it worthwhile
> to retain the knowledge of God, so God gave them over to a depraved mind,
> so that they do what ought not to be done.
>
> Romans 1:28 NIV

So your father and I decided early on not to allow our children to go to PG rated movies. Were they set apart? Yes. But since they have become adults, some of their friends have actually told us that they were going to do the same thing with their children—no cable TV and no PG movies. They recognized something good was happening at our house.

If you are a Christian, you know that God bought you with a price, and that price was His Son, Jesus. This radical news means that it is no longer a law that you are trying to obey, because that law was fulfilled in Jesus. Love is the key now, and love covers all of the laws.

So it's not that I am telling you that you must learn to follow ten thousand laws. Legalism is wrong. You are no longer bound by the laws that no one was able to keep.

> There is therefore now no condemnation for those who are in Christ Jesus.
> For the law of the Spirit of life has set you free in Christ Jesus
> from the law of sin and death. For God has done what the law,
> weakened by the flesh, could not do.
> By sending his own Son in the likeness of sinful flesh and for sin,
> he condemned sin in the flesh,
> in order that the righteous requirement of the law might be fulfilled in us,
> who walk not according to the flesh but according to the Spirit.
>
> Romans 8:1–4 ESV

If you love someone, you are automatically going to do what you perceive is best for them. You will not ask them to live with you before you have committed to them in marriage, because you know that in God's wisdom, He instituted marriage as a protection for both people. It also provides protection for any children that result from that union. It ensures commitment and loyalty and stability. It is the glue that keeps the mother and father together for the successful nurturing and provision of their children. It does so many other things too, mirroring the relationship between Christ and the church. Anyone who argues with this is just not being truthful.

True love would also prevent you from having sex outside of marriage, exposing yourself and your partner to so many dangers—disease, the risk of a child being conceived without the commitment of a father, and the probable poverty that would likely result from this. Or even worse, you may feel pressured to destroy the life that your careless union produced even though you both knew you were not nearly prepared for that responsibility. This is not God's design, and you need to talk to your children about this before they find themselves making these life-altering decisions in the heat of the moment. Inspire them to be intentional and to have a plan, which includes the purposeful choice of first getting an education, then getting married, and then having children. If they follow this path, they will be mature enough to guide their children to a hope-filled life, and they will have the financial means to nurture and provide for their many needs.

When it comes time for your children to head off to college, let them know that you are aware of the casual nature of things. I have been told that college students routinely meet people they know nothing about at bars and go home with them (to spend the night—to sleep with them). This behavior is appalling in so many ways that I just can't for the life of me believe it is actually true. How dangerous this would be just from the standpoint of possibly going home with a serial killer who happens to know that this is what college students do.

Sexually transmitted diseases, pregnancy, and regret are also looming possibilities. I could go on and on, but the main thing is that it goes against God's principles. And regardless of what I think, God made it clear that in His eyes, it is wrong. So if you love God and care what He thinks, you will obey Him. If you fear Him, you will follow Him. God's clear principles are there to protect us. While one of my children was in college, a student on this prominent college campus was raped and killed, and her house was set on fire with her in it. I believe she was a premed student with a promising future. I don't know if they ever caught the person who committed that crime. All it takes is going home with the wrong person, or letting them come home with you, just one time.

Sadly, you will have another issue to address, and one to discuss that was not even an issue when you were a child. That topic is homosexuality. I am sickened by the very idea, but again, it is not my opinion or your opinion that counts, and I would approach the subject from that perspective. It is the Creator who has made it crystal clear how He feels about it in multiple passages in the Bible.

> Or do you not know that the unrighteous will not inherit the kingdom of God?
> Do not be deceived:

neither the sexually immoral, nor idolaters, nor adulterers,
nor men who practice homosexuality,
nor thieves, nor the greedy, nor drunkards, nor revilers, nor swindlers
will inherit the kingdom of God.

1 Corinthians 6:9–10 ESV

For this reason God gave them up to vile passions. For even their women exchanged the natural use for what is against nature. Likewise also the men, leaving the natural use of the woman, burned in their lust for one another, men with men committing what is shameful, and receiving in themselves the penalty of their error which was due. And even as they did not like to retain God in *their* knowledge, God gave them over to a debased mind, to do those things which are not fitting; being filled with all unrighteousness, sexual immorality, wickedness, covetousness, maliciousness; full of envy, murder, strife, deceit, evil-mindedness; *they* are whisperers, backbiters, haters of God, violent, proud, boasters, inventors of evil things, disobedient to parents, undiscerning, untrustworthy, unloving, unforgiving, unmerciful; who, knowing the righteous judgment of God, that those who practice such things are deserving of death, not only do the same
but also approve of those who practice them.

Romans 1:26-32 NKJV

I have watched this issue go from being taboo and never mentioned, to being whispered about as a disgusting and perverted act that almost everyone abhorred, to a shameful thing people were forced to acknowledge, to a condition people tolerated, to something a person couldn't help, to an acceptable practice, to an almost "in" thing to be, and finally to a norm that we are all supposed to embrace. This was accomplished in record time by pushing an agenda to normalize this perversion. I have watched people, especially in Hollywood who have no fear of God, push homosexuality into nearly every movie and most television shows, making it appear to be much more prevalent in society than it actually is and making it seem so normal. The goal is to desensitize everyone so that finally they are accustomed, accepting, and okay with it. I think they have accomplished their goal.

Your generation has certainly been numbed to this perversion and would probably be offended by the sheer perversion reference. You see, the arrow hit its mark. I'm not saying you shouldn't love someone who is a homosexual, but you shouldn't tell them it's fine either, any more than you should tell a thief it's okay to steal. This desensitization is going to mean that your children will grow up thinking nothing of it unless you tell them that it is wrong in the eyes of God. They will hear from every corner and every front page how normal and how acceptable it is. And if you express a different opinion, you will be shunned like a person with the plague. But that's where the rubber meets the road. Are your convictions lining up with the Word of God? And you see, it is likely just a matter of time before they begin to put out there that polygamy, sex with children, and incest are all fine. Just watch. Natural progression. Just as marriage was sacred and now divorce is fine. Living together outside of marriage was absolutely low down and unacceptable when I was growing up—unheard of and wrong. Now it is considered wise, so you will know whether or not you are compatible. An open marriage is just great. It's a slippery slope when you step away from God. The farther away you get from God, the closer you think you are. You don't realize how far you have strayed. God is holy, and He says that these things are wrong, that homosexuality is an abomination to Him.

One argument that always seems to come to the forefront (to make us all feel guilty) is that you should be open-minded and live and let live. Well, the Creator of the universe was not open-minded at all about this issue, no matter what we think. There are verses to back this up. You should love the sinner but hate the sin. If it's true that some people are actually born with this tendency, it is a sad thing. But if you were born with a disease, you would not embrace it and tell others they should embrace it too. Everyone has their struggles in life, and according to the Bible, this is one God never expects you to give in to. Is all sin equal? Are gluttony, jealously, envy, adultery, fornication, pride, idolatry, and homosexuality all the same in God's eyes? I don't know. I suspect the answer is yes, because God is holy. We're all guilty and fall short of His glory. We are all faced with the call to surrender to God and to turn away from our sins. God calls homosexuality an abomination to Him.

Be careful to ask God to help you and your descendants walk in His ways through His love. To me, homosexuality has been one of the hardest areas to take a stand in. It's hit so close to home for so many people, and you feel like you're going to hurt someone you love by saying what you believe to be the truth. People whose families have been touched by this, whose children have come out of the closet and declared they are gay, have had to choose to continue to love those children or ostracize them. They've had to decide to understand, even to accept and embrace this lifestyle or stand against it and not condone it. I don't know what I would do or even what the right thing is to do. I know we are to love everyone and still reject sin. And I know I would love my children no matter what. This is such a difficult thing to wrestle with, and I grieve for parents who have been faced with this. No doubt the devil would love for this issue to come between parent and child. Though I am not sure how to handle all of this, I am sure that the Bible makes it clear that God abhors homosexuality. It is not a gray area or a maybe area or open in any way for alternate translations. Love the person, but stand by the truth.

An important issue may arise when your child reaches those teenage years, especially the college years. That is the issue of other religions and the question of whether or not they are all equal, whether or not they all worship the same God. If your child believes that Jesus Christ is the only way to the Father, it will be insinuated that your child is either uninformed or just needs to be more open-minded. Nice, well-intentioned people will argue that many religions actually worship the same God but just call Him something different. The truth, according to the Bible, is that our God is a jealous God, and He is in no way open-minded about this issue. "Jesus said to him, 'I am the Way, the Truth, and the Life. No one comes to the father except by me.'" John 14:6 ESV So, before you fall for that, or before you get so compassionate and so benevolent toward the validity of other faiths, think twice. There is a huge difference between Christianity and any other religion. Other religions are not worshiping your God. Period. Don't be deceived. If Satan can get a foothold here, the battle is almost won. If this argument were true, it would negate what Christ did for us on the cross. Saying this to God is serious business.

If you look around at nature, you can see that flowers don't usually just grow into a beautifully arranged garden without diligent training, manicuring, and loving guidance by a gardener. I have known people who foolishly believed that they should just let their children decide for themselves what they believed once they became adults. Now granted, you cannot dictate or demand that your child follow your faith. That would be meaningless. However, to avoid telling them why you believe what you believe so as not to sway them would be like leaving the garden untended. You will have confused children who may be open to any philosophy that comes their way. So in order to prepare for the eventuality of this argument that all religions are the same, explain to your children how Christianity is different. Then, when they are older, they will have an answer and a security. If you love God and are yourself a believer, you will walk on hot coals to make sure your child knows all about your faith.

I'm well aware that I keep going back to some of the same issues, but there are some things that undergird everything else. If you don't get them right, you lose your foundation. It's all about conviction and control. You must be convicted that what you believe is true, and that what you want for them is the best, and what you are asking them to do is right. And then the issue is control. In some ways, you need to start gradually loosening your control over your children when they reach their teen years, and in other ways, you need to be even more in control (behind the scenes). I can hear the sirens going off right now! 'Georgia is completely irrational! She has lost her mind, and this approach is just downright scary!' That's what I thought when I read over this paragraph. I sound like a complete nut, but still, it's true! I found it necessary to keep tabs on what was happening. I did it in a positive way, and it worked. This is where the rubber meets the road, and many parents just do not have the determination or the resolve to stick with the task. I have seen plenty of wrecked lives that came about because parents weren't willing to exercise control and pay attention to their children. It was too much trouble, so they let things slide. I was determined that was not going to happen to my children. It wasn't that I wanted to be overbearing (I think that overbearing mothers can have seriously negative effects on especially male children), and I hope I wasn't overbearing, but I wanted to do all I could to keep you off of that road that leads to destruction. And that meant knowing what was going on, which sometimes required covert operations. It meant clever approaches and nonthreatening approaches and, especially, fun approaches. It meant winsome, creative approaches and conversations that kept you on my team and off of the opponent's. My children thought I had eyes in the back of my head, and they were seriously perplexed sometimes when I knew about things they had no idea I knew. It was funny.

When it comes to dating, stick to your guns. Do not cave in to the pressure to let them go on a date at twelve, thirteen, or fourteen—that is, if there is such a thing as dating. When our children were in high school, dating was almost a thing of the past, and going out in groups had taken over. Sadly, the young ladies were not courted in the traditional way. They weren't asked out on a date and treated to a nice night with a special boy in an effort to win her affection. Lost was the time when different young men vied for a girl's attention. Now it seems they have been given a pass, and they don't have to put forth any effort. Perhaps that's because it's gotten so easy to get the favor of a girl. Or maybe it's just gotten too expensive. In any event, it's a sad turn of events for girls. I will concede that it's possible this change has inadvertently brought about more protection, although I'm not sure about this.

I assure you that my grandmother, Clara, had a lot more fun, as she enjoyed being wooed by many young suitors at the same time. In those days, a girl dated many boys at the same time, all trying to win her favor. And in those days, high school boys would try to get the girl they liked to wear their football letterman jacket or their class ring on a necklace chain to signify a steady relationship. In college, a boy who was in a fraternity had a lavalier pin with the letters of his fraternity on it. When he wanted to express his love for a girl, he would ask her to wear his lavalier, and if she accepted, she was then pinned to that young man. My grandmother was popular and was pinned to a lot of different boys, probably at the same time. She was pretty and fun, and she clearly had a good time! Joe's mother was much the same, and we still have some of her scrapbooks with dance cards filled with the names of boys who wanted to dance with her. These southern rituals seemed to elevate the courting process, and added a degree of significance and excitement that all of the young people enjoyed. It encouraged young men to put their best foot forward, and the young ladies to be on their toes.

You would look your best, act your best, be your best.

When I was growing up, and when my children were growing up, it was a great honor for a young girl (after her first year in college), to be chosen to be a debutante in her hometown of Columbus, Georgia, and an even greater honor to be asked to be in the Mardi Gras court or be crowned Mardi Gras Queen. At that time, only the girls whose families were old Columbus families were asked to be in Cotillion, and this is the way it was in most southern towns. Being chosen to be a maid in the Mardi Gras court, was a recognition of your family's contribution to the community. The Cotillion Ball was a momentous event, at which the young debs were introduced to society. It was, in actuality, a fundraising event that benefited the local hospital. But the original idea was that the young ladies had reached maturity and were being presented to society as eligible candidates for marriage. As a debutante, you would be honored with multiple (sometimes as many as 10) parties given by friends of your family, and then your family, in turn, would host a big party that usually had a theme, elaborate decorations, and a band. This all originated with a group of friends wanting to celebrate their children coming of age, and at the same time, raise money for a charity. It presented a grand reason to throw lavish parties while doing good, but it also afforded the parents the opportunity to supervise their children and further model proper etiquette. The young men and women learned social graces, how to talk confidently to adults, and how to handle themselves in varied settings and gatherings. Sadly, many towns in the south are no longer embracing this tradition, as it is considered politically incorrect. The political correctness watchdogs have pressured fine folks into doing away with another fun thing. In truth, even my own children worry that feelings are hurt because only a select few are asked to participate. I understand this, and appreciate it. I know that this happens and that they are right. Unfortunately, so often, such is life. People form groups with friends, and so it goes. All I know is that it was a lot of fun, and I believe served a legitimate purpose! My year, we had dances, house boat parties, wine tastings, luncheons, and luncheons, and luncheons. I learned a lot about life and adulthood, graciousness, and grace. One of the things I love about the south is that when there is an event, such as coming of age, or marriage, we want to make it special, and we make sure we do it in a big way! Another example of this is my parents' wedding. They each had sixteen attendants! Daddy always joked that he had to go out on the street to find people to be in his wedding!

We like to celebrate anything we can turn into a special event, and we teach our children the ins and outs of how to have fun the proper way. In my day, that included dating. If dating suddenly comes back in vogue, and your child is asked out on a date, use your best judgment concerning the appropriate age for a daughter to go out alone with a boy. I'd say probably sixteen, though under certain circumstances, fifteen may be all right. Just remember, you may be putting your child in the car with an inexperienced sixteen-year-old driver who may be drinking and driving, on top of wanting to impress his date with his hot rod driving abilities. Be sure your child knows how to call someone for a ride home—either you or a friend. And be sure your child has the confidence to say, "Stop the car!" Have a serious talk about drunk driving and its implications before that first date. If your child is a boy, remind him that if he is driving, he is responsible for someone else's beloved child.

Split-second decisions that your children will make can determine the course of their lives for years to come. So what can you do to help them? Help them understand what it means to put on the full armor of God. If they have this armor, they will be protected from so many bad decisions. Study Ephesians 6:10–17 (you can buy books that will explain this passage fully) until you understand what it means and how to apply it. The New International Version says the following:

> Finally, be strong in the Lord and in his mighty power. Put on the full armor of God, so that you can take your stand against the devil's schemes.
> For our struggle is not against flesh and blood, but against the rulers, against the authorities, against the powers of this dark world and against the spiritual forces of evil in the heavenly realms.
> Therefore, put on the full armor of God, so that when the day of evil comes, you may be able to stand your ground, and after you have done everything, to stand. Stand firm then, with the belt of truth buckled around your waist, with the breastplate of righteousness in place, and with your feet fitted

> with the readiness that comes from the gospel of peace. In addition to all this,
> take up the shield of faith, with which you can extinguish
> all the flaming arrows of the evil one. Take the helmet of salvation
> and the sword of the Spirit, which is the word of God.

You're going to need that armor too, so that you can stand your ground. As a parent, there will be moments when you might think, *It would be so much easier to walk away, either emotionally or even physically, than to have to deal with this situation.* And something deep inside you will want to run in the opposite direction. Or you might just want to look away for a minute when you know you shouldn't. This may seem all the more logical if you (Jonathan) have a tendency to be more passive and easygoing. You may think I am overstating the point, but you have to stick with it and keep your head out of the sand. I had all of these feelings, if only fleetingly, and I didn't even have difficult children. If you want the end result to be excellent, now is the time to double down on your efforts.

Love is much more than a feeling. *Love is an act of the will.* And practicing love, especially at this stage of the game, takes discipline. Running and hiding is pretty attractive when the alternative is to persevere through trials. Listen! This is the time to find your reserves and dig in your heels. If you know something is about to happen that will not be really good for your child, and you have the opportunity to intervene, by all means, make whatever effort is necessary to accomplish this. Don't wait, and don't hesitate.

Your response is critical and will also have a direct effect on the life path your child takes. Don't allow yourself to be lazy when you need to be taking action. Jonathan, you are so laid back, which I think is what makes you such a wonderful doctor. I used to worry, however, that your reaction time might be too slow if someone was really in trouble—that is, until I saw you go into action to save a child who was choking at a restaurant. I was amazed and blindsided by your swift response. Well, that's what you have to do here.

For instance, if your child has been invited to do something that you believe will, in some way, be detrimental to him or her, find a way to head it off at the pass. If you are feeling convicted about it, even if other parents are ignoring it and it appears to be somewhat justifiable, do something. If nothing else, just take your child out of the equation. Dream up a trip to take them on, an excursion, or some type of diversion that is fifty times more exciting and enticing than the undesirable activity. Use your imagination and creativity to do something. Find a way to accomplish this without embarrassing your child or another parent. For instance, if your elementary-aged child was invited to a birthday party where the parent is taking the children to a movie that is questionable, it is imperative that your first research the movie and make sure it is appropriate for your child to see. Sometimes the titles of movies can be deceiving, such as the PG-13 movie *Kindergarten Cop*. Of course, the PG-13 rating would have automatically disqualified it as an option for my children, but it is easy to read reviews for family viewing online. In the case of this innocuous-sounding movie, Common Sense Media describes it in this shocking way:

Parents need to know that Kindergarten Cop is a hybrid of slapstick comedy, character comedy, and the story of a violent, obsessed killer on the loose. Scenes of adorable little kids connecting with their unusually muscle-bound new teacher and his pet ferret are framed by gunfire and suspense and culminate in scenes with children in danger. Action includes (spoiler alerts): point-blank killings, a father holding his son hostage with a gun to his head, a little boy precariously hanging from a tower, and gunfire in a school. Numerous fistfights, head bashings, and a car purposefully hitting a lead character are among other violent sequences. The film is peppered with salty language, … Several of the kindergarten kids are children of divorce; some of the stories may be unsettling to sensitive viewers. A bizarre relationship between the killer and his mother (with sexual overtones), a warm kiss between lovers, and a silly scene in which a couple having sex are interrupted account for the sexual content. Drugs are referenced; the villain is a narcotics dealer, and we see a motley assortment of his young people who appear to be under the influence.

The title was deceiving, to say the least. You have to do your research. In all cases, if the movie or activity threatens to destroy your child's innocence, protect your child. When you can, though, avoid hurting feelings. You can do this by simply dreaming up something special and fun to take the place of the event you are trying to avoid. Come up with a trip and take it. Make sure it is enticing enough for your child to be happy about it, and make it happen so your reason is an honest one. This just helps to keep your child on your team.

The same types of problems will arise with your teenagers. People will ask them to do things that you know are not going to be good for them. The parents will want to let couples all stay at their house together after prom, or they will allow them to all meet there and drink at their house (because, they will say, it is safer than letting them drive around after drinking). You have a sinking feeling that something isn't right, but you are up against a tide of parents saying it's fine. Your child will be the only one who can't go. Now is the time to exercise (yourself) the old adage, "If Johnny jumps off a bridge, are you going to jump too?" Be strong and stick to your convictions. I am not saying that you should always try to be the standout, stick-in-the-mud, obstruction-loving, problem mom. I am saying use wisdom and make sure that your child's path is filled with wholesome fun that would please God.

It is imperative that you do the right thing because your children are watching you. If you recognize immediately that the answer needs to be no, say so without reservation and with conviction in your voice. Your child will be more apt to respect it and recognize your decision as a wise one. A child will sense hesitation and weakness and then try with everything they have to dissuade you from your mealy-mouthed decision. Conversely, they immediately recognize it when you are sure that something is wrong and you make it clear that you will not tolerate it, and they will accept it with little or no rebellion (or nagging and discussion).

Even if it becomes necessary to remove your child from a group completely (for instance, a school or a sport), stand firm for what you think is right, but do it with love and without bringing judgment on others, if at all possible. However delicate or difficult the operation, it is simply imperative that you not look the other way. All that said, remember what I said early on in this book: say yes to everything you can say yes to. Be fun but be firm when it comes to your child's welfare and God's ways.

CHAPTER 13

Beware! Both Volunteering and Paying Jobs Can Preoccupy Your Mind and Your Heart

Everyone thinks that volunteerism is so important in our culture today, but too much of it can have a harmful effect on your family. Be very careful not to volunteer for too many jobs. You can quickly become distracted by, if not consumed by, those opportunities to serve. Volunteer jobs can be just as demanding as paid jobs, and as your daddy pointed out to me when we were young parents, your first responsibility is to your children. That is your ministry. You want to get that right, first and foremost. If you fail at that, the importance of any other accomplishment will dim in comparison. So guard your time for your family. If you are able to lead your children to a victorious life in Christ, you have accomplished a mighty goal. I cannot tell you how many people I know who were incredibly community minded and impressive in their commitment to help others, who ended up with lost children. I have sat through funerals of prominent people whose accomplishments in the community were overwhelming and astonishing, but I knew their children had gotten the short end of the stick. I'm telling you, successfully raising children is a full-time job. So don't be deceived about what's important.

    I sometimes felt guilty because I would do more for my own family than for anyone else. I felt selfish because I lavished my attention, finances, and love on them. But I've considered this over the years and have come to the conclusion that if you spread yourself too thin, whether in an official volunteer role or by always being available to help a friend, you sometimes cut off your nose to spite your face. Your husband gets the short end of that stick, or your children get fussed at because you are at the end of your rope, overwhelmed, and exhausted. So be careful not to fall into this trap. Don't be deceived into thinking that God wants you to sacrifice your family for some other noble task. I feel certain this would rarely, if ever, be the case. So be sure you are hearing God before you act.

It is difficult for me to give my opinion on whether a mother should work or not because even though I was happy staying at home, I know that many women expect to use the education they received to accomplish lofty goals. They feel that if they don't use their talents and their education, they are failing or missing something important—maybe missing God's plan. Just being a mother does not seem like enough; they want to accomplish more. I know that, in other cases, it is just financially imperative that a mother work to help support the family. But if you feel you must work for financial reasons, be sure to sit down and count the costs and the benefits before you take that step. The costs of childcare, a working wardrobe, transportation, eating out, and taxes usually cancel out the financial benefits. Although it may not be inevitable (if you are willing to nearly kill yourself following through with the demands of a family and a job outside of the home), it is almost always true that *something* will suffer. It would be a challenge not to be somewhat preoccupied with even a part-time job if you are to accomplish something meaningful. Your children and your husband will stand to lose a powerful experience that would have come from your being consistently in the home. It makes perfect sense to me, however, that many women yearn to follow their professional pursuits or the talents they feel God has given them. I understand that, and I know that if God is leading you to do something outside of the home, He will give you the means to do it and still fulfill your role as a mother impeccably. So I know what I would do, but I don't know what you should do. Ask God to guide you in this important decision, but always keep in mind that if you elect to have a job away from your family, you will likely miss a lot of firsts, and you might not be there to guide them with your advice. If you decide to work, be sure you find someone who thinks like you do to be there with your impressionable little ones.

Former First Lady Barbara Bush passed away a few days ago, and I was so impressed with her life and with something she said in a commencement speech at Wellesley College. She never worked a day in her life and yet was so accomplished. She said in the speech, "At the end of your life, you will never regret not having passed one more test, winning one more verdict, or not closing one more deal. You will regret time not spent with a husband, a child, a friend or a parent." She lost a little girl at the age of three to leukemia and I'm sure was acutely aware of how important it is to seize the opportunity to spend time with your children. That time is fleeting and precious. None of the firsts will ever come around again, and the lost teachable moments will dissolve into years of uninvested time. Those are the facts, which I write here not to condemn but to arm you because you need to consider some realities in order to make this decision with wisdom and with your eyes wide open. If there are going to be regrets, choose wisely what you are willing to let those be.

Early in our marriage, your father and I decided to do whatever was necessary for me to be able to stay home to raise our children. That decision meant giving up many material things that most other couples our age enjoyed. New cars, bigger and better houses, decorating those houses with expensive drapes and furnishings, nice clothes, travel, and entertainment. (Now that I think about it, we sacrificed a lot.) Without a shadow of a doubt, when we look back on our lives, we both agree that it was the best decision we ever made. The blessings continue to rain down on all of us, and I absolutely expect that decision to affect generations upon generations. Maybe God just knew that I was not equipped to have a profession and be fully present with my children at the same time. I was going to be distracted, detached, and less focused. I don't think I had what it took to do both. Maybe I have a one-track mind, and the fact that I was not driven to explore a great talent made my decision easy.

My daughter and my daughters-in-law are so much more together than I have ever been. They are smarter beyond compare and immensely gifted and talented, so I'm sure they have aspirations that might make my opinion of having a full-time job outside of the home seem strange. Still, I do believe that a mother's presence in the home is an irreplaceable gift to her children and an even more amazing gift to herself. Who else in the whole world is going to treasure, care for, and teach your children the way you would? No one. Absolutely no one. And witnessing the firsts of your child can never be relived or revisited. There are no do-overs. Children grow up so fast—and *poof,* they are gone! All of those precious moments are then either precious memories or opportunities that are lost forever. Being there offers the family cohesiveness as you live these experiences together.

Just knowing that you are there provides a great deal of security for your child. Knowing that you will be there every day when they get home from school offers them security, support, commitment, and love. You are there to listen to their stories and hear about their day and give advice and heal broken hearts and build them up. As I said, I realize that you may feel a leading from God to pursue a calling, a talent, or a career. We are all different, and God's plan is unique for each of us. This is just my take on it and my experience. I am not trying to tell you not to do what you feel God has set before you. You will know what you are supposed to do, you will do it well, and I will be happy for you.

As hard as this is to believe, your child's homework may be a consideration when deciding whether to work or not. Helping with homework at night can be exhausting, and it requires energy from a parent who is not already spent. It takes a great deal of time and effort, especially as the child gets older—that is, if you do it the way we did. When a child (and I had three!) was studying for a test, I would have them go through the material, and then I would read every word of each chapter with the child. Then I would go back through the material and ask questions about every fact contained therein. I made sure they knew it. Of course, by junior high school, they did most of this on their own, though I did offer to help in any way I could. But for many years, we would do this with each child, and that is time-consuming.

Each of you will decide how best to help with homework. Most people think that what I did was way overboard and apt to create a problem for the child. They would say it would be more beneficial for the child to do it all on their own and learn to study without aid. Some parents believe the child should be "responsible" enough to do it themselves without help, and they find that this produces excellent results. I understand this, and I think your approach needs to be based on your knowledge of the child's personality. You will have to decide. The different approaches may also stem from a parent's own experience as a child. My parents did not emphasize grades. They told us to do our best and assumed we would. I must have overcompensated with my children for what I perceived to be lacking in my own childhood. I've always thought I would have done much better if someone had come alongside me and stayed beside me to make sure I understood and learned the material and did the work. Consequently, I wanted to make sure that my children understood the material before they faltered on a test. I believed that if I got them on the right track in the beginning—that is, making straight A's—they would want to continue on that track. I guess I was afraid that if they got behind or off the track, it would be very hard, if not impossible, for them to catch up. I have seen this happen to children I know who were in a challenging private school. It was almost a nightmare as high school unfolded, since they had not taken lower school seriously and were woefully behind. They just could not catch up. College choices, as well as professional options, were all very limited.

So this approach worked for us. They all did stay on that track of excelling. I will admit, however, that Katherine told me recently that she felt when she got to high school, she was unprepared to study for herself and to deal with her own tendency to procrastinate. I'm not sure how I could have helped her learn to read the assigned material when it was assigned (I thought we did this). Clearly, no approach is perfect.

Children learn in different ways. One child's logic makes little sense to another child. So study your children and teach them in a way they can understand. Figure out what their way is. It may just be a matter of phrasing an explanation in a different way. They may learn visually better than auditorily. You will have to decide what's right for you; just make sure your approach is working and that the child understands before moving ahead.

Clara and Caroline on the Beach

CHAPTER 14

Making Memories That Will Last a Lifetime

When we think back on our childhoods, it's sometimes surprising what pops up as memorable moments. It seems like the most wonderful memories are of the more commonplace occurrences. In my case, I remember being with my grandmother in her big front yard, just sitting in her wrought iron chairs. In my eyes, she was a very elegant person, and in this moment, she was just sitting with me. She was wearing a light blue, knit, shirtwaist dress and had streams of perspiration running down the sides of her face, probably from cutting roses in her garden in the hot Alabama summer sun (or maybe she was having a hot flash!). I guess, because of the tranquility of the moment, and because I liked her so much, this is a most pleasant memory for me and one that I cherish. We weren't at Disney World or a concert or a play or a museum. We weren't playing a game. We were just sitting together talking. Another vivid memory is of a warm, starry summer night when I was a little girl, just lying beside my father on a chaise lounge on our back patio, gazing up at a million stars. These special moments were unplanned but imprinted themselves on my soul and have never left me. These memories are comforting, and in quiet moments they catch me and confirm the love of parents, friends and even my creator.

I know my children have memories like these that occurred impromptu, but I also know they have many wonderful memories of occasions that became meaningful because Joe and I worked hard to make them so.

A French Café

When my children were young, we did not have computers, and believe it or not, we had never heard of an app store or Google or Siri or Alexa. We didn't have access to Pinterest or Duolingo or Babble. Little Passports was not around to broaden our children's horizons and familiarize them with different worlds. Back then, a mama had to come up with creative ways to teach whatever she wanted her preschool children to learn or be entertained by. So, one day I came up with the idea to teach my children something about other countries, and I decided France would be a fascinating and colorful place to start. I was great at dreaming up all sorts of ways to make a project fun, but the more I thought about it, the more involved it got. It usually ended up being complicated, time consuming, and expensive, but it was almost always fun! So, I tried to think of all the things relating to France that would be fun to explore. Language, food, music and landmarks. I decided that we would make it very educational, and the children would participate in the creation of a French Café. So, we made a mad dash to the local library (all of us!), and collected books on France. The children helped me find age-appropriate books on the country's history and landmarks, as well as books on French cuisine, the French language, and French Music. The search at the library was an exciting adventure in and of itself, and we came out with a treasure trove of ideas. We were able to find a stack of good books to take home with us, along with cassette tapes of French music. We invited some neighborhood children to come to our French Café that night, and we all had a ball exploring the possibilities for our café. The children made tall chef's hats out of construction paper for everyone, menus for our café, and chose very *French* dishes to prepare. Everyone was all in. I don't think any one of us has forgotten that night because it really was so much fun. When each guest sat down with their own chef's hat on, they found a hand-drawn menu listing our café's fancy French fare, and French music transported them to another world where everyone had to speak French at the table. The children were delighted to be introduced to all kinds of fondue and crepes that we had made using a recipe written by the famous French chef, Jacques Pepin. We all learned a lot about France, but even more about how to have fun. And now, that's a cherished memory that brings smiles to our faces every time we remember that special day.

Mud Pies, Garden Rivers, Moo Cows and Camping

There are a lot of ways to make memories in a garden. I used to let the children make streams with villages alongside them in the back yard that were quite amazing and required considerable ingenuity and creativity. On their grandmother's back patio, they spent hours making mud pies in old tin pie pans. I have a picture of my two sons in the back yard, half naked, and covered with mud. They had probably loved every minute of pouring mud on each other. Sometimes you just have to get down and dirty to make a memory.

Admittedly, I was not much on camping out. I liked the idea and wanted my children to experience it, but I just wasn't excited about being cold and dirty and not having modern conveniences. However, I did consent to roughing it one night at our country place. We have a building there that is referred to as 'The Shelter.' My grandfather built this structure to house water ski equipment and provide bathrooms when we were at the lake, and it had a large room upstairs for recreation. This is where we decided to sleep that night. It was cold outside, and although we were behind locked doors, we were exposed to the elements. There was no central heat and air, just a large fireplace. I'm sure we had a fire early on, but all I remember is how cold I was that night. About midnight, I woke up to the sound of shots being fired out on the water close by, and all I could think about was the movie, *Deliverance*. There we were with our three little children, like sitting ducks, waiting for them to come get us. I woke up my husband, Joe, panic-stricken, and he assured me that he had a gun. *In his sleeping bag!* If I was panicked before, I was nearing a stroke to find this out, but could not convince him to move the gun. He insisted it was locked, which he double-checked. My C.P.A. husband is a very methodical, rational person. He is smart, and typically cautious and wise, but I thought he had lost his mind that night. I have never been so glad to see the light of day. Now we all look back on that night and laugh at my fear of the scary woods and dislike of all things that are in any way uncomfortable, and no one tries to take me camping these days. Glamping, maybe. Or, maybe not.

No doubt memories *of some kind* will result from being out in God's natural world, witnessing the amazing sights, sounds and wonders of it, so make regular dates with nature, and your children will love you for it. Even if it's in the garden, climbing a Magnolia tree or making boats out of leaves and sticks. Let them help you build a fort or a treehouse or hang a swing from a big tree.

Chasing Fireflies, or Lightning Bugs, as we called them, on a warm summer night in the south is nothing short of magical. And if you should muster the courage to spend the night in a sleeping bag in the middle of a field out in the country, away from the city lights, when you look up you will see what appears to be millions of tiny Lightning Bugs flung out into the night sky. This sight is simply unimaginable as long as you are sitting safely in your civilized living room. All those stars twinkling in the night sky will take your breath away. You and your children will ponder the enormity and expanse of what God has made, marvel at the complexity of the universe, and experience a profound humility knowing how small you are in the midst of it and yet how important you are to the Creator. It will even make you forget that your toes are freezing or that coyotes are howling in the fields nearby!

There are a lot of cows living on our farm in the country and whenever we took our young children there, we would always stop to Moo at the cows. We would have a contest to see who mooed the best, and we would watch as the large herd of cows came closer and closer to investigate their uninvited guests, until the bull with big horns stared us down and made sure we took our leave. That's okay Mr. bull, we'll leave your family alone. We have paths to walk down and fires to build and graham crackers and marshmallows and chocolate in our knapsacks.

Subways, Elevators, Museums and Factories

Not to bore you to death, but the obvious is not always the obvious. When we were young, we could not afford to go flitting across the country or flying to other continents to expose our children to things they would never see in our hometown. So, I tried to take advantage of whatever I could that would help them envision what might be around the bend. We toured a candy factory (one of my absolute favorite days!), rode the subway in Atlanta (with Joe and I looking at each other with fear in our eyes, wondering if we would make it off alive because of some of the characters riding with us), and we visited the newest hotel in Atlanta that sported an outside glass elevator. The elevator's view was spectacular and a thrill to our children. I have taken my grandchildren on a similar glass elevator to the top of the Westin Peachtree Plaza to dine in their revolving restaurant. We've been to puppet shows and museums and plays and aquariums and zoos and ice-skating rinks and to Tea with Santa at the St. Regis. We have made a lot of memories, and we're just getting started. In these different settings, they not only form precious memories, but they learn how to behave with appropriate manners and curtesy, and they learn how to get around in the world.

Valentine's Day

One memory that I adored creating was the Valentine's Day scavenger hunt. Valentine's Day is about love, and through this scavenger hunt, we were able to teach our children in a special way just how much we loved them and how to love one another. Because of this hunt, Valentine's Day became one of our family's most cherished holidays. Every Valentine's Day, I would have a scavenger hunt prepared for each child. When the children were small, I would use little children's Valentine's cards for clue cards (or sometimes make my own), and when they were older (we did this through college), I used something larger. I would write three things on each Valentine's card:

- a reason why Joe and I loved that child
- a Bible verse that corresponded to that reason
- a clue telling them where to find the next card

Their last clue would lead them to a gift, especially for them. Joe and I made a big deal out of each hunt, and usually Joe would read out loud what I had written. Everyone listened to the reading of the cards to hear what was said about themselves or their siblings. With wide eyes, the child being spoken about would listen, spellbound by what was singled out as a reason why they were loved. It was a magical way to affirm them, to build up their confidence, and to make them aware of their gifts and talents. And with everyone listening, it served to strengthen our bonds and our love for each other. It reinforced our children's perception and assurance of our commitment to them and their commitment to one another. And it encouraged them to love one another and look for things to love in other people. What I wrote about them would vary from a physical attribute, to a style, to a habit, to personality traits, to matters of the heart. I often talked about the spiritual, such as the fruits of the spirit that I saw in them. I always reminded my children that they were beautiful inside and out, but I also reminded them that beauty is as beauty does. Your overall message to your children should be filled with joy, but every now and then, a dose of reality is important in balancing your message, and truth is a part of love. In these little messages of love, you never have to come out and say anything negative, but you can encourage children to be better in an area they're struggling with. I definitely did not make correction a focus of these letters but more so inspirations.

These Valentine's scavenger hunts for my children took time to prepare, but they were worth every minute I spent searching for the right message and the right words and the right Bible verses. There are so many things to teach your children about love, but one key thing they will learn incidentally from these scavenger hunts is that love begets love. My children's response to all of this love was indeed to love one another. I am including some of the notes they found written on their Valentine's cards in part because this book is primarily for them and because I believe that what is written about who they are is remarkable.

We are All Excited to Have Oliver, an amazingly Big Boy!

Katherine
A Greek Name Meaning
Pure

Dear Katherine Kimbrough,
I love your rosebud lips and blue eyes! They are so striking—no wonder a little boy told you today, "You know I love you, don't you?" How could he resist? I know he's just the first of a long string of boys who will fall in love with your outside and inside beauty. I can't lay claim to having anything to do with it. God made you and you are really *His*. Be sure that you are responsible with what God has given you. He sure loves you more than any boy ever will!

There was a rich man who had a manager,
and charges were brought to him that this man was wasting his possessions.
Luke 16:1 ESV

Dear Katherine,
Thank you for telling me so often that you love me. I can't tell you how much I appreciate you for that. When those words come from the lips of your 16-year-old, it is very special. They are words I take with me every day. They live with me and stay with me when I have to say goodbye to you. They bring you close to me every time I remember them. Don't stop saying 'I love you!' And always remember, 'I love you too!'

But the fruit of the Spirit is love, joy, peace, patience, kindness, goodness, faithfulness,
gentleness, self-control; against such things there is no law.
Galatians 5:22, 23 ESV

Dear Sweet Katherine,
The excitement with which you are approaching life is contagious! I know your friends must feel it because I do. I saw you come into Caroline's deb party and move exuberantly across

the floor with such a look of anticipation on your face. You looked so happy and expectant and full of fun. You have approached life at UGA that way, adapting but not conforming to ways that you know are out of God's will, yet finding ways to work around them and still have a great time. You've reached out and made a zillion new friends, found Bible studies, had dates with great guys, found a wonderful church, and made sure to support and love your old friends too. That takes real zeal and passion. It's very becoming of you!

> Because your steadfast love is better than life, my lips will praise you.
>
> Psalm 63:3 ESV

Katherine, My Valentine,

I love you so much for giving your mama someone to shop with, to share ideas and dreams with, to pray with, to be happy and sad with, to share emotions that only girls seem to feel, to share clothes with, to compare notes with, to hug, to appreciate ballet with, to decorate with, to tell jokes with, to understand others together. Thank you, Thank you, Thank you! Just think! I did nothing to deserve it, and though I am the most useless Christian there is, I was the one chosen for this special joy.

> Every good gift and every perfect gift is from above,
> coming down from the Father of lights,
> with whom there is no variation or shadow due to change.
> James 1:17 ESV

Dear Katherine,

I love you because you're a great shopping partner. Silly. Wacko. Expensive! But fun. We have a good time together and both of us being girls, we understand each other. We like a lot of the same things and you're a great friend. I love to go to Atlanta with you and wind up cracking up laughing over something ridiculous. We're proof that you really don't have to have drugs or be drunk to have fun. Thanks for putting up with a mom who behaves like a teenager half the time.

> Let what you say be simply "Yes" or "No"; anything more than this comes from evil.
> Matthew 5:37 ESV

> Do not be conformed to this world, but be transformed by the renewal of your mind, that by testing you may discern what is the will of God, what is good and acceptable and perfect.
> Romans 12:2 ESV

Dear Katherine,

Happy Valentine's Day! O heart of mine, I love you so much! Thank you for being my daughter. I don't know how God found it in his heart to bless me so deeply with a little girl like you. You probably were supposed to go to a queen to be a princess. (Sorry!) But somehow, I got you and I can't tell you how thankful I have always been. (Can you tell that I don't want to let you go now that I have you?)

    You have adjusted so beautifully to being off at school. I can't believe you are 19! Your childhood *zipped* by for me, and left me standing in my tracks, in awe, wondering how it all went so fast. You grow up, get married, and have children and believe that *that* is your life. But you find out it was just a stage in your life. Your children begin to leave home one by one, and you're back where you started. But not really. You're richer than ever, and parents see each other in a new light: the light of having watched each other accomplish a great deal. I am so proud of you for seeking God when everyone else ran out on him and did their own thing. I know how hard it's been, but once you find out that God really is the answer to contentment and peace, doing things his way is sheer joy. It's just a matter of keeping your eyes on him in the midst of all the confusion this world sets before us.

Thanks for letting your light shine in the middle of the darkness. Sometimes that light can certainly attract unfavorable attention, but you've risked that and I believe God is really blessing you for that very thing.

As Aunt Emily would say, you're a great gal!

Dear Heavenly Father, please help my children understand your word, that they are your workmanship, created in Christ Jesus, and that their self-image should be strong.

> For we are his workmanship,
> created in Christ Jesus for good works,
> which God prepared beforehand, that we should walk in them.
> Ephesians 2:10 ESV

Dear Lord, help all of my children not to be like many others around them who are out of control and dulled to the things of the Spirit.
Let them be alert and sober as they walk through their lives.

> So then let us not sleep, as others do, but let us keep awake and be sober.
> 1 Thessalonians 5:6 ESV

My Dearest Katherine,

I love you for sharing your day with me! I'm well aware that many children would not do this, and it has been a tremendous blessing. I've had so much fun talking to you about all the many things that happen to a teenager throughout the day, the week, and the year. Thanks so much for sharing it with me. I'm excited about what your future holds, and about the many roses that I know will be yours on Valentine's Days to come. What makes it so exciting is that I know while you wait for those things that you long for now, you are becoming this amazing person. God is shaping you into the most interesting, wonderfully capable person. I really envy what I see happening in your life. I mean, I wish I had been more aware of the importance of preparing for life as an adult. It means so much to develop talents, to seize opportunities, to look for open doors. It's maturing and growing and creating more and more worthwhile offerings within yourself for God, the world, and for your sweetheart. God's given you this time and protected this time for you. It's precious and so are you.

> The spirit of man is the lamp of the Lord,
> searching all his innermost parts.
> Proverbs 20:27 ESV

Dear Katherine,

Thank you, Katherine, for not being some *wild hellion*. I think I should tell you how much I love you for not causing the heartbreak that some children do. I know that you really yearn to be free of authority right now, which is *so* normal. You're getting that freedom gradually. And I thank you for being so responsible. It won't be long before you're at college and totally on your own. You're going to love that! It'll come with responsibility, as you continue to live within certain parameters that give life meaning--standards that God commands from us all, and rules that govern us all as adults. And also rules that the world imposes, that sometimes go unnoticed until we're on our own. I guess that's one reason you have parents. God kind of eases you into the situation and gives you some back up in case you're not quite up to the task. But I can see that you are indeed going to be up to the task of handling independence, and you're gaining momentum every day. I love, love, love you, and am so proud of how you are handling this time in your life.

> When I was a child, I spoke like a child, I thought like a child, I reasoned like a child.
> When I became a man, I gave up childish ways.
> 1 Corinthians 13:11 ESV

Dearest Katherine,

To me you are brilliant! You seem to be working so hard to keep good grades and I appreciate that so much. I never was a real brilliant student. I marvel at your organization and ability to piece unrelated facts together to make sense of something. It's something you are really good at. But more than that, I am struck by your creativity. Your ideas are so unique and you're always confident in the outcome. I have had ideas, but was often scared they would not turn out; I was scared to try them. I admire your boldness and certainty of the value of your ideas. That is what makes leaders great and innovators effective. You've got a lot to contribute to this world. Being able to throw your ideas out, no matter how bazaar, risking rejection, is invaluable. You've got the ideas, and you've got the confidence to own a restaurant or become the President. Your biggest ideas are really visions. I've always thought you were a visionary. A guy named Stanley just wrote a book about millionaires. He investigated their lives and found that about 80% of them were average students with average IQ's and made an average of 1190 on the SAT (you beat that by a mile!). They weren't able to get into the Ivy League Schools and had been told they weren't that smart—not smart enough to do anything that would make them millionaires—nothing that required genius. But they did become millionaires, and they all said the key was that they had good ideas, and worked harder than everyone else. I think you have one more thing going for you: you know that being a millionaire is not the peak of the mountain. And, you know the fellow who owns the peak!

>Dear Heavenly Father, I thank you for giving my children great talent, ability and intelligence, and for filling them with great hope that comes with believing.

>May the God of hope fill you will all joy and peace in believing,
>so that by the power of the Holy Spirit you may abound in hope.
>Romans 15:13 ESV

Dear Katherine,

I've seen a lot of positive changes in you this last year. You're one year away from being a teenager, and with every passing day you look more like a lady. And I praise God that you also behave like a lady. I'm so glad that God is letting me watch Him mold you and conform you to his image. Keep living true to God! I know you will. The love of God is so contagious. When you have God's love and His Spirit dwelling in you, you just glow, and everyone wants to know what makes you so different.

> This is my commandment, that you love one another as I have loved you.
> John 15:12 ESV

Dear Katherine,

I'll always be thankful for your giving spirit. You're always thoughtful and desiring to give and to share. You're always genuine in your ways. In other words, you never profess to believe something and yet try to get away with compromising that position even when you know it would make your life so much easier. No, you really do believe it and live it unhaltingly. Thank you for that.

> I press toward the mark for the prize of the high calling of God in Christ Jesus.
> Philippians 3:14 KJV

Dearest Katherine,

One thing I've noticed about my one and only daughter is your unwavering commitment to correctly managing your money. You are always quick to repay a debt, and you never insist on spending more than God has blessed you with. In other words, you're usually content with what you are able to buy with what He's given you. You're a good steward of your money. It's a witness to me, it really is.

> For you know the grace of our Lord Jesus Christ, that though he was rich, yet for your sake he became poor, so that you by his poverty might become rich.
> 2 Corinthians 8:9 ESV

Dear Katherine,

You are really a witness for Christ to me. I've never know a person so truly ad genuinely loving. When things don't go your way, you are still sweet and the love still shines through. Thanks for reminding us all of how Christ would have us behave.

> Beloved, let us love one another, for love is from God,
> and whoever loves has been born of God and knows God.
> 1 John 4:7 ESV

Dear Katherine,

You are a beautiful ballerina, and I love the grace God has given you! I have so enjoyed your ballet. I could watch you dance for hours and hours on end and never tire of it. I would have liked to have been a serious dancer and performed myself. In fact, when I used to watch musicals, I was thrilled by the dancing and longed to be doing that myself. But I never worked hard enough to do it, and I never really had the vision of myself being able to do it. But I think we got our love for this from Mammy, my grandmother. She loved the stage and would have been an actress if her mother had allowed her to stay in New York City where she was in college when her cousin, Sydney Blackmar (the actor), asked her to perform on stage. She no doubt had the talent, but her mother knew that taking that road held many snares and she brought her home immediately.

But Mammy had stage presence even when she wasn't on stage. She was always 'bigger than life' to me. But, you know, I'm so glad she didn't stay in New York to be on Broadway. Her life was a lot more 'normal' and 'wholesome' in Eufaula, Alabama, and we are here because she stayed in the south! She became my 'Mammy' and my *profoundly wonderful* grandmother!

You have a talent. God takes people different places with their talents. But one thing I will say. Mammy always seemed happy to me. She always had a cheery disposition and loved people. So no matter what you decide to do with your life, be happy with the outcome! Choose to be happy and content with what God gives you. Not to just have a façade of gaiety, but true contentment. You're always going to be a blessing to those around you—fun and filled with so much life that, like Mammy, you exude Presence. So I know that wherever God takes you, everyone will notice when you walk in the room and when you walk out. I love you and am so blessed by your talents.

As each of you has received a gift, use it to serve one another, as good stewards of God's varied grace: whoever speaks, as one who speaks oracles of God; whoever serves, as one who serves by the strength that God supplies—in order that in everything God may be glorified through Jesus Christ. To him belong glory and dominion forever and ever. Amen.
1 Peter 4:10–11 ESV

You are the light of the world. A city set on a hill cannot be hidden.
Nor do people light a lamp and put it under a basket, but on a stand,
and it gives light to all in the house. In the same way,
let your light shine before others, so that they may see your good works and give glory to your Father who is in heaven.
Matthew 5:14–16 ESV

Dear Katherine,

In all of your busyness, you do not forget to spend time with God in prayer and Bible study. That's amazing to me. Going to Bible studies and church is important, but the rubber meets the road when you really devote solitary time just to be with God—to hear Him, which I know you are trying to learn how to do. I called you the other night and you did not answer. I found out later that you were there, but in the middle of a Bible study. You witness to others without planning to, because of the way you live and relate to Jesus. Because He really is the center of your life. I appreciate your efforts to keep Him front and center. I pray, too, that I will do the same.

Dear Lord, I thank you that my child's life
is marked by prayerfulness, and that she is attempting to keep
You in the center of her life.
Fill her prayer life with your Spirit so that she will know what to pray.

Praying at all times in the Spirit, with all prayer and supplication. To that end keep alert
with all perseverance, making supplication for all the saints.
Ephesians 6:18 ESV

Zadie Dressed Up for her First Halloween!

Jonathan
A Hebrew Name Meaning
God's Gift

My Dear First-Born Son, Jonathan,

I have watched you this year set your mind on learning how to play the guitar. You have worked hard to achieve this goal. I am amazed at how you have been able to teach yourself, and how God has made this possible for you. I am mesmerized with your abilities! Already you are able to play fairly complicated songs that require sharp, quick finger movements. I know that it has taken hard work, time, and concentration. You can't know now what that effort will mean to you in the future. It is not often that someone has a talent, recognizes it, and devotes the necessary time to develop it. God places these strengths in you, but He gives you the option of exploring and perfecting them. Wasting your time or redeeming the time. I know that this interest will serve you in many ways in the coming years. It will make you more interesting, and you will have something to offer in a myriad of situations that others may be profoundly affected by. You can minister to people through music. Almost always. No matter where you are or who you are with. Music is a universal language and one that God values greatly. So learn to play songs about Jesus! You never know where your talent will take you!

> I will sing a new song unto thee, O God: upon a psaltery
> and an instrument of ten strings will I sing praises unto thee.
> Psalm 144:9 KJV

Dearest Jonathan,

You cannot imagine how much it means to me to have you come find me at night when you're ready for bed, and say, 'Goodnight, I love you." Those are the sweetest sounds ever to my ears. Not just the words, but the fact that you go out of your way to find me, in order to say those things to me. I will always love you for doing that. As a parent of a teenager, it's hard to know how much to say before your child wishes you would talk to someone else. I just love you so much and would like to talk to you all the time and tell you how much I love you 99,000 times every day. So remember, if you're ever wondering if I care about you, I've thought about how much I love you and how wonderful I think you are at least 150 times before I get up in the morning, and I manage to keep my mouth shut so I don't become a bother. But you melt my heart when you think to tell me that you love me at the end of the day. Thanks a million!

> These things I have spoken to you, that my joy may be in you,
> and that your joy may be full.
> John 15:11 ESV

Dear Jonathan,
I just want to thank you for being a good friend. I think you are kind to others and respectful of them but that you generally stand up for them. I imagine you would be willing to help anyone who needed help, even if this meant expending physical energy! You are smart and fun, so you make other people's lives more interesting and happier. I know that you and I have such a good time together that I would never be able to trade you in! Keep this up—be sacrificial for your friends. Be willing to get your feet wet and your hands dirty. Work up a good sweat any opportunity you have. I think that sweating makes a better and stronger man and I know it builds the world and relationships and makes dreams realities and puts roofs over families. You are exceptionally smart, Jonathan, and I've noticed that you enjoy taking time to think, which is great. Remember that dreaming about a thing in order to do it properly is right, but dreaming about it when we should be doing it is wrong. So don't hesitate or waste time on thinking when you should be acting with the necessary effort required to be a standout friend.

> But whoever would be great among you must be your servant,
> and whoever would be first among you must be your slave,
> even as the Son of Man came not to be served but to serve,
> and to give his life as a ransom for many.
> Matthew 20:26, 28 ESV

Do you not know that in a race all the runners compete, but only one receives the prize? So run that you may obtain it … But I discipline my body and keep it under control lest after preaching to others I myself should be disqualified.

1 Corinthians 9:24, 27 ESV

Dear Jonathan,

You have reached a crossroad. Being a freshman in high school is a milestone. It's a marker in the road, and beside this marker there is a measuring stick that measures several things. Your physical height, which has changed considerably; your progress in school, which has been exceptional; your commitment to your convictions and beliefs, which seems genuine and steadfast, and your gradual maturation into a man, which I am witnessing before my very eyes. I am proud of your accomplishments at the desk, but I am prouder of you because you Love Jesus and want to do His will. Nothing else you accomplish in this life can measure up to a life lived for its Creator. Nothing. Not grades. Not good jobs. Not friendships. Absolutely Nothing. And as you know, a life that is lived with and for Christ is the most abundant life available. Everything you give up for Him is replaced with something much, much better. It's like exchanging garbage for gold. And who wouldn't do that? The only thing is, a lot of times the garbage is wrapped up in a beautiful and enticing package. Satan loves to distract our attention from the truth, and this is one way he does that. He makes garbage tempting and it appears to be soooooo much fun, or soooooo harmless. But in reality, it leads to destruction. And it's ultimately very unfulfilling. But I see you now being smart and aware of these trappings. That's something that comes with being spiritually mature. I love you and am so proud of you. You've lifted me and I think others to a higher standard. Make sure that when the rubber meets the road, you're always genuinely on the high road. You're our leader, don't forget. I love you! The world wants your best, but God wants your ALL.

And he said to him, you shall love the Lord your God
with all your heart and with all your soul and with all your mind.

Matthew 22:37 ESV

Dear Jonathan,

Your name means 'Gift of God,' and you are such a special gift. God has blessed us so much through you. Believe it or not, you have taught me many things and for that I love you. You have taught me patience and faith—two important things to learn. I have learned these things while training you!

> Love is patient, love is kind; love does not envy or boast; it is not arrogant or rude.
> It does not insist on its own way; it is not irritable or resentful;
> it does not rejoice at wrongdoing, but rejoices with the truth.
> Love bears all things, believes all things, hopes all things, endures all things.
> 1 Corinthians 13:4 ESV

My Handsome Jonathan,

I am so glad that I don't have to worry about your knowing exactly who you are. You know Jesus. You know He died for you. You know how He wants you to live. And you are able to look out at the world and see that men, in many cases, are lost, and that their philosophies of selfishness, lust, and greed destroy the spirit. You are able to turn away from those things and follow the truth. I am so proud of you; you just don't know. You, Katherine, and Matthew are all witnesses to me of Christ. I look at you and am in awe of what you have done with your lives. You are tributes to Him, seriously. Thank you for knowing what God wants you to be and being it. It is so easy these days to convince yourself that you are doing fine, headed the right direction because you look around and most everybody else is going the same way. But be careful! Sometimes it seems that the only time you can know for sure that you are alright is when you feel like you're heading the *wrong* direction on the freeway. Then you know!

O Lord, you have searched me and known me! You know when I sit down and when I rise up; you discern my thoughts from afar. You search out my path and my lying down and are acquainted with all my ways. Even before a word is on my tongue, behold, O Lord, you know it altogether. You hem me in, behind and before, and lay you hand upon me. Such knowledge is too wonderful for me; it is high; I cannot attain it. Where shall I go from your Spirit? Or

where shall I flee from your presence? If I ascend to heaven, you are there! If I make my bed in Sheol, you are there. If I take the wings of the morning and dwell in the uttermost parts of the sea, even there your hand shall lead me, and your right hand shall hold me.
Psalm 139:1–10 ESV

Dear Jonathan,

One thing I love about you is your quiet thoughtfulness. I can sit alone with you and talk quietly, and when we talk, I love to hear what you have to say because it is always so interesting! You are so good at remembering! You always remember things that the rest of us have forgotten. God can surely use that talent when you begin to study His word. I've already seen great possibilities and promise in you. You have an uncanny ability to remember places and people in the Bible and what happened in their lives. You can be like a guiding light to other people when they want to learn more about God and how to be close to Him. This is a gift.

All scripture is God-breathed and is useful for teaching, rebuking,
correcting and training in righteousness, so that the servant of God may be thoroughly
equipped for every good work.
2 Timothy 3:16, 17 NIV

Do your best to present yourself to God as one approved,
a worker who has no need to be ashamed, rightly handling the word of truth.
2 Timothy 2:15 ESV

Dear Jonathan,

I'm very impressed with your taking the lead at school this year. I saw a bumper sticker recently that said, 'If you're not the leader, the scenery never changes.' I think that being a leader is exciting because it puts the reins in your hands. You have the opportunity to do the steering and therefore the decision making about what tack to take. And boy does this give you a better view than everybody else. The future of those you are leading in some way rests with you. Including whether they will have much of a view. So with leadership comes awesome responsibility.

The real objective is to draw out the talents and abilities of everyone you're leading. You have to be observant and recognize immediately who's got what strengths and encourage them to maximize them. That's the mark of true leadership. You're learning that being chosen to be president is a lot more than being hailed 'chief'; more than being given a title. It's realizing that something is then expected of and from you. And what you deliver to those who elected you is critical. Anyone can sit on a throne and look regal and important. If you aren't willing to get off the throne and dig the dirty ditch yourself, you're really worthless to everyone, and they may as well have elected a donkey to carry out the duties of the office. If you aren't up to the task of using your mind, and being creative, innovative, instigative and insightful, you aren't worth the paper they used to cast their ballots. So you're learning this early, and I'm proud of how you've handled your first lead role. I believe there are many more to come.

> A good name is rather to be chosen than great riches,
> and loving favor rather than silver and gold.
> Proverbs 22:1 KJV

Dear Jonathan,

You have the most handsome face of any six-year-old I've ever seen. God has blessed you with fine features. I look in your face and I love what I see. Your clear blue eyes are like open windows to a deep soul full of intellect and understanding. I marvel at this, because all of my children seem to have this—and it's something *I* don't have. I am amazed. You have a face that tells of strength and sensitivity. *God given! God given! God given!* When I look at you and when I talk to you, this is what I think. By God's grace you have many gifts; talents galore. And I praise God that He made you who you are. And I praise Him that you know who you are in Christ. You are not haughty or, in a bad way, self-aware. You are just very comfortable with yourself, and you know what you know! I love to be around you!

> I will praise You, for I am fearfully and wonderfully made;
> Marvelous are Your works, and that my soul knows very well.
> Psalm 139:14 NKJV

Dear Jonathan,

I want to tell you a few things I love about you that I haven't taken the time to share with you lately. First, I love your calmness in the middle of a storm. It's wonderful to have someone around who can have the pressure of two or three tests, an essay to write, baseball practice, and daily chores and just take a deep breath and get to it. It's difficult to do that, and I believe that in the last year or two you have taught yourself how to do just that. God sure never wants us to lose our cool in the midst of trials or panic in the midst of the storm. We all know It's easy to maintain your cool when everything is fine, but much more difficult when things are going haywire. Miraculously, you seem to take the chaos in stride, and never have one ruffled feather! I love that about you. You work hard until the job is done. You stay up late to study (if necessary) and are organized and ready to go in the morning.

Second, I love the way you can imitate people—it is so funny. We have had so much fun laughing! Humor is such a great thing to possess.

And finally, I've noted your desire to pay for part of your new jacket and how you felt bad that we spent so much money on it. Not too many children would have realized or appreciated the significance of handing someone that much money for an item of clothing. Daddy works hard to provide for each of you and it's nice when someone recognizes a gift. Thanks for not taking gifts for granted.

> Give, and it shall be given to you. Good measure, pressed down,
> shaken together, running over, will be put into your lap.
> For with the measure you use it will be measured back to you.
> Luke 6:38 ESV

Dear Jonathan,

I can't tell you how amazed I am that you are my child! You are wonderful and awesome in so many ways. You have already accomplished more than I could even have dreamed for you. As you continue to reach for your many aspirations, don't forget that there are many things in life that warrant your attention. Your schoolwork is very important, but so are some other things. Your devotion to God, who is, and always will be, your first love, is paramount to anything you ever do or accomplish in your life. Whether you put Jesus first; whether you keep your eyes keenly on Jesus, *will determine the entire course of your life.* Think about who you want to be and what you will be able to claim about the facts of your life when all is said and done. I love you!

> Therefore be imitators of God, as beloved children.
> And walk in love, as Christ loved us and gave himself up for us,
> a fragrant offering and sacrifice to God.
> But sexual immorality and all impurity or covetousness
> must not even be named among you, as is proper among saints.
> Let there be no filthiness nor foolish talk nor crude joking,
> which are out of place, but instead let there be thanksgiving.
> Ephesians 5:1–4 ESV

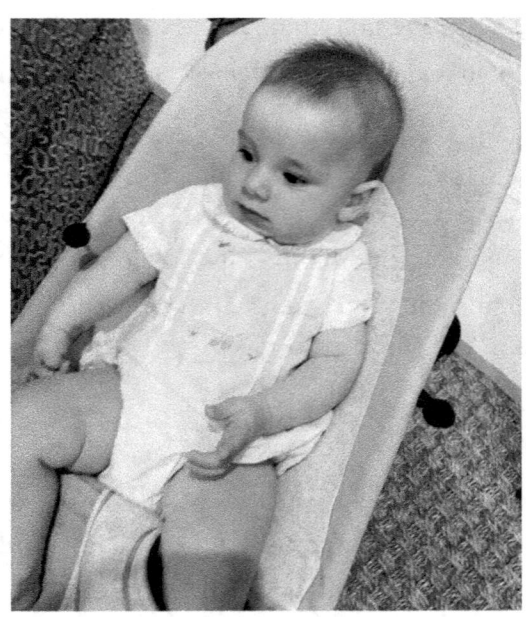

Oliver May Be Big Enough to Play for the Dawgs!

Matthew
A Hebrew Name Meaning
Gift of God

Dear Matthew Full of Strength,

The whole family marvels at your physical strength and agility. God really made you a showy miracle. Nobody can be around you long without seeing that you are extraordinarily talented physically. God took a very, very weak baby and made him very healthy and strong. I love seeing you begin to use your abilities in disciplined ways that are meaningful and fun, such as playing sports and helping others. There is just something about watching someone with natural physical talent and ability that points us all to our Maker. He alone could have made you like you are, and we are all amazed by it.

> Do you not know that your bodies
> are temples of the Holy Spirit, who is in you,
> whom you have received from God?
> You are not your own; you were bought at a price.
> Therefore honor God with your bodies.
> 1 Corinthians 6:19–20 NIV

Dear Matthew,
I sure do love you! You will never know how many times I have thanked God for your life. Of course, I consider all of my children miracles, but I feel like God gave us an extra miracle with you. And to look at you! Matthew, Daddy and I prayed that you would be perfectly healed and that you would be not just smart but brilliant. And I truly believe God gave you those things that we asked Him to. I love to see how strong you are and how really bright you are. I've never told you this before, but thank you for hanging in there and being strong when the going was tough when you were a baby. That is a quality that you have obviously honed and carried with you all these years and it has already served you well. Thank you again. Thank you!

> Jesus looked at them and said, "With man this is impossible,
> but not with God; all things are possible with God."
> Mark 10:27 NIV

Dear Matthew,

As I told you in your last clue, you have more energy than all of the monkeys in the jungles of Asia. And I know that at times it must be difficult to know just how to handle so much energy. But you have beautifully managed it in school. Your teachers consistently inform me that you are '*so well behaved*,' and it is obvious that you are attentive and do excellent work. I want to encourage you to do the same though your life. Set goals. Harness that energy and make it work for you and for God's kingdom. Explore the possibilities for someone with all that energy. Think what can be done with it. You are very fortunate. I know you will bridle and conc=troll it to make it productive and fruitful. I can't wait to see what you do with all that energy. What a blessing it could be.

> He made my feet like the feet of a deer and set me secure on the heights.
> Psalm 18:33 ESV

My Dearest Matthew,

Thank you for providing so much excitement around our house! Things are rarely dull when you are around. Yes, you tend to keep us excited and a little topsy turvy, but I know we are all glad that you do because otherwise life could become boring and hum drum. You keep us on our toes, and keep us looking around to see what's going to happen next--thinking that something may come flying out of nowhere—and sometimes it does—you! But we love you because you are such an interesting person and you infuse our lives with your zest. It's been a great 15 years with you. One thing that goes beyond your exuberant personality is your solid character. I always have felt confident that you were one person that knew what he knew to be right and would always stick to his convictions. Thank you for the witness you have displayed for your family.

> Create in me a clean heart, O Lord; and renew a right spirit in me.
> Psalm 51:10 KJV

Dear Matthew,

    I am so proud of you for taking a stand for Jesus. You have been intentional about attending the 'Warriors for Christ' meetings and you have told your friends about salvation with a boldness that is so refreshing. I can't tell you what it means to have a son who loves Jesus and loves to do things for Jesus. You are a witness to me and I love you for that. My prayer is that you will continue to walk through your life with this desire to be God's instrument—a voice and a life available for His use—without fear of the opinions of other people. If you do this, there is no telling what will happen. But whatever it is, it will be great!

> For they loved the praise of men more than the praise of God.
> John 12:43 KJV

> Don't let anyone look down on you because you are young,
> set an example for the believers
> in speech, in conduct, in love, in faith and in purity.
> 1 Timothy 4:12 NIV

Dear Matthew,

I am so glad that God gave us people like you who love animals so much and want to protect them. It is one way you demonstrate your tender heart and your extraordinary compassion and love for God's creation. You are very sensitive, and I believe that you will love and protect your family in the same big way. So I hope that you will remain sensitive, but at the same time be a strong man who can balance emotion with reality and the acceptance that many things are in God's control and realm where they should be. And He is all knowing and understands all mysteries. He knows us each intimately because He created each one of us. He made you to have this conviction in your heart and place you in this imperfect world. He will also help you to work through those strong feelings that you have when you think no one else understands. You know I share your love of animals and am just as burdened with compassion for them as you are. So if one day you become a zoo keeper, or run Sea World, or take charge of a wild life preserve, or teach monkeys sign language, or raise endangered animals I will be your biggest cheerleader. But who knows, you might decide they don't SMELL too good! And as we all know, that would be the end of that!

> Look at the birds of the air: they neither sow nor reap
> nor gather into barns, and yet your heavenly Father feeds them …
> Matthew 6:26 ESV

Dear Darling Matthew,

How I admire you for going out for football! Being the smallest one on the team would have been enough to turn most people away. But not my Matthew! He was undaunted. You aren't afraid to give it your all, even when the all might really be the all! And the end. I was so proud of you for facing guys at least twice your size and bigger on that football field. Courage. Man, that's courage! I'd be scared to death I was going to be killed. But what's also wonderful is that they all had respect for you, which is why they all called you *Phenom*. That's a great tribute to your spirit! And your spirit is a great tribute to your faith, that God is directing your path, going before you in every endeavor, and that you know you will be strong through Him.

> No, in all these things we are more than conquerors through him who loved us.
> Romans 8:37 ESV

Dear Matthew,

 I have to compliment you on some things that I've noticed lately that I love about you. I love the way you support your friends. I've heard you talking to friends when you've said things like, 'I bet you did really good on the test,' or 'I know you can do that better than I can.' I've noticed that when you outdo someone—either on a test academically or physically as in P.E., you don't take that opportunity to rub it in. You emphasize their strengths and at times point out legitimate excuses for their poorer performance. You seem to realize, too, that God doesn't make people perfect. Some people are just great at one thing and not so great at something else. You told me several times that you just weren't made to write well or be still for a long time. You are aware of and OK with your own weaknesses. But I really am impressed when I see you trying to lift others up. When you do this, it always lifts you up in the eyes of other people. You are thoughtful. You usually are careful to thank me when we go out to eat or I buy you something. That is so important. It makes me want to do things for you because I know it's appreciated. It makes me adore you!

> If either of them falls down, one can help the other up.
> But pity anyone who falls and has no one to help them up.
> Ecclesiastes 4:10 NIV

Dear *Mattalu,*

You have such an effervescent personality! It's such fun to be around you! God can so use this trait for His good. You can easily be the salt and light that God commands us to be. Turn your personality over to God and let it rip! No telling what great things will happen. Can't wait to see your life unfold in the light of His presence. I love you Matthew!

> Let your speech always be gracious, seasoned with salt,
> so that you may know how you ought to answer each person.
> Colossians 4:6 ESV

> No one after lighting a lamp puts it in a cellar or under a basket,
> but on a stand, so that those who enter may see the light.
> Luke 11:33 ESV

> Again Jesus spoke to them, saying, "I am the light of the world.
> Whoever follows me will not walk in darkness, but will have the light of life."
> John 8:12 ESV

Dear Matthew,

I love to see how conscientious you've been about your school work. You are always careful to make sure your work is in order before school and you always study hard for tests. Mama and Daddy really appreciate that diligence and I know God does too. It will mean more than you can now imagine for your future. God's plan for you will certainly require diligence. You have that! Always remember to draw on Jesus's awesome wisdom and power.

> But without faith it is impossible to please him,
> for he that cometh to God must believe that he is,
> and that he is a rewarder of them that diligently seek him.
> Hebrews 11:6 KJV

Dearest Matthew,

It's hard not to notice that you really do a good job befriending people. To start a brand-new school; to start high school with almost all new people, and be voted President is a real accomplishment. I think it is a real testament to the fact that you love people and they respond to that love. Not to mention that you are extremely good looking and have a quick wit and a darling personality (you don't reckon your mother is a bit prejudiced, do you?). I just really like you, and obviously other people do too. I'm sure they appreciate your boldness and willingness to speak your own mind without reservation. You're not scared of what others will think or of diminishing your self-worth if you catch a little flack over something. You seem so confident of who you are. I love that about you. I was so proud of the way you automatically offered to serve as President of your class with no hesitation. That speaks volumes about who you are and what you're all about.

For if anyone thinks he is something, when he is nothing, he deceives himself. But let each one test his own work, and then his reason to boast will be in himself alone and not in his neighbor. For each will have to bear his own load.
Galatians 6:3–5 ESV

Dear Matthew,

This past year I have seen you take big steps for Christ. At nine years old, you have told your friends about Him and I really believe that your witness will be something they never forget. I'm proud of you for being bold in telling others about your savior. You have an unbelievable testimony of healing and mercy that will one day shake a lot of people's lives and bring them to their knees. I'm so glad you're letting God use you in such a special way.

Whosoever therefore shall confess me before men,
him will I confess also before my Father which is in heaven.
Matthew 10:32 KJV

My Precious Matthew,

I'm glad to see you're helping out with the Bible Study and what's really neat to see is your wonderful ability on your feet. You can lead a prayer group in a very effective way with bright ideas and insights even when you aren't really prepared. I love that about you. You have a very spontaneous personality that is full of imagination and creativity. Give that talent to God and He will show you great things!

You shall be a crown of beauty in the hand of the Lord,
and a royal diadem in the hand of your God.
Isaiah 62:3 ESV

Dear Matthew,

    I love your energy. You are the most 'alive' person I've ever met. Except maybe Mankme, who runs a close second. You are vibrant and expressive and rarely content to just sit. This means that you have an exciting life ahead of you. You want to do so many things with your life—it astounds me. You are 13, and yet you love, love, love, gaining knowledge. You know about 15 things you really want to commit your life's work to—and if anyone has the energy to see it come to pass—YOU DO! You're interested in people and I think you will find that this one special ingredient of your personality, along with persistence and love and energy, will make you very usable to God. If you let Him do the leading—which I admit will be difficult since you are a strong leader yourself—He will take you on a magnificent journey through this world. I'm excited to know that God allowed me to give birth to a person that will shake up the world. I know what I know. And I know you. Get ready for a big adventure!

> Your word is a lamp to my feet and a light to my path.
> Psalm 119:105 ESV

Dear Matthew,

You sure do keep me hopping! Your body and your brain move about the same speed and it's always *Fast!* I honestly have always thought that the average person has a hard time keeping up with you. Your thoughts and your physical activity level. We just weren't blessed with the energy that you were. It's incredible. What are you going to do with that gift? I am confident that you could run the pony express mail company on foot—and by yourself! God must have something important for you to do that requires speed. I know it's not clean up your room or get ready for school. That's the only category of your life that is not in fast gear—that and getting out of bed in the morning! But you know, that figures. You started out slow when you were born but you've been picking up momentum ever since. I love you. Will you pleeease loan me some energy?

> God has given each of us the ability to do certain things well.
> Romans 12:6 TLB

The content of the cards may be simple for the youngest child and more involved and lengthier for the older children. Whatever God leads you to say is appropriate. This is a fantastic tool for telling your children who they are, who you want them to be, and how much Christ loves them.

Clara, Caroline and Georgia

Christmas

Years ago, I wrote this letter to my children for them to read on Christmas Day, after receiving the many gifts I showered on them, which my husband declared every year to be sinful!

>Children, we have a Southern tradition on Christmas morning, and that is to call everyone we love and try to be the first person to say 'Christmas Gift!' The one who says it first supposedly gets a gift from the other. So, this Christmas I am saying 'Christmas Gift' first and asking you to give me a specific gift.
>
>Since Christmas is all about Jesus and nothing about materialism, and since I have spent so much time gathering material things to give each of you, I want you to take a moment to think about a few things Jesus said.
>
>The first is this: 'Lay not up for yourselves treasures upon earth, where moth and rust doth corrupt, and where thieves break through and steal: But lay up for yourselves treasures in heaven, where neither moth nor rust doth corrupt, and where thieves do not break through nor steal: For where you treasure is, there will your heart be also.' Matthew 6:19–21 KJV
>
>You know that the things I have given you will one day be corrupted—they will rust and break and fall apart. They are not lasting. Some things are temporal and some are eternal. A relationship with Jesus will be with you forever.
>
>Another thing Jesus said is this: 'And again I say unto you, it is easier for a camel to go through the eye of a needle, than for a rich man to enter the kingdom of God.' Matthew 19:24 KJV
>
>There are so many things in this world that distract us from developing a deep relationship with Christ. Our eyes and ears go straight to them. Music, food, alcohol, academics, as well as any other type of self-indulgence from which we derive pleasure. But the focus on gathering wealth—material possessions—is a very dangerous focus, as this verse points out.

Jesus actually said this to some people about your age: "If any man come to me, and hate not his father, and mother, and wife, and children, and brethren, and sisters, yea, and his own life also, he cannot be my disciple.' Luke 14:26 KJV This is a verse that is easily misconstrued. Jesus is making a comparison of sorts. 'Hate' in this verse means 'love less' than Jesus. In other words, God must always come first; be loved most. You can't let another interest or another person, or another thing take precedence. He has to be supreme, and you have to guard that place for Him diligently. Only then will all of the other relationships be worth gold.

Read this verse from the Bible: 'Every good gift and every perfect gift is from above, and cometh down from the Father of lights, with whom is no variableness, neither shadow of turning.' James 1:17 KJV

At Christmas, when we are so focused on what we are getting, it is so easy to forget what we've already got. Jesus! And at times we all look at the world and ask, 'What has this world come to?' We forget altogether what has come into the world. Focus on the good and perfect gift!

This verse reaches the heart of what I am trying to say: 'Love not the world, neither the things that are in the world. If any man love the world, the love of the Father is not in him. For all that is in the world, the lust of the flesh, and the lust of the eyes, and the pride of life, is not of the Father, but is of the world. And the world passeth away, and the lust thereof: but he that doeth the will of God abideth for ever. I John 2:15–17 KJV

Are you willing, even anxious, to toss out every THING you got for Christmas in order to give everything to Christ? Would you want the things you own too badly to open your hand and give them up if that was required? Strengthen your relationship with Jesus—not your grip on this world.

And Jesus said this thing: 'If ye then, being evil, know how to give good gifts unto your children, how much more shall your Father, which is in heaven give good things to them that ask him?' Matthew 7:11 KJV

> Nothing I have given you since the day you were born can compare in any measure to the unbelievable riches that God wants to give you. Things are really just things. Christ is something else entirely. Be smart enough to know which one to grab hold of with your strongest hand.
>
> Your most precious gift to me is a few minutes of time to wander around these verses—to meditate on them and lock them away in your heart. I love you and Merry Christmas!

To say that Christmas was a big celebration in our family is an understatement. I have so many memories surrounding this day. My own traditions and memories began with my mother's parents, who lived in Eufaula, Alabama. They were such characters, as were most of the people I knew from Eufaula. My grandparents would walk across Country Club Road to our house at dawn on Christmas morning to see what we got from Santa, and after we hooped and hollered over our new toys, we would get dressed up and walk back across Country Club Road to my grandparents' house for Christmas lunch. My grandmother's cook, Mary Lou (Lulu), and Daisy (my mother's housekeeper and mine and my siblings' nurse), would be there to serve the traditional meal of turkey and dressing, rice and gravy, sweet potatoes in little orange cups topped with marshmallows, oyster casserole, English pea and asparagus casserole, butter beans, homemade rolls, and beautiful desserts. There were always Spanish peanuts on the table along with homemade artichoke relish. In Mammy and Pa's living room, there was always a beautiful cedar tree that had been cut from their farmland just outside of town and delivered by Scholtz, a beloved workman on my grandfather's farm. Outside, my grandmother's gardener, Henry, would hang string after string of big colored Christmas lights all the way to the top of a huge tree. Everything was so festive!

One of the things I looked forward to more than anything else was gathering around Daisy after lunch in the kitchen. We all wanted to watch her unwrap her Christmas presents because her reaction just *made* Christmas! Daisy is one of those precious people who everyone loves because her love for everyone is so attractive. She would alternately laugh hysterically her contagious laugh and cry tears of joy and appreciation as she opened each gift. I think back on this memory every Christmas and feel privileged to have been there and to have known a person like Daisy. Few people in this world are as humble and grateful as she is. It was the most poignant and unforgettable scene. It seems these days that most of us think we deserve everything and if others have more than we do, we are resentful and bitter. Not Daisy.

My father's parents lived in Columbus, Georgia, and after we moved to Columbus (when I was nine years old), we began to go to their Christmas Eve party. A huge pine tree that had been taken from the woods around their house was fabulously decorated, awaiting the large family gathering in the parlor. We continued this tradition into adulthood, and as my siblings and I married and had our own children, we all made the trek to either my grandparents' house, my parents' house, or one of the aunt's and uncle's houses for Christmas Eve.

I remember one particular Christmas Eve when our families had grown so large that we had gathered at Mama and Daddy's house with just my siblings and their families. It was the most festive Christmas Eve I remember, with my brother, George, and my daddy shucking oysters on the patio. December nights in Georgia are not always cold, but I remember this night being chillier than usual, so I stayed inside by the fire and enjoyed boiled shrimp and a glass of wine or a cup of Eggnog anticipating our celebration the next day. It was a wonderful night and one of my favorite memories. I love having such a large family, and most of the Adams live in Columbus.

This year, we reverted back to our old tradition and held a Christmas Eve party at our grandparents' home, an old farmhouse that our family donated to Historic Columbus and is now being used as the home of the Columbus Botanical Garden. Most of the Adams family came (nearly 70 people), and everyone loved the musician we found who played the violin and the guitar while singing Christmas songs. I'll never forget Mama's face as they brought her into the parlor and she heard the violin. She just lit up with her beautiful smile. It was a great night, and it reminded us all of how precious family is. These family gatherings are important, and are worth the little bit of effort required to pull them off. (We were smart this year. We had the food catered!)

A day or so before Christmas, if all of the gifts were wrapped and the other preparations were handled, and if I still had a little energy left, I loved taking a moment to actually celebrate

Jesus's birthday with the children. We would bake a birthday cake and sing Happy Birthday. It was a fun way to make sure the children understood that the day was sacred and set aside for the world to reflect on, and be amazed by, the birth of its Savior, Jesus Christ. And on that cake, the candles were ablaze, symbolic of The Christ, the light of the world! This can be one of the desserts served at lunch, and with it the reading of the Christmas story.

> And in the same region there were shepherds out in the field,
> keeping watch over their flock by night. And an angel of the Lord appeared to them, and the glory of the Lord shone around them, and they were filled with great fear. And the angel said to them, "Fear not, for behold, I bring you good news of great joy that will be for all the people. For unto you is born this day in the city of David a savior, who is Christ the Lord. And this will be a sign for you:
> you will find a baby wrapped in swaddling cloths and lying in a manger."
> And suddenly there was with the angel a multitude of the heavenly host
> praising God and saying, "Glory to God in the highest,
> and on earth peace among those with whom he is pleased!"
> When the angels went away from them into heaven,
> the shepherds said to one another, "Let us go over to Bethlehem
> and see this thing that has happened, which the Lord has made known to us."
> And they went with haste and found Mary and Joseph, and the baby
> lying in a manger. And when they saw it, they made known
> the saying that had been told them concerning this child.
> And all who heard it wondered at what the shepherds told them.
> But Mary treasured up all these things, pondering them in her heart.
> And the shepherds returned, glorifying and praising God
> for all they had heard and seen, as it had been told them.
>
> Luke 2:8–20 ESV

On Christmas Eve, Joe and I and the children have made it a tradition to pile into the car and head out to look at the Christmas lights and decorations before going to church. We started this when the children were very young, and we would return every year to the most lit up houses. Joe found several that were beyond belief, and each year they prompted screams and squeals and hysteria. There were two or three that beat all the competition. All was not calm, but all was definitely bright! Somehow these 'sights to see' set the stage for the calm of worship. There were several services on Christmas Eve, but when the children were older, we would endeavor to hold out for the 11:00 p.m. candlelight service, when they would have communion, and the whole congregation of this large downtown church would light candles and sing the last song of the night, "O Come, All Ye Faithful." The church was never so beautiful, with spirits rejoicing over the birth of the Savior of the world. This really was a blessed time for me, when I was finally through with all of my exhausting attempts to make everything perfect, and I could allow myself to breathe and let the Spirit take over my heart and soul while I contemplated the real meaning of Christmas, the divine birth. I loved that time!

We listened for reindeer on the rooftop while tucking the children in bed. They knew the truth about Santa, as we had told our young children that Santa was not real, hoping that we could avert the misconception that Jesus was also not real. We told them that we gave them the gifts because we loved them so much, just like God gave us the greatest gift, Jesus. We made sure they understood that other children's parents wanted their children to believe in Santa Claus, so they could not tell anyone. It was our secret! But we all played along anyway, anticipating Santa and his reindeer with the children. We had great fun, without lying. And to my knowledge, they never told a soul!

On Christmas morning, we would have the children line up at the door to the living room, waiting for the signal from their daddy that all was as it should be in that room. My father began the tradition that Joe continued, going into the living room and returning from inspecting the scene with an exclamation that the presents weren't there, and that someone must have taken them! Or saying, "The only thing that's out there is coal!" At first, their eyes were as big as saucers with disbelief, but they quickly caught on and expected this outrageous observation from their father each year. The whole routine elicited giggles mixed with squeals of anticipation. (Remember, I said you should be the most fun of anyone your child knows, because you want them to find you to be a person they delight in being with!) When they entered the room at last, they were screaming with excitement over the sight of so many toys. Santa's sleigh had been too, too full, and they were lavished with more than they would ever have imagined to ask for. However, I will caution you here. If you are not financially secure enough to spend much, don't! When your children are very young, they will consider one toy (or even the paper it's wrapped in) a real thrill. As they get older, they will prize even more the security that comes from having a responsible parent who is providing a more stable future. Material things are not the point, but the overwhelming, lavishing love of Jesus is. Don't be persuaded that all the material things will take the place of the gift of God's Son in your children's lives.

Whenever we entertained, and especially on holidays, I was terrible about preparing too much food and spending way too much time and money decorating the house and the tables—at least according to my dear husband. I am convinced that he would be just fine with the everyday meal and the everyday table for the highest celebration of the year. It just did not compute to him (or my male children) as being important, and he just could not appreciate it or the trouble it took to produce it. But I just could not scale it back, and I felt guilty for the seeming waste I was creating, even though I believed that it made the day special and it made each person who came to my house feel special. At least that was the intention and the hope. That's just the only way I knew to do hospitality. A last-minute hosting job was always a calamity. I just could not pull off the unplanned event. I had to have a plan and a recipe and, if possible, a florist and a caterer. And my great fear would be of running out of food!

Then one day, when reading John 2:1–12, I began to understand just how lavishly Jesus showers us with everything good, even ordinary things that are just for our enjoyment. This passage is the story of the first miracle, when Jesus turned water into wine at a wedding. The wine was about to run out, which would have been a social catastrophe. Jesus intervened to rescue the couple from certain shame, and even though the wedding was almost over, Jesus turned the water in six stone water jars to wine. Each jar held about thirty gallons, so that is the equivalent of about 180 gallons, or eleven kegs. When the master of the feast tasted the wine (not knowing where the wine came from), he told the bridegroom that everyone always served the good wine first, and he could not understand why they had saved the best wine for last. Jesus had lavished them with much more than they could ever have needed of the very best wine. In this story of Jesus's lavish love, I found my justification for being lavish in my hospitality and my gifts to my children and grandchildren. Jesus didn't just do what He *had* to do; He went way overboard and *lavished* them. He did this too when he shed his blood for the sins of the world.

> See what great love the Father has lavished on us,
> That we should be called children of God!
>
> I John 3:1 NIV

> In him we have redemption through his blood,
> the forgiveness of sins,
> in accordance with the riches of God's grace
> that He lavished on us.
> With all wisdom and understanding.
>
> Ephesians 1:7 NIV

> May mercy, peace, and love
> be lavished on you!
>
> Jude 1:2 NET

> May grace and peace
> be lavished on you
> as you grow in the rich knowledge of God and of Jesus our Lord!
>
> 2 Peter 1:2 NET

> He gives lavishly
> to the needy; his righteousness endures forever.
>
> Psalm 112:9 NET

The children were thrilled that Joe's mother (his father had died when he was seventeen) would show up at the crack of dawn on Christmas morning to see what they had gotten from Santa. After the excitement of showing off their presents died down a bit, we would gather at the table for a special Christmas breakfast. It always included a breakfast casserole, baked cheese grits, and cinnamon rolls. This would be the first of several indulgent meals on Christmas Day. Afterward, we'd get everyone dressed, and our family would join my siblings' families at my parents' home for opening yet more presents and having *more* Eggnog. When our second unwrapping was over and everyone had had a cup of cheer, we would have a formal lunch at Mama's or my sister's or at my house. Whichever house it was, it was decorated and adorned for a king, and rightly so, because a King *was* ever-present with us because of what took place on that first Christmas morning.

This was so much fun, and the Eggnog was so good that I have decided to record the recipe for my grandmother's Eggnog as well as an even older (and maybe even better) recipe in the book. You will not regret making Eggnog every Christmas and using a beautiful silver punch bowl to serve it in. Serve it on Christmas Eve, Christmas morning while opening presents, or for dessert after dinner on Christmas Day. The first Eggnog recipe takes a long time; the second is shorter, but just as good or better! Follow the recipes closely, especially adding the Bourbon *one drop* at a time. I cheat a little with this, but be careful, because the whole thing will fall apart if you add the Bourbon too quickly! I will also include our typical southern Thanksgiving and Christmas Dinner Menus and some key recipes that make these holidays so special.

Our Traditional Southern Thanksgiving Meal

Hos d'oeuvres
Cheese Stuffed Celery

Entrée
Roasted or Fried Turkey, Sliced and Arranged on a silver tray

Rice and Gravy

Dressing

Sweet Potato Souffle (a version of which was always served in orange cups with toasted marshmallows on top when I was a child)

English Pea and Asparagus Casserole

Squash Casserole

Butter Beans

Oyster Casserole

Cranberry Salad

Ambrosia

Cranberry Sauce (Whole Berry Sauce from a can, if not homemade)

Rolls

Embellishments
Spanish Nuts

Artichoke Relish

Desserts
Bakery Cake Decorated with a Whimsical Buttercream Turkey

Frozen Chocolate Torte

Caramel Cake

Chocolate Wafers Layered with Homemade Whipped Cream and Topped with a Cherry (so pretty at Christmas!)

Christmas Menu

Christmas Dinner Menu

Hos d'oeuvres
Cheese Ring
Cheese Straws
Mixed Nuts

Entrée
Beef Tenderloin with Horseradish Sauce
Mashed Potatoes Rachael or Feathered Rice
Caribbean Salad
Asparagus
Green Beans with Toasted Pecans and Blue Cheese Crumbles
Butter Beans for the children
Rolls
(Instead of Beef Tenderloin, we sometimes have Country Captain with Caribbean Salad and Asparagus.)

Desserts
Lemon Meringue Pie
Buttermilk Pie
Turtle Cheesecake
Meringue Kisses
Bakery Cake Decorated with a Buttercream Santa

Clara Alderman Foy Roberts' Eggnog

Clara was my mother's mother, who we called 'Mammy.' This recipe dates from about the year 1928, if not before.

3 Mixing Bowls
Electric Mixer
1 Silver Punch Bowl and Cups
1 Quart Whipping Cream
12 Eggs (for Safety, Pasteurized)
12 Tablespoons Sugar (or 3/4 Cup)
12 Tablespoons Whiskey (Bourbon)
1 Tablespoon Whiskey for pot (extra)
Vanilla Ice Cream
Nutmeg

Beat the egg yolks on medium high for 1 1/2 hours until real thick. After 3 minutes beating, add one-third of the sugar. Finish beating yolks. Mixing on low, slowly add the whiskey. In a separate bowl, beat the cream until stiff. Slowly add one-third of the sugar. In still a separate bowl, beat the egg whites until stiff. Slowly add remaining sugar. Mix together the cream, egg yolks, and egg whites. To serve, put a little ice cream in the bottom of a sliver cup (if you have one). Add the Eggnog and sprinkle a little nutmeg on top. Merry Christmas!

Natalie Petry Stewart's Eggnog

Natalie was a Eufaula, Alabama, resident around 1900.
This recipe takes less time than the previous one,
and may be even better than Mammy's!

3 Mixing Bowls
Electric Mixer
Silver Punch Bowl and Cups
1 Egg Per Serving (for safety, Pasteurized)
Sugar (1 Heaping Tablespoon per Egg)
Whiskey (1/2 Ounce Bourbon per cup served)
½ Pint Whipping Cream per Six Eggs
Vanilla Ice Cream
Nutmeg

Beginning with the yolks (because they take longer), beat the egg yolks and the egg whites separately, both for a long time (15-25 minutes). While beating, add 1/2 *heaping* tablespoon sugar per egg to the yellows, and 1/2 heaping tablespoon sugar per egg to the whites (for instance, one egg equals 1/2 *heaping* tablespoon sugar in the egg whites and 1/2 *heaping* tablespoon sugar in the yellows). When beating the egg whites, beat till stiff. Beat whipping cream, just before serving, till stiff, but do not overbeat (or you'll make butter!). At end of beating the yellows, add the whiskey *one drop at a time*. (*This is very important. If you add the whiskey too quickly, the mixture will break down. I confess that I did not add it exactly one drop at a time, but be careful to use a lot of restraint and patience!*) To the large serving bowl (preferably a large silver punch bowl), add the whipped cream and the egg whites. On top, put yellows. Do *not* stir. Instead, fold, spooning up from bottom to mix. To serve, put two heaping tablespoons of ice cream in each silver cup. Spoon Eggnog over this. Sprinkle with nutmeg. Divine!

Breakfast Casserole

Our traditional Christmas and Easter breakfast menus are always the same. Breakfast Casserole, Baked Cheese Grits, Pillsbury Cinnamon Rolls, and sometimes Cheese Danishes.

Two Small Loaves of French Bread (Rolls)—enough to cover the bottom of a 9x13 Pyrex dish, Torn into bite size pieces
4 T Butter
6 Eggs
2 Cups Milk
1 Pound Sausage (Mild)
1 Cup Sharp Cheddar Cheese, Grated
1 Teaspoon Salt
1 Teaspoon Prepared Mustard
Pam Non-stick Cooking Spray
9x13 Pyrex dish

Preheat the oven to 350 degrees. Sauté the torn bread in butter. Sprinkle the bread over the bottom of the Pyrex dish that has been sprayed with non-stick cooking spray. Brown and drain the sausage. Mix the eggs, milk, salt and mustard in a bowl. Pour some of the mixture over the bread. Layer the sausage, then the cheese on top of the bread. Pour the rest of the milk and egg mixture on top of the cheese. Refrigerate overnight. Remove from over the next morning about 30-45 minutes before putting in the oven so the dish can come to room temperature (or warm in the microwave a few minutes). Bake for 40-50 minutes. You may need to place a little loose aluminum foil over it the last 10 minutes or so to avoid having it brown too much.

Baked Cheese Grits
Margaret Lewis

1 ½ Cups Grits (Quick Grits)
6 Cups Water
½ Cup Butter or Margarine
3 Teaspoons Lawry's Seasoned Salt
8 Ounces Velveeta Cheese
8 Ounces Sharp Cheddar Cheese (grated)
3 Eggs, Beaten

Preheat the oven to 350 degrees. Cook the grits in the water, as directed on the box. Do *not* add salt to the water at this time. Add the remaining ingredients, cutting up the butter and cheese into small pieces that will melt easier. Blend well, and pour all into a buttered baking dish. Cook, covered, for 1 ½ hours until center is set. It may take a little longer than this to set up, and you may have to put a tent of foil over it the last 10-15 minutes to avoid having it brown.

Louisiana Grits
Margaret Lewis

This recipe just adds a little to the basic Baked Cheese Grits recipe and is dynamite with a fillet, hot curried fruit, asparagus and a salad.

1 ½ Cups Grits (Instant or Stone Ground)
6 Cups Water
1 Stick Butter or Margarine
3 Teaspoons Lawry's Seasoned Salt
½ Pound Velveeta Cheese
8 Ounces Sharp Cheddar Cheese

3 Eggs, Beaten
½ Cup slightly Browned Chopped onions
2 T Pimentos, Chopped (optional)
Pam Non-stick Cooking Spray or Butter

Preheat oven to 350 degrees. Cook the grits in the water as directed on the box. Do Not add salt to the water at this time. Add all of the ingredients to the grits, cutting up the butter and cheese into small pieces for better melting. Blend together and pour into buttered baking dish. Bake for 1-1 1/2 hours or until center is set. Cook uncovered, but when it is finished baking, cover until ready to serve.

Cheese Stuffed Celery

This hors d'oeuvre has been served at our family's Christmas Dinners for as long as I can remember, probably some 60 years. You can make your own pimento cheese, as we have done for years, or you can purchase Palmetto Pimento Cheese with or without Jalapeños at the grocery store, as a perfectly wonderful substitute. It is almost as good, and it is much easier!

Celery Sticks
1 Block Cracker Barrel Extra Sharp Cheddar Cheese, Coarsely Grated
Mayonnaise
Tabasco
Worcestershire Sauce
Onion Salt, optional
Onion, Coarsely Grated
Electric Hand Mixer

Wash the celery thoroughly and pat dry with paper towels. Trim any bad looking ends. Cut into 4-inch sticks. Grate the cheese coarsely. Add a little mayonnaise (don't add too much at the time), a little Tabasco, the onion, and *a very little bit of* Worcestershire Sauce to the cheese. If you add too much Worcestershire Sauce it will turn the mixture brown. You don't want that! Adjust the seasonings to suit your crowd. We like for it to have a good bit of Onion and enough Tabasco to make it tasty. You can mix this all together with an electric mixer, but you *do not* want it to be over-mixed or to have a smooth consistency. You want it to be a little chunky and to have a little bite. Fill the ribs of celery with this mixture and place on a tray to be served before dinner as your guests arrive.

Roasted Turkey

1 ½ Pounds of Turkey per person if you want leftovers (Fresh Turkey is preferred)
Salt
Pepper
Garlic Powder, optional
Butter, Softened or slightly Melted
Bacon, optional
Parsley
Roasting Pan with a Rack
Aluminum Foil

This is a simple recipe for roasting a turkey, and with just this little bit of effort, it turns out great. For the last five years or so, we have fried our turkey, and it is always delicious. However, aside from being slightly dangerous for the chef, it yields no gravy, so roasting is sometimes a better option. When you have a fried turkey, you will have to purchase the gravy from a restaurant or grocery store, and doctor it up with seasonings.

Preheat oven to 325 degrees and place the oven rack in the lowest position of the oven. Remove the turkey neck and giblets, and rinse the turkey well. Pat the turkey dry with paper towels, and position the turkey, breast up, on the rack. Rub the skin with the butter. Put one or two tablespoons of butter inside the cavity of the turkey. Sprinkle salt and pepper liberally on the skin and in the cavity of the turkey. Sprinkle on a little garlic powder if desired. It is optional to place two strips of bacon over the top of the turkey. Cover the turkey with a loose tent of aluminum foil. Roast for about four hours (for an 18-pound turkey), or until meat thermometer, inserted in thickest part of the breast, reads 165 degrees. I often cook a turkey breast also in order to be sure there is enough and that we have left overs. If I have the turkey breast and it looks pretty, I might place it on the tray and put slices of turkey around it. Garnish with parsley.

Fluffy White Rice

My mother was very good at cooking rice that ended up being fluffy! We all know, you don't want gummy rice unless you're eating it with chopsticks! I will try to write the directions here.

Long Grain Rice
Parsley

Boil whatever amount of rice you need for your crowd according to directions without salt or butter. Pour rice into colander and drain. Add a small amount of water to the same pan. Put the colander with the rice on top of the boiler and do not cover. Heat water to simmer and let stand about 10 minutes. Remove from heat and let cool. Rice may be stored in Ziploc bags in the refrigerator or freezer until ready to serve. When serving, garnish with a little parsley sprinkled on top.

Corn Bread Dressing

Corn Bread for the Dressing

2 Cups Self-Rising (Yellow Hot Rize) Cornmeal
¼ Cup Vegetable Oil
1 Egg
Buttermilk (enough to make it soupy)
Vegetable Oil for Pan
Cast Iron Muffin Pan or Skillet

Dressing

6-7 Pieces White Bread, Torn into small pieces
6 Eggs
2-3 Cups Chicken Stock (I always use 3 Cups so it won't be dry.)
2 Medium Yellow Onions, Chopped
3-4 Stalks of Celery, Chopped
Butter for Sautéing
Salt
Pepper
Worcestershire Sauce
Butter for greasing Pyrex dish
9x13 Pyrex dish
Pam Non-stick Cooking Spray

Heat oven to 450 degrees. Put about a ½ teaspoon of oil in each muffin cup. While oven is heating, mix together above ingredients, making the mixture the consistency of pancake mix or soupier (or, as Mama would say, sloppy). Put the pan in the oven and heat until a drop of water that is dripped into a muffin cup sizzles. Do not allow it to get too hot, because it will catch on fire! Bake about 20 minutes or until tops are golden brown. Remove from the oven and use a knife to loosen each muffin and stand them on their sides to cool. Reset the oven temperature to 350 degrees. Spray the Pyrex dish with Pam. Sauté the onions and celery in butter. Crumble the Corn Bread in large bowl. Add all other ingredients, making sure to add a lot of salt and pepper, but only *a little* Worcestershire Sauce (too much will darken the color of the mixture). Stir to combine and pour in the Pyrex dish. At this point, you may want to bake a small single portion to make sure it has enough seasoning. It can be frozen to be used at a later date. When ready to serve, bake about 30 minutes until set and slightly browned. Do not over-cook as it will be dry. If you find that it seems too dry, you may add a little chicken stock during cooking.

Sweet Potato Souffle

5 Large Sweet Potatoes (I use the largest and reddest Potatoes I can find, but if using smaller Potatoes, just use more.)
1 ½ Cups Sugar
2 Eggs
1 Teaspoon Vanilla
½ Cup Milk
½ Cup Margarine or Butter, Softened
Pam Non-stick Cooking Spray

Boil the potatoes in skins until they are tender. Preheat the oven (if planning to cook immediately) to 350 degrees. Spray a 9x13 Pyrex dish with Pam or grease with butter. Remove jackets of the potatoes and discard. Place the potatoes in a large mixing bowl and beat while they are still hot, stopping the mixer (unplug the mixer!) two or three times to clean the beaters. The object is to get rid of the strings that will accumulate around the beaters. I usually run water over the beaters to clean them. Dry the beaters before continuing to beat the potatoes. When you feel you have gotten most of the strings, mix, or even whip, the potatoes while adding the other ingredients. Pour mixture into the Pyrex dish.

Topping

1 Cup of Light Brown Sugar
1/3 Cup Butter, Softened
1 Cup Chopped Pecans
1/3 Cup Flour

Mix the ingredients until crumbly. Don't overmix. Sprinkle on top of the potatoes. Bake for 30-60 minutes until puffed up and heated through. You may need to cover with foil the last 10 or 15 minutes so the topping will not get too brown.

Asparagus and English Pea Casserole

2 Cans Asparagus Spears
2 Cans Le Sueur English Peas
2 Cans Cream of Mushroom Soup
2 Small Cans Sliced Mushrooms
2 Small to Medium Onions, Diced
Extra Sharp Cracker Barrel Cheese, Grated (enough to cover top)
Butter
Salt
Pepper
Worcestershire Sauce
Garlic Salt, optional (I don't use much)
Pam Non-stick Cooking Spray

Preheat oven to 350 degrees if you plan to cook immediately. Grease 9x13 Pyrex dish with Pam. Sauté the onions and mushrooms in butter. Lightly salt. Combine with the mushroom soup. Add a little Worcestershire Sauce if desired. Layer the asparagus, then the English peas. Sprinkle with a little salt, then top with the soup mixture. You may repeat the layers, if desired. Sprinkle plenty of cheese on top of this. Use a spoon or a knife to poke holes or make slits in the casserole to allow the soup mixture to seep down into the bottom ingredients and spread the flavor.

Cranberry Salad

1 Large Raspberry Jell-O
1 Can (15 ½ Ounce) Crushed Pineapple
1 Large Can Whole Cranberry Sauce
1 Cup Orange Juice
1 Cup Chopped Celery
1 Cup Chopped Pecans,

½ Pint Sour Cream (or more)
Jell-O Mold
Red or Curly Lettuce

I usually double this recipe for our crowd, and put one recipe in a mold that will be placed on the center of a silver tray with pretty lettuce sticking out from under it. I put the other recipe in a 9x13 Pyrex dish to be cut in squares when congealed, and placed around the molded salad, each on its own piece of pretty lettuce. When using a mold, I have, a time or two, lined the mold with saran wrap before pouring in the Jell-O, so that it would be easier to get out of the mold. If using a different cranberry salad recipe that does not include sour cream, it is pretty to put the first recipe in a mold that has a hole in the middle so that you can put a little dish with homemade mayonnaise there, which can then be put on top of salad.

Heat the orange juice. Dissolve Jell-O in orange juice and cool. Add other ingredients except sour cream. Pour half into the mold or Pyrex dish and put in refrigerator until soft-set. Spread sour cream on top. Add the rest of the Jell-O mixture and place in refrigerator to congeal. Unmold and place on a silver or glass tray as described above.

Farmhouse Squash Casserole
The Farmhouse Restaurant, Ellerslie, Georgia

2 Pounds of Squash, Washed, Cleaned, and Sliced
2 Eggs
1 Large Chopped Yellow Onion
6 Tablespoons Margarine
½ Cup of Canned Evaporated Milk
3 Tablespoons of Sugar
1 Teaspoon Salt
3 Shakes of Crushed Red Pepper
1 ½ Cups Shredded Cheddar Cheese

1 Cup Ritz Cracker Crumbs
3 Tablespoons Melted Butter
Pam Non-stick Cooking Spray

Preheat oven to 350 degrees. Boil squash till tender. Sauté onions in six tablespoons of butter. Drain the squash in a colander and mash. Add the eggs, milk, sugar, salt, onions, red pepper and cheese. Pour into a Pyrex dish that has been sprayed with Pam. Mix melted butter and crackers. Sprinkle on top of the casserole. Bake for 30 minutes or until heated through.

Mammy's Artichoke Relish

My grandmother grew her own artichokes, and as I recall, this was quite a task for her gardener, who had to dig up all those artichokes. The artichokes then had to be cleaned and cut up. The end result of this effort is a relish that compliments almost any food, whether meats or vegetables (it pairs well with butter beans and rice). I have never had anything else quite like it. This recipe makes quite a lot of relish, and I believe Mammy canned it and during the Thanksgiving and Christmas holidays, gifted it to family and friends. It was like receiving gold!

6 Quarts Jerusalem Artichokes, Cut Up
6 Pounds Cabbage, Cut Up
3 Pounds Onion, Cut Up
12 Bell Peppers, Seeded and Cut Up
6 Tablespoons Black Pepper
6 Tablespoons Mustard Seeds
4 Tablespoons Turmeric
3 Pounds Brown Sugar (9 Cups)
3 Pounds White Sugar (9 Cups)
2 Cups Flour
2-24 Ounce Jars of French Mustard
4 Quarts Vinegar

Soak the bell pepper, onion, and cabbage in water and salt (1-gallon water to 1 cup of salt). Wash and cut up artichokes. Soak in water overnight. Drain and squeeze water out of vegetables. In a bowl, make a paste out of the flour, mustard, vinegar, pepper, turmeric, mustard seed and sugar. Cook 10 minutes. Add the vegetables and cook 25 minutes. Add the artichokes. This old recipe ends here, with no instructions about whether or not to cook the artichokes. I don't believe you do, however. The artichokes remain crunchy.

Christmas Table

Frozen Chocolate Torte
Anita Eaton

This is the best dessert! Whenever we have it, it is the chosen one! To make it even prettier, double the recipe and make three layers.

The Meringue

3 Egg Whites
½ Teaspoon Cream of Tartar
¾ Cup Sugar
¾ Cup Pecans, Chopped
1-2 Brown Paper Grocery Bag or Parchment Paper (depending on how many layers you are making)

Preheat oven to 275 degrees. Beat the egg whites until frothy. Add the cream of tartar, and beat until soft peaks form. Add the sugar, 1 tablespoon at a time, and continue beating until stiff peaks form. Fold in half of the pecans. Cover two baking sheets with brown paper. Cut a brown paper grocery bag in half so that you have two pieces on which to trace two 8-inch circles. Use an 8" cake pan to trace the circles. Spread half of the meringue on each circle to make a flat shell. Sprinkle the tops of each shell with the remaining pecans. Bake for 45 minutes. Check at 30 minutes if your oven tends to cook hot.

The Filling

2 Cups Whipping Cream
¾ Cup Hershey Chocolate Syrup
1 Teaspoon Vanilla
Shaved Chocolate, or little extra Chocolate Syrup to decorate the top

In a mixing bowl, beat the cream until stiff. Fold in the chocolate syrup and vanilla. To assemble, spread one meringue with half of the cream mixture. Top with the second layer of meringue. End with the other half of the whipped cream mixture. Sprinkle with shaved chocolate or drizzle top with chocolate syrup. It's best to freeze uncovered, then cover with Saran Wrap. Remove half hour before serving and let stand at room temperature. Serves 8 to 10 if you are lucky! To add a third layer, double recipe and divide to make the three layers.

Mammy's Caramel Cake Icing

1 Cup Sugar
3 Cups Whole Milk
1 Stick Butter
1 Teaspoon Vanilla
Cast Iron Frying Pan
Electric Mixer
Candy Thermometer
Box of Yellow Cake Mix (or a homemade cake)

Bake a yellow cake and place on racks to cool while you make the icing. Brown 1 cup of sugar in a heavy iron frying pan *VERY SLOWLY*. Heat 3 cups milk, also *VERY SLOWLY*. Bring to a good boil until sugar browns lightly. Remove from the heat. Pour the browned sugar into the milk. Place back on the burner and cook until it reaches the 'soft ball' stage. Use a candy thermometer, but the 'soft ball' stage is when you can pick it up in a ball with your fingers after it's been dropped into a cup of cold water. It should not look milky or cloudy. At this point, remove from the heat. Add 1 stick of butter and 1 teaspoon of vanilla. Let it sit while the butter melts. Do not mix. When melted, beat it with a mixer until it is thick. If it gets *too* thick and dry, add ½ teaspoon of milk. This will keep the icing from cracking on the cake,

Mammy's Divine Divinity Candy

2 ½ Cups Sugar
1/3 Cup Karo Syrup
½ Cup Water
2 Egg Whites
Pecans, Chopped, optional
Food Coloring
Electric Mixer
Candy Thermometer
Sheet Pan Lined with Wax Paper

Combine the sugar, Karo Syrup and water in a boiler and bring slowly to a boil. Boil until it forms a good thread (make sure it reaches 250-260 degrees, even though the thread stage is supposed to be between 223 and 235 degrees). If you live in a high-altitude location, subtract one-degree Fahrenheit from the stage's required temperature for each 500 feet above sea level. The thread stage is reached when you lift your spoon out of the boiling mixture and a thread descends from your spoon. However, to be sure, use a candy thermometer. While it's cooking, beat the egg whites until stiff. When the syrup reaches the thread stage, pour ½ of the syrup into the egg whites and beat. Cook the other half of the syrup about one minute, then pour into the egg whites and continue beating. To determine if you have beaten the mixture long enough, turn off the mixer and lift the beaters. If the candy falls into the bowl in long ribbons that quickly merge together it is *not* done. Continue beating. It should lose its glossiness and stickiness. To test another way, drop a teaspoonful of candy onto the wax paper and see if it puddles like a melting snowman. It *should not,* rather it should hold a peak and stay in a mound. When it is done, mix in nuts and food coloring, if desired. Drop by spoonfuls onto the wax paper. Store in an airtight container lined with wax paper. The divinity is pretty if it is white, light pink, or light green.

Ambrosia

Fresh Navel Oranges, Segmented
Coconut, Shredded and Sweetened
Maraschino Cherries, Drained

Adjust quantities for the number in your crowd. This simple version of Ambrosia is all you need if the oranges are sweet. It will be heaven in your mouth.

Country Captain

This recipe is enough for four people. In order to make sure you have plenty of sauce, *double the recipe for the sauce.*

1 ½ Medium Onion, Chopped
2 T Butter
2-3 Large Cans of Whole Tomatoes, Cut Up
1 ½ Large Green Pepper, Chopped
1 Garlic Clove, Crushed
1 ¼ Teaspoons Salt
½ Teaspoon White Pepper
1 ½ Teaspoons Curry Powder (add more if desired)
1 ½ Teaspoons Parsley, Chopped (or flakes)
1 Teaspoon Thyme
¼ Pound Slivered Almonds, Toasted
3 Large Tablespoons Currants, plus more for serving
2 Cups Fluffy Rice
2-3 Pounds of Fried Chicken (Traditionally, this is bone-in Chicken, but you can use Chicken Tenders. To make it healthier, you can also use Skinless, Baked Chicken or Grilled Chicken Tenders.)

Fry chicken as usual or purchase it already fried. In either case, keep the chicken hot! This is the key to the dish's success. In this day of health consciousness, feel free to use grilled or baked, skinless chicken, but it won't be quite as good (although almost!). Sauté the onion in butter. Add to this, green peppers and garlic clove. Stir constantly while cooking very slowly. Add the salt, white pepper and curry powder. Check the taste and adjust the seasonings, especially the curry. Add the tomatoes, parsley, and thyme. Cook for approximately 15 minutes. Mix the currants with the sauce, reserving some for garnish. Put the chicken in a Pyrex dish and pour some of the sauce over the chicken, reserving some for the rice and gravy boat. Cover the sauce-coated chicken with foil and cook in a 350-degree pre-heated oven for 45 minutes. To serve on a buffet, place the Chicken in the center of a silver tray with the rice around it. Pour sauce over the rice, reserving some sauce for a gravy boat. Scatter Almonds and Currants on top, reserving some of each for your guests to add as they desire.

Mashed Potatoes Rachael
Rachael Peek
This is such an easy recipe and yet it *always* gets rave reviews!

2 Family Size Packages of Simply Potatoes (regular flavor)
¾ of a 16 Ounce Carton of Sour Cream
½ + Stick of Butter, Melted
½ Cup of Chives, Chopped
Salt
Pepper
Fresh Grated Parmesan Cheese for top
Pam Non-stick Cooking Spray

Preheat oven to 350 degrees. Spray 9x13 Pyrex dish with Pam. Heat potatoes in the microwave before adding ingredients. Add all ingredients except cheese and mix. Make sure you add enough salt. Spread in the Pyrex dish which has been coated with Pam. Top with a lot of parmesan cheese. Bake until the cheese melts and it is browning a little, around 30 minutes.

Feather Rice

1 Stick Butter or Margarine
1 ½ Cups White or Brown Rice
1 ½ Cups Beef Bullion
1 ½ Cups French Onion Soup (Undiluted)
1 ½ Quart Pyrex dish
Pam Non-stick Cooking Spray

Preheat oven to 350 degrees. Spray the Pyrex dish with Pam. Melt the butter and toss the rice in it. Put the rice in a 1 ½ quart Pyrex dish, and add all other ingredients. Cook for 1 hour 15 minutes.

Caribbean Salad
Margie Richardson

¼ Cup Vinegar
2 Tablespoons Water
1 Package Good Seasons Italian Dressing Mix
2 ¾ Tablespoons Brown Sugar
2 Teaspoons Dijon Mustard
2 ¾ Tablespoons Fresh Lemon Juice
2/3 Cup Salad Oil
9-10 Ounces Fresh Spinach
1/8 Cup Red Onion, Thinly Sliced
1 Avocado, Cubed
1 Cup Fresh Grapefruit Sections (We usually just purchase this in a jar.)
Sunflower Seeds

For the dressing, mix the vinegar, water, and dressing mix together. Add brown sugar, mustard, lemon juice and oil and whisk. Tear the spinach into bite size pieces and place in bowl or on individual salad plates. Layer on top of the spinach the onion, avocado, grapefruit and seeds. Drizzle dressing over.

Buttermilk Pie

This is an easy but *winning* dessert that is loved by almost everyone!

2 Heaping Tablespoons All Purpose Flour
½ Teaspoon Baking Powder
1 ½ Cups Sugar
1/8 Teaspoon Salt
3 Eggs
5 Tablespoons Buttermilk
¾ Stick Margarine or Butter, Melted
½ Teaspoon Vanilla Extract
Deep Dish Pie Shell, Thawed, and Brushed with Egg Wash. Use a fork to Pierce holes in the bottom and sides of the Pie Shell to prevent bubbles.

Preheat the oven to 350 degrees. Mix the dry ingredients by hand. Beat the eggs slightly by hand. Add the milk mixture to the eggs. Add this to the dry ingredients. Add the margarine. Mix. Add the vanilla. Pour into an unbaked pie shell. Bake for 45 minutes or until set and the middle is no longer jiggly. You may need to cover with a loose tent of aluminum foil for the last few minutes to avoid over-browning.

Lemon Meringue Pie

Vanilla Wafer Pie Crust (Use a Graham Cracker Pie Crust if you can't find a Vanilla Wafer Pie Crust.)

Filling

2 Cans Sweetened Condensed Milk
3 Egg Yolks
¾ Cup Fresh Lemon Juice
1 Teaspoon Lemon Zest

Combine all by hand. Pour in the pie crust.

Meringue

4 Egg Whites
¼ Teaspoon Cream of Tartar
4 T Sugar

Preheat oven to 325 degrees. Beat the egg whites with the cream of tartar until a little more than frothy. Add the sugar, 1 tablespoon at the time. Beat well after each tablespoon. Continue to beat until stiff peaks form. Top pie. Bake for 12-15 minutes or until peaks begin to brown. If you find that the egg whites in the meringue 'weeps,' drain off before serving.

Easter Desserts

Easter

Easter memories for my children definitely included dying Easter eggs. However, the eggs were *not* boiled. Instead, I would use a spoon to tap a little circle around the top of the raw eggs, take the tops off (about a dime-size piece of the shell), and drain the eggs directly into the frying pan or into a bowl for later use. I rinsed out the egg shells, both inside and out, very well, and stood them up (hole side down) on paper towels to dry. Before we dyed the eggs, we would sometimes use the clear crayon that came with the dyes and draw crosses or write Bible verses and Easter exclamations (like, 'He is Risen!') on them. Once we dyed them, we again stood them on paper towels to dry. Later, I would fill them with candy and use scotch tape to seal them. They were so pretty just sitting in a silver, pottery, or glass bowl waiting for the Easter egg hunt. The egg symbolizes the resurrection of Jesus Christ for a Christian, and has long been associated with rebirth and renewal. I even use the egg to explain how the Father, Son, and Holy Ghost are one. There are three obvious parts of an egg. The yolk, the white, and the shell. But it's all one egg.

It was always a treat when someone we knew would have an Easter egg hunt in their yard for all of the little children we knew. Often the Spring flowers were blooming, an amazing backdrop for all of the precious children dressed in their Easter outfits. It made for quite a sight. By Easter morning, the children had been to several hunts at private homes and churches, and to the annual Wynn House Easter Egg Hunt. The Wynn House is a beautiful, antebellum home in Columbus with a huge lawn where thousands of colorful eggs were scattered. The children became quite skilled at hunting and finding Easter eggs, so they needed big, beautiful baskets with pink, yellow, and green grass lining them, and ribbon adorning them. I love Easter baskets, and I always made sure each child had the prettiest chocolate bunny I could find, along with other special candy in their basket when they woke up on Easter morning. And they always got a bathing suit on Easter, since in the south, warm weather was just around the corner.

Early, early, on Easter morning, our children would wake up ready to go after that Golden Egg. They knew the Easter Bunny had come, but once again, we were honest about who the Easter Bunny was. That fact did not affect our day one little bit, except to let them know just how much we loved them. The children were ecstatic about Jesus's resurrection, about the gifts they received, and about finding the eggs filled with candy, especially the Golden Egg. This hunt took place in our home, and then we gathered with grandparents, aunts, uncles, and cousins for lunch. We might go to Twin Springs for a picnic, or we might just all gather at someone's house in town. Easter lunch was and is always casual, though the little children were usually dressed in the beautiful Easter clothes they wore to church. We almost always picked up fried chicken and prepared picnic food to go along with it. Stuffed eggs, ham with tiny little, perfectly round biscuits (that I did not make), baked beans, and a colorful Cole slaw. Once or twice I followed my inclination to try to make Easter a little fancier and maybe prettier, by having things like chicken salad instead of fried chicken, and Beehive Butter instead of honey mustard for the ham biscuits. But the picnic is easier, so we usually let that rule the day.

Once we finished lunch, we would have two more egg hunts where eggs were strategically hidden around the lawn, in the flower bushes, and at the base of trees. The first hunt was for the children, and the second one was for the adults. I have enough Easter baskets for everyone, so everyone gets to run around with the excitement of a child gathering the colorful eggs. The children's eggs might have a little change in some of them, and there was always (and still are) a golden and a silver egg that were filled with as much candy as I could stuff in them, along with a little money. The adults had a golden egg too, but with a little more serious money in it—enough money for those adult children and their spouses to get pretty excited about it so that it was (and is) a real competition. I am always afraid someone is going to break their leg trying to run all over the sometime uneven terrain looking for that egg!

I always tried to talk to the children, and later the grandchildren, about the spiritual meaning and symbolism of Easter *before* Easter, while we were eating together, praying, reading books, and dying eggs, instead of during all of the hoopla of racing around looking for eggs. There are many things you can do to demonstrate the resurrection of Christ. Again, look at Pinterest!

A favorite thing that my children made when they were very small attending a little church nursery school was a clay bird's nest with eggs. I still have the nests and eggs that they painted pastel colors. They are captivatingly perfect with all of their hand-shaped imperfections. Beautiful. I pull these out every year at Easter and place them where I can see them often, reminding me of my children, their precious innocence and the promise that we received from the Word. "Therefore, if anyone is in Christ, he is a new creation. The old has passed away; behold, the new has come." 2 Corinthians 5:17 ESV

A friend recently gave me a recipe for a Strawberry English Trifle that her family has made for Christmas for years and years. I know it would be just perfect for our Easter dessert.

Easter Table

Strawberry English Trifle
Martha Flournoy

2 Packages Plain Ladyfingers
¾ Cup Sherry, Divided
1 ½ Cups Fresh Strawberries, Hulled and Halved
Trifle Custard
1 Cup Strawberry Preserves
Toasted Almond Slices
1 ½ Cups Whipping Cream
¼ Cup plus 2 Tablespoons Sifted Powdered Sugar
Fresh Cut Strawberries
Mint Leaves
16-Ounce Trifle Bowl

Line the bottom of a 16-ounce trifle bowl with 1/3 of the Ladyfingers. Sprinkle with ¼ cup sherry. Arrange the strawberry halves, cut side out, around the lower edge of the bowl. Spoon 2 cups trifle custard over the Ladyfingers. Place half of the remaining Ladyfingers over the custard. Gently spread the strawberry preserves over the Ladyfingers. Sprinkle the toasted almonds on top. Top with the remaining Ladyfingers. Pour the remaining ½ cup sherry over the trifle. Spoon the remaining trifle custard on top of this. Cover and chill 3 to 4 hours. Beat whipping cream until foamy. Gradually add powdered sugar, beating until soft peaks form. Spread over trifle. Top with fresh cut strawberries and mint leaves. Serves 14-16.

Custard

2 Cups Milk
2/3 Cup Whipping Cream
4 Eggs
Electric Mixer

Combine the milk and the whipping cream in a medium saucepan. Cook over low heat until it is warm. Combine the eggs and sugar, beating well with an electric mixer. Gradually stir about ¼ of the warm mixture into the eggs to temper them so they will not cook and become scrambled eggs. Then add the eggs to the saucepan, stirring constantly. Cook over low heat, continuing to stir until mixture thickens and coats the spoon. Remove from the heat. Stir in the vanilla. Cool to room temperature. Chill.

The Fourth of July

The Fourth of July celebration is great fun for everyone! Take your children to the best fireworks display you can find! We took our children to the celebration at Ft. Benning, and the year we went they had a band playing patriotic music as the fireworks popped and swirled so majestically into the heavens. It was exciting and inspirational. I've never been so impressed by any other fireworks show. We all thought the millions of sparks were going to rain right down on top of us, we were so close. But it was an incredibly beautiful, heart pounding experience.

This holiday presents a wonderful opportunity for the children to learn a lot about our country's founding, it's amazing liberty, and what makes it so great. While celebrating our country's independence, teach your children about the faith of our founding fathers, the reason our forefathers came here in the first place, and what it means to be free. Talk to them about our capital, Washington, D.C., about the White House, and about how our government works. The Preamble to the Declaration of Independence and the Preamble to the Constitution are both great documents to read and memorize. Teach them to pray for our country, for peace, and for those who are protecting us. If you know stories of patriotism, service, or other significant contributions made by any of your ancestors to America, now is the time to tell those stories to your children. Ask your parents if they know any stories. It may also be an appropriate time to acknowledge that, just as we make mistakes in our personal lives, our country has at times strayed from God's perfect will, and that we need to pray for renewal and recommitment.

Blessed is the nation whose God is the Lord; the people he has chosen as his own inheritance. The Lord looks from heaven; He sees all the sons of men.
Psalm 33:12, 13 NKJV

Your children need to know what God expects and how He will bless our country if our country follows Him. You are the only one who will teach them these things. When I was a little girl, every school day began with a prayer and the Pledge of Allegiance. We would always sing two patriotic songs, usually "God Bless America" and "America the Beautiful." This was such an important first step in the day, reminding us of what God had blessed us with and inspiring us to be great Americans. It made us appreciate and honor our country and its flag. It helped us understand the sacrifices that so many Americans have made for our freedom. Yours and mine.

It's important to me to pass this on to our children and grandchildren, as they may not learn it in school. America has been a beacon of light in this world, blessed by God in so many ways. I'm proud of my country, and I want my children to be as well. Being proud means that you will treat her right, stand up for her, and defend her. If you ever begin to take your blessings for granted, take a trip to almost any other country, and you will appreciate all the more what we have right here. Especially our freedom.

So, as July brought us the heat we were so familiar with, it also reminded us to celebrate the country we love. I tried to capitalize on the time that my children and I spent in the car by playing a CD that featured children singing one great patriotic song after the other. The name of this terrific little CD is *Wee Sing America*. In the last few years, I have given it to my grandchildren, and it's still wonderful! My children and grandchildren have loved singing along with the CD and everyone (including myself) really learned a lot from the songs about the country we pledge our allegiance to. Music makes learning fun and easy, and learning the words to a few of our country's most important documents is inspiring.

Preamble to the Declaration of Independence

When, in the course of human events, it becomes necessary for one people
to dissolve the political bands which have connected them with another,
and to assume among the powers of the earth the separate and equal station
to which the laws of nature and of nature's God entitle them, a decent respect
to the opinions of mankind requires that they should
declare the causes which impel them to the separation.
We hold these truths to be self-evident; that all men are created equal;
that they are endowed by their creator with certain unalienable rights;
that to secure these rights, governments are instituted among men,
deriving their just powers from the consent of the governed;
that whenever any form of government becomes destructive to these ends,
it is the right of the people to alter or to abolish it, and to institute a new government, laying
its foundation on such principles, and organizing its powers
as to them shall seem most likely to effect their safety and happiness.
Prudence, indeed, will dictate that governments long established should not be changed for
light and transient causes; and accordingly all experience hath shown
that mankind are more disposed to suffer, while evils are sufferable,
than to right themselves by abolishing the forms to which they are accustomed.

The Pledge of Allegiance
Francis Bellamy

I pledge allegiance to the flag of the United States of America
and to the Republic for which it stands,
one Nation under God, indivisible,
with liberty and justice for all.

You're a Grand Old Flag
George M. Cohan

You're a grand old flag,
You're a high-flying flag
And forever in peace may you wave.
You're the emblem of
The land I love,
The home of the free and the brave.
Ev'ry heart beats true
'Neath the red, white and blue
Where there's never a boast or brag.
But should auld acquaintance be forgot,
Keep your eye on the grand old flag.

America
Samuel F. Smith

My country, 'tis of thee,
Sweet land of liberty,
Of thee I sing;
Land where my fathers died,

Land of the pilgrims' pride,
From every mountain side
Let freedom ring!
My native country, thee,
Land of the noble free,
Thy name I love;
I love thy rocks and rills,
Thy woods and templed hills;
My heart with rapture thrills,
Like that above.
Let music swell the breeze,
And ring from all the trees
Sweet freedom's song;
Let mortal tongues awake;
Let all that breathe partake;
Let rocks their silence break,
The sound prolong.
Our fathers' God, to Thee,
Author of liberty,
To thee we sing;
Long may our land be bright
With freedom's holy light;
Protect us by Thy might,
Great God, our King!

America the Beautiful
Katharine Lee Bates

O beautiful for spacious skies,

For amber waves of grain,
For purple mountain majesties
Above the fruited plain!
America! America!
God shed His grace on thee
And crown thy good with brotherhood
From sea to shining sea!
O beautiful for pilgrim feet,
Whose stern, impassioned stress
A thoroughfare for freedom beat
Across the wilderness!
America! America!
God mend thine every flaw,
Confirm thy soul in self-control,
Thy liberty in law!
O beautiful for heroes proved
In liberating strife,
Who more than self their country loved,
And mercy more than life!
America! America!
May God thy gold refine,
Till all success be nobleness
And every gain divine!
O beautiful for patriot dream
That sees beyond the years
Thine alabaster cities gleam
Undimmed by human tears!
America! America!
God shed His grace on thee

And crown thy good with
Brotherhood
From sea to shining sea!

The Star-Spangled Banner
Francis Scott Key

O say, can you see, by the dawn's early light,
What so proudly we hailed at the
twilight's last gleaming,
Whose broad stripes and bright stars,
through the perilous fight,
O'er the ramparts we watched
were so gallantly streaming!
And the rockets' red glare, the
bombs bursting in air,
Gave proof through the night that
our flag was still there.
O say, does that star-spangled
banner yet wave
O'er the land of the free and the
home of the brave?

Preamble to the Constitution of the United States
We the people of the United States, in order to form a more perfect Union, establish justice, insure domestic tranquility provide for the common defense, promote the general welfare, and secure the blessings of liberty to ourselves and our posterity, do ordain and establish this Constitution for the United States of America.

CHAPTER 15

Mind Your Manners

Teach your children manners. Southern women especially appreciate polished manners. Southern men, on the other hand, are not as easily convinced that manners matter and generally only adopt them because their mothers insist on their importance. Still, I'm pretty sure it's true that a southern man would think twice before becoming too interested in a girl without them. And a refined southern girl would think thrice about going out with a man who lacks proper gentility.

So, teach your children to say, "Yes, ma'am," "No, ma'am," "Yes, sir," "No, sir," and just plain *ma'am* and *sir*. Teach them to say please (and "Pretty please with sugar on top!") and to always say, "Thank you, ma'am" and "Thank you, sir." This is imperative for the southern child and should be for all children. You are forthwith teaching them to respect their elders and other people in general. In the South, this is what you do. Period.

Teach them to look a person in the eye when they are talking to them, to speak distinctly, and to have good posture. They should stand up straight and sit up straight with good form, shoulders back. Little ladies should learn to be poised and to cross their ankles when seated. Older girls need to know to cross their legs. Make them practice posture and remind them regularly how important it is not to slouch. A strong handshake is important, especially for a young man. Staring at another person is rude. Explain to your children that when not speaking, they should be aware of keeping their mouths closed. Remember Mary Poppins telling Michael to close his mouth and saying, "We are not codfish!"? Do not chew gum when you are on stage or in a conversation with others—in whatever capacity. Teach them that burping in public and blowing their nose at the dinner table is unattractive if not downright rude (although this cannot always be helped, they should try to avoid it). A yawn should be covered with your hand. My absolute pet peeve has to be seeing a person use a toothpick to remove food from their teeth after a meal. Retreat to a restroom to handle such problems. Even if the person is not removing food from their teeth, a toothpick hanging out of someone's mouth at the end of meal is really not a very pleasant sight!

One thing that is very significant, though sometimes overlooked as such, is the introduction. There is a right way and a wrong way to introduce two people who do not know each other, but there is a simple way to remember what the right way is. *In an introduction, look at and say the name of the most important person first.* For instance, "Grandmother, I'd like for you to meet my roommate, Sam." Then turn to look at Sam and say, "Sam, this is my grandmother, Mrs. Adams." It is fairly easy to determine the more important person. A woman is given the curtesy of being more important than a man, and an older person would be more important than a younger person. A friend would be more important than a family member, and an adult more important than a child. Try to say the last names of those you are introducing. Repeat their first names while mentioning something interesting about at least one, if not both, of them in order to stimulate the conversation between two new friends. Tell your child, since they may not think about the necessity of it, that they should say their first *and* last names whenever introducing themselves to someone new.

If you have a son (which may be unlikely for my children since I now have five granddaughters and no grandsons, and my sister has seven granddaughters and no grandsons), you must teach him to be a gentleman, and to always honor a lady. If that sounds like lunacy to the equality-conscious members of the twenty-first century, I beg you to consider my argument. This book, after all, is written with those in mind whose faith is in the living God, who created us, male and female. I don't think many would argue against the predication that the male is generally, and almost without exception, the stronger of the two sexes, and it is precisely because of this God-given trait that the male should take the role of protector. In that vein, over the years, certain social norms have come to bear. I have not taken a poll, but I can tell you that most women I know would nearly swoon having a man treat them with such care and deference. This treatment indicates much more than meets the eye. If sincere, it will carry over into a marriage. It will extend to faithfulness based on a desire to please God and to honor and respect the one he loves. While training your son to be a gentleman, you are afforded the opportunity to discuss the fact that you expect him to always be courageous and do the right thing. Tell him that anyone can follow the crowd, taking the common road, but it takes courage, strength, and conviction to be honorable. In doing so, he may have to walk away from a friend or two or even a friend group if they are behaving badly, in order to stick by his convictions. Whether the issue is drinking, smoking, using drugs, having sex outside of marriage, being unfaithful to a spouse, or mistreating someone through thievery, bribery, or deceit, his decision at those critical moments will reflect his character. And he needs to have thought about what he wants his character to be. In this case, being protective of someone weaker than he.

A gentleman, (a strong, protective figure not to be confused with a sissy), will be aware of the comings and goings of the ladies at his table. When everyone is coming to the table, he will always pull the chair out for his date or for any unaccompanied lady sitting beside him. He then helps her reposition her chair so that she is comfortable at the table. If a lady at the table excuses herself for a trip to the powder room, the man stands when she leaves and when she returns. Once again, he seats her at the table (if she is his date or is unaccompanied and sitting next to him). This should be done as naturally as possible, and not with ceremony or awkwardness. Actually, it is polite and correct manners for a gentleman to stand anytime a woman enters or leaves a room. I know a man who consistently does this very thing with sincerity, and believe me, it is impressive. He stands out in the crowd, particularly because this man is in a social position whereby he could easily expect all around him to grovel at his very appearance. Instead, he is the epitome of humility and grace. This type of deference to another human being speaks volumes to those who are watching and those who are on the receiving end, and it clearly demonstrates God's love. It is not overblown or done in an ingratiating way, but with grace. With these manners, it becomes clear that he was raised properly with appropriate concern for the welfare of others.

I was at a party last night, and a man stood when his wife was leaving the table to go to the powder room. I overheard a lady at the table talking to the person sitting next to her about how nice that was. She took note of this chivalrous act, probably wishing the man in her life treated her this way. So rare is the sight of it these days. It is a small act that costs the man little, but makes the woman feel like a million dollars. Fathers, set the example! Treat the women in your life this way. Your son will emulate you, and one day he will amaze someone when he shows this degree of respect to a date, or maybe a lady entering the boardroom. *If that offends someone, I say 'pooh' to the new concept of equality.*

Table manners are another matter. It takes some time to get table manners right. For instance, especially to a hungry child, it is counterintuitive to wait until everyone is at the table to actually sit down, but when at a party or a more formal setting, this is appropriate, even for children. They should be instructed to stand behind their chair until all guests are at the table and the host or hostess is seated. The first thing they will do when they sit down for a meal is put their napkin in their lap. If it is a large napkin, it is not to be completely unfolded but rather can remain folded in half. Again, it is counterintuitive to wait to eat until everyone at the table has been served and the blessing has been said to eat, but this is exactly what they must learn to do. They take their first bite only after the host or hostess lifts his or her fork. Little ladies (and grown women) should use their napkin to dab away food from the corners of their mouths rather than wipe their mouths like they are swabbing a floor!

Teach your children to set the table correctly by insisting they do it when they are very young (of course supervising the handling of the knife). Make it a game, and make it as much fun as you can. This little task will make them feel important and useful, and proud when they get it right. Teach them the fundamentals, that is, that the fork is placed to the left of the plate, and knives belong on the right of the plate. The blade of the knife always faces the plate and may be tucked slightly underneath it. (The children will find it fascinating that this careful placement was instituted in bygone days when knives were used for the first time at the table and were considered weapons!) The spoon goes on the outside of the knife. *Teach your children to use the acronym FORKS to help them remember where everything goes. Facing the placemat, think "F" for fork, O for plate, "K" for knife, and last, "S" for spoon. If you tell them the fork goes on the left side of the plate, and if they tend to forget which way is their left, have them hold up their hands, making an L with their pointer finger and thumb. This will only work with their left hand, making it easy to tell which is their right and which is their left.* When they get a handle on this, offer a little more information. Tell them that if dessert silver is used, it is to be placed in logical fashion above the dinner plate. The dessert fork (or cake fork) is closest to the plate pointing right, since it then makes sense to draw it down (with its handle) to its correct position on the left side of the plate. The dessert spoon is above that pointing left, so that it may be easily drawn down (with its handle) to the right side of the plate. Explain that it is most common, however, for guests to simply lift the proper utensil from its position above the plate to begin the dessert course. There actually is a common-sense reason for most of our formalities.

Knowing the proper American etiquette when it comes to holding your knife and fork is important to me even if the Europeans do it a different way, and even if you are just as comfortable holding chopsticks. We live in America, and there are certain cultural mores that have been handed down through the generations that have been deemed socially acceptable. Unfortunately, many people have either neglected to teach their children these mores or they never learned them themselves. I'm sure there are just as many people who do not think these formalities are important at all, so they don't bother even trying to ascribe to any particular form. On top of this, one thing that has come with today's ease of travel is a desire to be internationally literate when it comes to other customs and cultures, and I believe the consequence has been a diminished desire to hold on to our own American customs. It may even be more of a disdain for our customs, although I'm not sure I understand why. I hope you will see the significance and consider the value of adhering to your own culture's long-held traditions. Your children will need this polish and knowhow, especially as long as they are living in America.

So it is my hope that your children will master the art of holding their knife and fork *the American way*. The fork should be cradled between the thumb and the index finger, resting on the middle finger. When cutting, the fork is in the left hand, tines down, held between the thumb and middle finger, with the index finger resting on top of it. The knife is in the right hand, with the index finger resting on the back of it. After cutting the food, the fork is transferred back to the right hand, and the food is then brought to the mouth.

Instruct your child *not* to cut their food into a dozen tiny pieces as if they were a baby. Cut one piece, eat it, then cut another and eat it, and so on. Their knife should rest across the edge of the plate when it is not being used to cut food (don't continue to hold it in your hand). To avoid the ravenous appearance of someone who hasn't eaten in a month of Sundays, take breaks during the meal by placing your fork down diagonally on the plate. Otherwise, someone might think when they see your appetite, "She ate like a field hand!"

One thing that you will want to teach your children is that when bread is served on a bread plate and butter is passed, they should take a slice of butter with the master butter knife (the one passed with the butter) and place it on their bread plate, then return that knife to the butter plate. When they are ready to eat the bread, it is most polite to break off a piece of their roll or biscuit and butter it with their own butter knife (or dinner knife if a butter knife is not provided). If they are not taught this, they will end up 'stealing' the master butter knife and the other guests will be looking for it! The more important and logical reason for this custom is that if the master butter knife were used by each guest, that knife, being returned to the butter, would contaminate it.

Teach your children to keep their elbows off of the table. No matter why this custom originated, whether for practicality or formality, I cannot say. But it is important! Every mother says to her children, "Mabel, Mabel, strong and able, take your elbows off the table!" I think the best explanation is that in our civilized society, it really is unappetizing to see someone at the table leaning forward over their food in an overindulgent stance. We get nervous that they are about to shovel their food into their mouth as if they haven't eaten in days. This explains, too, why your children should learn the importance of lifting their fork to their mouth rather than leaning down toward the plate to reach the fork. And of course, it goes without saying that no one wants to be subjected to a fellow diner who does not know to keep their mouth closed when they are eating. When finished with any meal, whether formal or casual, they should place their utensils together diagonally across their plate, pointing toward the center of the plate, so that the person removing the plate will not encounter problems with the silver falling off of the plate.

Although I do feel strongly about the importance of table manners, I feel just as strongly about the importance of enjoying your children and having a good time around the family table. So make it as interesting, fun, and painless as possible, while making sure the children attempt to use manners. Accept the fact that they will make mistakes over and over again but also expect progress as they mature. Gathering around the family table should be one of the most pleasant parts of any day, so use humor and lightheartedness as you teach. The table should be like a sanctuary, with an emphasis on interesting conversation, a chance for the children to express themselves and to learn social skills, and it should be full of praise for God's goodness. It should be a happy time and place, not a stressful one. As the children get older, you will be able to insist that they use the proper manners that you have spent years training them to use, but even then, make sure you refrain from making everyone miserable. You will gradually figure out how to best handle this, but I'll tell you it's not always so easy. If you, yourself, display good manners, the likelihood is that your children will imitate you (though this is not always the case). Your children will need these skills when they go out into the world, the workplace, and on every important date. Help them learn to have a little polish.

When having a dinner party, invite people that will trigger conversation. Mix the ages of the people you invite, and try to invite people you think would be interesting to the other guests. Teach your children some basics of table service as well. Hostesses with or without servers will need to have this information in order to have even an informal meal. Your children should know some simple rules. The guest of honor, traditionally, is seated to the right of the host. Always serve that person first. The host is the last person to be served. Service, therefore, proceeds counterclockwise. The host or server should place and remove plates from the left of their guest, and conversely, place and remove beverages from the right. This is easy to remember, since the glasses are stationed on the right of the plate. It is proper to leave the glasses on the table when refilling them.

The hostess (or at home, the mother) signals the beginning of the meal by lifting her fork and taking the first bite, and the end of the meal by placing her napkin to the left of her plate. Of course, if the one hosting a party is a man, one would watch for his signal to begin the meal. When one leaves the table but plans to return (for instance, to go to the powder room or to the buffet), one leaves the napkin on the chair, not the table.

When your children are young and the family finishes a meal, the children should tell their mother (or whoever prepared the meal) that they enjoyed it and ask politely if they may be excused. I am teaching my grandchildren just that and insisting they say, "Gigi, I enjoyed it! May I be excused?" They should be allowed to leave the table only once everyone has finished eating (unless, of course, they need to use the restroom or are too young to sit through the entire meal). Of course, adults should also thank the hostess when the meal is over and say, "Excuse me, please," when leaving the table to go to the powder room. "Please" and "Thank you" are words everyone appreciates. My daughter-in-law brought something up that I thought was a great idea. She teaches her child to say "please" and "thank you" to Alexa so that she doesn't get used to ordering people around. Smart.

While doing a little research for this section of the book, I found a few interesting facts that are helpful to know. Decanters were introduced at a time when corks were not used. At that time, wine was stored in barrels in the cellar. Now decanters are used for red wine, which attains a fullness of flavor when decanted. The wine is poured into the decanter for the purpose of allowing the wine to breathe and the sediments fall to the bottom of the bottle. Decanters are also used for liquors such as scotch and brandy. A decanter may be left on the table; a wine bottle is not to be left on a formal table. However, in these days of informality, this rule no longer seems to apply.

An old-fashioned glass is also called a rocks glass and is used for a beverage that is drunk on ice. A double old-fashioned is twice as big. Often this glass has the man's initials engraved in the glass and is used for many types of drinks.

Apparently, brides almost always received a silver punch bowl as a bridal gift in the 1950s, and they were used primarily to serve punch between courses. But today, it is most often used as a beautiful vessel for serving Eggnog at Christmas. This is how my family used theirs and how I use mine. It is a nonessential but an essential at the same time. A thing of beauty is a joy forever!

Here are a few of the technicalities of etiquette, some of which are basic, and some that you, yourself, may not know, but that are essential to know if you are entertaining or being entertained in a formal manner.

It is important to learn where the bread plate and the drinking glasses should be placed on the table. It's mighty awkward to be at a dinner party and realize you aren't sure which bread plate or salad plate is yours. Embarrassing! The salad plate should be above the forks and slightly to the left and the bread plate goes a little above this and between the bread plate and the cake fork. The stemware for drinking is positioned to the right of the dinner plate and slightly above the spoons. *To help your children (as well as yourself!) remember this, tell them to make the okay sign with both of their hands. The left hand forms a 'b' and the right hand forms a 'd.' Bread plate on the left, Drinks on the right.*

The placement of the crystal stemware for a formal meal can be confusing unless you know the reason behind this traditional setting. Each stem is placed according to when it is to be used, just as is the silverware. In a very formal meal, there can be as many as five glasses, and their position denotes when they are to be used. Although in this day of the relaxed, unceremonious, and laid-back, you may never find yourself in a situation with five glasses, it is still interesting. And should you ever have three glasses, you will know where to start and where to end.

The water goblet is always placed above and near the tip of the knife. The champagne flute is placed (in deference to space) above and to the right of the water goblet. The red wine (served with the meat) glass is positioned to the right and slightly below the water goblet. Then, slightly below that and to the right, is the white wine glass (served with fish or poultry). The sherry glass, if used, is placed below and to the right of the white wine glass, since sherry is served with the first course (soup). Therefore, it is simple to see when you are addressing your place setting that you use the glass farthest from the plate with the first course and end with the champagne flute during dessert.

You can easily remember that champagne is the last drink of a formal dinner because that lovely drink goes with dessert. And Gigi's favorite course is always dessert, the last course.

So the flute is at the top of the line of glasses, and you are obviously going to use the glass at the bottom first. Yes, I love dessert, and I love the way champagne looks. My grandmother, Mammy, loved champagne. It's so pretty, especially pink champagne with its beautiful pink bubbles. The person who supposedly invented the process for making champagne is a seventeenth-century monk named Dom Perignon. He would reportedly summon his confreres to partake of his discovery by saying, "Come quickly, brothers. I'm drinking the stars."

A long-stemmed flute is the preferred way of drinking this drink, so that your hand doesn't warm the champagne. In light of my exuberance over this pretty drink, I want to caution you to never overdo this drink. If you do, you will surely regret it. I will tell you again that I am not and have never been a big drinker. I don't even drink this lovely drink because it bothers my stomach. This discourse on champagne is included here to help you remember your crystal lineup.

The same logical lineup applies to the silverware. Use first the pieces farthest from the plate and work in. In other words, with the case of forks, use the fork farthest from the plate for the first course, and so on.

Manners and methods of communication have changed notably from pen and paper to telephone texting and email. I implore you, however, to teach your children how to write a proper thank-you note and to do it expediently. Starting with the millennials, the younger crowd no longer expects a handwritten thank-you note to be forthcoming when one gives a gift or helps another person in some way. It is more common now to get a quick text, and I guess that is acceptable. I am definitely guilty of doing just that a time or two in the recent past in response to something small that was done for me. But it is much more meaningful to know that someone has taken the time and made the effort to write a letter, put a stamp on it, and drop it in the mail. This also applies to writing someone who has just had a death in the family, had a baby, or has been in the hospital due to an illness. Once you have been in that situation, you realize how very much it means for someone to actually write you a thoughtful note. It feels like the proper thing to do, because it is. I just can't believe that it is common now for a company representative to email or text you saying you have or have not been given a job. That seems so rude and so cold and so uncaring. Why can't they pick up the phone and call the person and speak to them? I'll tell you why. That personal interaction is much more difficult to do. And with that level of communication, you are saying, in effect, that the person is not very important to you. If you do take the time to call or write a letter, you will stand out in a big way as a person of great value.

It is also quite rare, now, for anyone to ever send a formal RSVP note, but your child surely needs to know that a prompt reply to an invitation is expected and not to be neglected. A hostess who has honored you by requesting your presence at their party or event deserves the curtesy of a response. If you've ever hosted a party, you know how important it is to have a number, for planning, seating, menus, and amounts of food and drinks. So whether it's an enclosed response card, an email, a text, or a call, it is paramount that your child learn to respond in a timely manner.

Believe it or not, when I was young, the accepted response to an invitation was a handwritten, formal note!

Mr. and Mrs. Joseph Henry West accept with pleasure
your kind invitation to a luncheon on September 1, 1976.

or

Mr. and Mrs. Joseph Henry West decline with regrets your kind invitation
to a luncheon on September 1, 1976.

Ha! Ha! That formality is gone with the wind, and we've replaced it with whatever is the least amount of trouble, which is usually a quick text or a click of a button on an email. I'm not sure what the next step to even greater informality will be, but I know it will be less about the person and more about our convenience.

I hope I've convinced you to take a little time out of your busy life to let another human being know they are loved and appreciated. It can be important, and it can be a witness. When writing a note, consider a few things that will make it even nicer, more special, and meaningful. Use the heaviest stock paper you can afford with nothing on it except your personalization. Have your name or initials printed, engraved, or embossed on nice note paper. When possible, try not to resort to the less impressive preprinted notecard. If you cannot afford to have a personalized notecard, purchase a nice, cream or white blank card. If available, write with a black ink pen rather than a ballpoint pen. Make sure your letter is carefully written in cursive so that it does not convey the message that you were in a hurry. Never begin your letter with "I" and avoid saying things that clearly required little thought. If a person has given you a gift or has done something for you, it is worth a little effort on your part to make sure you communicate how kind they are, how great the gift is or how helpful the act, and your sincere appreciation. There are two letters I received that I will never forget. Both were from men. One was from a person whose brother had died. I had written him a note, and he had actually taken the time to write me back, thanking me for my note. This was especially meaningful, because this person conceivably had hundreds of notes and acts of sympathy to respond to. The other was from a busy doctor, who very unexpectedly took the time to write a letter, not a note, thanking me for something I'd done.

Aside from table manners and communication manners, your male children should be taught another form of chivalry. At least in the South, a man escorting a lady always walks on the outside of a sidewalk, by the street, to protect her from errant drivers. He should never let her lag behind, and he should never walk in front of her. He should always open the door for her when entering or exiting a building or a car. If you are a man and this seems old-fashioned, just try it and see how she responds to your genteel ways. She will appreciate greatly your genuine concern for her welfare and consequently be much more interested in you. That's not to say you should act like your date is unable to do a thing on her own. If you do, she will recoil from your affected, overdone manners.

You want your sons to be gentlemen, but you also want your daughters to be strong and confident of their own abilities to take care of themselves. There is a big difference between a man who is condensing to a woman and a man who is humble and trying to offer all he is to a lady.

Teach your children that when they are guests in someone's home, whether it be their grandparents' home or a friend's, they should be respectful of their host's possessions. Of course, they should not take food out of the dining areas or eat while seated on the den or living room furniture unless directed to do so by the host. Nor should they wallow on their hostess's furniture. They should treat their furniture and other belongings with care. If they are overnight guests, they should make their bed in the morning and make sure their clothes and any toys they have been playing with are picked up and put away. That is, unless they are instructed otherwise. This is just being courteous and considerate and respectful to the person who has graciously invited them to their home. As they mature, they should be taught that when visiting someone's home for a party or extended stay, they should not go empty-handed, but should take a little hostess gift as a thank you for the hostess's hospitality.

In the same vein, your daughters should learn about the niceties of true hospitality. They need to know the meaning of saying, "the hostess with the *mostest*!" I remember my grandmother saying this, and *she* really was the *hostess with the mostest*. Mammy had a lot of parties, and was known for wearing a gardenia in her hair to those parties. She was the consummate entertainer. But she also knew how to make her overnight guests feel welcome and want to come back. I remember her guest room well, especially the beds. The beds seemed like heaven to me. There were blanket warmers (sheets that covered the blankets), and pillows that were tightly rolled to form neck rolls. It made the bed look so perfect. Mammy was stylish, and she had decorated that room to make it nothing short of glorious to me. It was painted yellow and had yellow sheers on the windows. Now, that sounds so tacky, but it was beautiful! And when my sisters and I spent the night in Mammy's guest room, the sun would come up the next morning, filling the room with a shine that I cannot describe. About that time, Lulu would come in and ask if we wanted fresh-squeezed orange juice with our breakfast, which was a real treat, because after squeezing the oranges, she turned the juice into a frothy, frosty drink in the blender. What more could a guest ask for?

When entertaining overnight visitors in your home, make the person feel special by making them as comfortable as possible. Fresh flowers might be placed in their bedroom and bathroom, as well as throughout the house. A little bag of goodies in their bedroom is a thoughtful thing to do for your guest, perhaps filling it with snacks made in your town or area. Put a magazine, an interesting book, and possibly a pamphlet describing points of interest in your community on their bedside table. Make sure any toiletries they may need are available. Your guest will appreciate your attention to those details that will make their stay enjoyable and extra special. Your girls will learn about hospitality as you go the extra mile to love your guests and lavish them with these nice thoughts and things.

Zadie's First Birthday!

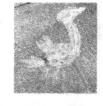

CHAPTER 16

Recognize the Truth and Act on It

I found these quotes, poems, and verses insightful and encouraging as I endeavored to keep looking forward in my parenting efforts. They have inspired me to be my best, and in some cases, have helped me to understand better the God I love.

> Knowing is not enough; we must apply. Willing is not enough; we must do.
> Goethe
> *My* good intentions will accomplish little without *my* action.

> For God in his wisdom saw to it that the world
> would never find God through human brilliance,
> and then he stepped in and saved all those who believed his message,
> which the world calls foolish and silly.
> 1 Corinthians 1:21 TLB
> The world will *call foolish* many of my decisions.

> Wisdom is knowing what to do next; virtue is doing it.
> David Starr Jordan
> I *must* do what I know I should!

It is better to be wise and not seem so,

than to seem wise and not be so.

Plato

I will be intentional about looking for God's wisdom, even when no one else is.

Parents can only give good advice

or put children on the right paths,

but the final forming of a person's character

lies in their own hands.

Anne Frank, *Diary of a Young Girl*

I am only responsible to my children, not for them.

You cannot make yourself feel something you do not feel,

but you can make yourself do right in spite of your feelings.

Pearl S. Buck

I will know what is right, and I will do right by my children even when I don't feel like it. Love is an act of the will.

That which seems the height of absurdity in one generation

often becomes the height of wisdom in the next.

John Stuart Mill

We are fickle. Fads and philosophies come and go. But God's Word is unchanging. I will not be swayed by the ever-changing words of my generation and I will teach my children to know the difference.

Trust in the Lord with all your heart,

and do not lean on your own understanding.

In all your ways acknowledge him, and he will make straight your paths.

Proverbs 3:5–6 ESV

If I don't understand, God does. His ways are higher than mine. I can rely on God to direct my paths!

Oh, the joys of those who do not follow evil men's advice,
who do not hang around with sinners, scoffing at the things of God:
But they delight in doing everything God wants them to,
and day and night are always meditating on his laws
and thinking about ways to follow him more closely.
They are like trees along a river bank bearing luscious fruit each season without fail.
Their leaves shall never wither, and all they do shall prosper.
But for sinners, what a different story! They blow away like chaff before the wind.
They are not safe on Judgment Day; they shall not stand among the godly.
For the Lord watches over all the plans and paths of godly men,
but the paths of the godless lead to doom.
Psalm 1:1–6 TBL

God sees me as godly only because when He looks at me, He sees Jesus. I will pray that my children and grandchildren seek that same Savior with their whole hearts, and that because of that, blessings upon blessings will be passed
down for generations upon generations in our family.

The Lord is my shepherd; I shall not want.
He makes me lie down in green pastures.
He leads me beside still waters.
He restores my soul.
He leads me in paths of righteousness for his name's sake.
Even though I walk through the valley of the shadow of death,
I will fear no evil, for you are with me;
your rod and your staff, they comfort me.
You prepare a table before me in the presence of my enemies;
you anoint my head with oil; my cup overflows.
Surely goodness and mercy shall follow me all the days of my life,
and I shall dwell in the house of the Lord forever.
Psalm 23 ESV

I have a shepherd who is leading me along paths of righteousness.
His name is not important to the world,
but He says that the reason He does this for me is
for his name's sake, which is all important to Him.
His name is so precious to Him
that in the Old Testament, His people did not dare say His name,
much less use His holy name profanely or in vain.
I hear friends and strangers throwing around
that name that means so little to them
because they do not know the one behind the name.
Lord, help me to know you so intimately
that I will treasure your name as you do, and
have every reason to protect and honor your name
through my actions and my words.

Names of God and Their Meanings

Elohim, God my Creator
El Elyon, the Sovereign One
El Roi, the God Who Sees
El Shaddai, the All-Sufficient One
Jehovah Y'Shua, the Lord my Savior
Adonai, the Lord my Master
Jehovah-Jireh, the Lord will Provide
Johovah-Rapha, the Lord that Healeth
Jehovah-Nissi, the Lord my Banner
Jehovah-Mekoddishkem, the Lord who Sanctifies
Jehovah-Shalom, the Lord is Peace
Jehovah-Sabaoth, the Lord of Hosts

Johovah-Raah, the Lord my Shepherd
Jehovah-Sidkenu, the Lord my Righteousness
Jehovah-Shammah, the Lord is There
Qanna, the Jealous One
Yahweh, Lord Jehovah
El Olam, the Everlasting One

And those who know your name will put their trust in you, for you, O Lord, have not forsaken those who seek you.
Psalm 9:10 ESV

The Sermon on the Mount

Seeing the crowds, he went up on the mountain,
and when he sat down, his disciples came to him.
And he opened his mouth and taught them, saying:
Blessed are the poor in spirit, for theirs is the kingdom of heaven.
Blessed are those who mourn, for they shall be comforted.
Blessed are the meek, for they shall inherit the earth.
Blessed are those who hunger and thirst for righteousness,
for they shall be satisfied.
Blessed are the merciful, for they shall receive mercy.
Blessed are the pure in heart, for they shall see God.
Blessed are the peacemakers, for they shall be called sons of God.
Blessed are those who are persecuted for righteousness' sake,
for theirs is the kingdom of heaven.
Blessed are you when others revile you and persecute you
and utter all kinds of evil against you falsely on my account.
Rejoice and be glad, for your reward is great in heaven,

for so they persecuted the prophets who were before you.
Matthew 5:1–11 ESV
I can pretend I am sitting on that mountain and that Jesus Christ
is speaking just to me. His compassion encompasses me.
I have felt poor. I have mourned. I have felt meek and friendless.

If
Rudyard Kipling

If you can keep your head when all about you
Are losing theirs and blaming it on you;
If you can trust yourself when all men doubt you,
But make allowance for their doubting too;
If you can wait and not be tired by waiting,
Or, being lied about, don't deal in lies,
Or, being hated, don't give way to hating,
And yet don't look too good, nor talk too wise;
If you can dream – and not make dreams your master;
If you can think -- and not make thoughts your aim;
If you can meet with triumph and disaster
And treat those two impostors just the same;
If you can bear to hear the truth you've spoken
Twisted by knaves to make a trap for fools,
Or watch the things you gave your life to broken,
And stoop and build 'em up with worn-out tools;
If you can make one heap of all your winnings
And risk it on one turn of pitch-and-toss,
And lose, and start again at your beginnings
And never breathe a word about your loss;

If you can force your heart and nerve and sinew
To serve your turn long after they are gone,
And so hold on when there is nothing in you
Except the Will which says to them: "Hold on";
If you can talk with crowds and keep your virtue,
Or walk with kings—nor lose the common touch;
If neither foes nor loving friends can hurt you;
If all men count with you, but none too much;
If you can fill the unforgiving minute
With six seconds' worth of distance run—
Yours is the Earth and everything that's in it,
And—which is more—you'll be a Man, my son!

Even a child is known by his doings,
whether his work be pure, and whether it be right.
Proverbs 20:11 KJV

Honor your father and your mother,
that your days may be long upon the land that the Lord your God is giving you.
Exodus 20:12 ESV

So whatever you wish that others would do to you, do also to them,
for this is the Law and the Prophets.
Matthew 7:12 ESV

Enter by the narrow gate.
For the gate is wide and the way is easy that leads to destruction,
and those who enter by it are many. For the gate is narrow and

the way is hard that leads to life, and those who find it are few.
Matthew 7:13 ESV

A soft answer turns away wrath, but a harsh word stirs up anger.
Proverbs 15:1 ESV

Whoever is slow to anger is better than the mighty,
And he who rules his spirit than he who takes a city.
Proverbs 16:32,33 ESV

The Ten Commandments

You shall have no other gods before me.
You shall not make for yourself a carved image, or any likeness of anything that is in heaven above, or that is in the earth beneath, or that is in the water under the earth.
You shall not take the name of
the Lord your God in vain, for the Lord will not hold him guiltless
who takes his name in vain.
Remember the Sabbath day, to keep it holy.
Honor your father and your mother.
You shall not murder.
You shall not commit adultery.
You shall not steal.
You shall not bear false witness against your neighbor.
You shall not covet.
Exodus 20:3, 4, 7, 8, 12 ESV

Daffodils
By William Wordsworth

I wandered lonely as a cloud
That floats on high o'er vales and hills,
When all at once I saw a crowd,
A host, of golden daffodils;
Beside the lake, beneath the trees,
Fluttering and dancing in the breeze.

Continuous as the stars that shine
And twinkle on the Milky Way,
They stretched in never-ending line
Along the margin of a bay;
Ten thousand saw I at a glance,
Tossing their heads in sprightly dance.

The waves beside them danced, but they
Out-did the sparkling waves in glee;
A poet could not but be gay,
In such a jocund company:
I gazed—and gazed—but little thought
What wealth the show to me had brought:

For oft, when on my couch I lie
In vacant or in pensive mood,
They flash upon that inward eye
Which is the bliss of solitude;
And then my heart with pleasure fills,
And dances with the daffodils.

But they who wait for the Lord shall renew their strength;
They shall mount up with wings as eagles;
they shall run, and not be weary;
they shall walk, and not faint.
Isaiah 40:31 ESV

Be Like the Bird
Victor Hugo

Be like the bird,
Who Halting in his flight
On limb too slight
Feels it give way beneath him,
Yet sings
Knowing he hath wings.

My Kingdom
Louisa May Alcott

A little kingdom I possess
Where thoughts and feelings dwell;
And very hard the task I find
Of governing it well.
I do not ask for any crown
But that which all may win;
Nor try to conquer any world
Except the one within.

CHAPTER 17

Your Southern Heritage

There is so much about the South that I love. And since I am writing this book in response to my child's request, and primarily for my southern-born and southern-raised children, I will take this opportunity to encourage my children to pass along that love to their children. Forgive me if this offends anyone, especially our northern neighbors. It is not meant to. I have children and their spouses who have lived as far north as Washington, D.C., Boston, Massachusetts, and Michigan, and they loved and got along just fine with the natives there. But there is a difference, and we all know it. How you see that difference just depends on whether you are from north or south of the Mason Dixon Line.

To southerners, there is indeed a line in the sand. Whether that line has been blurred beyond recognition in places by the footsteps of those crossing over it is debatable, but I am writing this to remind you of what you have been given by being born here. I want my grandchildren to know what they otherwise may not. The legacy passed down by their ancestors is rich and not to be forgotten.

So I will tell you what I experienced and what my parents experienced to the extent that I know it. That does not mean that there were not events or episodes or challenges or disgraces that happened in Dixie for which I would not be proud. But that is everywhere. People will occasionally disappoint you. Only God is perfect. But I will tell you that this land is beautiful, and as a child, I fell in love with it. People in the South, and thereby in my life, have been intertwined with the land, the heat, and the humidity. The white sand and the red Georgia clay, the Spanish moss, the sweet-scented magnolias and gardenias, and again, the heat. Southerners are somehow like those things. Rich in character like the clay, graceful like the moss, and winsome and sweet smelling like the flowers. But we're tough like the heat. Maybe because of the heat. These characteristics melded together make southerners more than just interesting.

Southerners' toughness is belied by our soft-spoken, easy nature. We don't like to deliver bad news, even if the news is not *so* bad. We will find ways to make it sound a little better by tiptoeing around unpleasant subjects with cushioned speech and softened words (both in meaning and in how they are pronounced) because we never want to hurt anyone's feelings. We will carefully craft our words to hide any disconcerting feelings, knowing, however, that our audience reads that coverup like a book, because they do the same thing. Women are especially true to this rule, but if the need arises, we can and will speak directly, and we will defend our families, friends, and ideals with the scrappiness of a hurt animal. More often than not, however, our menfolk sometime find themselves confused, bewildered, and frustrated trying to get to the bottom of an issue. They need a straight answer, but that straight answer has a hard time finding its way out of a sweet southern girl's pretty mouth. We just can't help it! We long to comfort and not disturb, which may also be the reason we talk with drawn-out syllables that sound kind and calm. We accentuate the softness of each word, exchanging a's, ah's, and uh's for letters that sound too harsh. You will hear southerners say *windah*, *pillah*, *nevah*, and *evah*. It may just be the southern heat that slows us down in speech and action, and makes us say words with less precision (because we're about to pass out from the heat!). But I believe that this is really our way of communicating love. We can spot a northerner a mile away by their directness. To us, their approach lacks tact, friendliness, kindness, compassion, and love, though this is surely not their intent. The harsh sound of their language, for some reason, just doesn't *sound* sweet to us a'tall!

If a child was raised in the North, we know it the very minute they say "yes" to an adult. Our manners are sacred to us. We consider it shameful if your children do not say "yes, ma'am" and "no, ma'am," "yes, sir" and "no, sir," because that would be an indication that they are terribly ill-mannered and have not been raised properly. They must always say "ma'am" and "sir" out of respect for their elders, and if they don't, they have not had good training. The South is just different from anywhere else. And we're proud of those differences.

But, in all fairness, the North isn't the South. It is much colder in the North. The South is rarely so, and its warmth has been ingrained in our southern nature, southern smile, and southern drawl. Most everything moves slower because of the heat in the South, (including our speech, as I said). And people are more highly concentrated up North. More people are strangers there, and in smaller southern towns, you are less afraid of the unknown because there is less unknown to contend with. Most of us have never met a stranger, and most southerners are friendly and open. I think, too, that because of the closeness people feel in the South, there is an accountability that may not exist in large cities. That, coupled with the fact that almost all southerners still believe in the Ten Commandments, or at least did as I was growing up, is probably the reason we tend to treat each other more graciously and more often with a smile. I love that about the South.

With so many foreigners moving into our area, and with most of us going far and away for our education, our acceptance of different foods and art and music has been eye opening. We've expanded our horizon in many good ways. We've realized there are worlds beyond our sanctuary, and worlds that have much to offer. With that realization comes the question, though, of whether or not we will also accept the ways of those other cultures that might not be so godly at all. I look around, and listen, and I know we have lost a little; we expect a little less virtue now. We seem to have decided that abandoning some of our southern ways so that we might be more 'opem'minded' and 'prugressive' and more 'suphistacated' is worth the trade-off. I guess we don't want to be politically incorrect or considered close-minded. We want to be, in the eyes of the world, more attractive and not so "backwuds." We're a little more jaded, and at the same time, we want to be up on the times and in on the fun. I'm afraid the consequence has been that we've at times forgotten what we were taught, and some of us have turned our backs on what we know to be right. We object less to the immoral, and we're beginning to buy into those more enlightened philosophies that insist we should never restrict anyone from doing anything they want to do. We're becoming very adept at blurring the lines of right and wrong, and we try not to hold anyone to account so that we, ourselves are free to do as we please without anyone raising an eyebrow.

We are worldlier, more carnal, and more accepting of the ungodly and perverse. We are becoming more desensitized to the ways of God, and once you head down those paths, you become less and less aware of how far you've gotten away from what you once cherished. The further away we get from God, the closer we think we are! Right becomes wrong, and wrong becomes right.

So, I hope you will do what is going to be the hardest thing to do. Keep your eyes on God. I wish we would all decide to go back to what we had years ago in the South, which perhaps is in some small ways a metaphor for going back to God. Character, morality, and answering to a higher authority. I hear people talk so casually about living together instead of marrying, as if it is just fine, but at the same time they say they are believers in Christ. What they fail to recognize is that for Christians, it doesn't matter if the world condones that lifestyle. What matters is what God Almighty says about it. Always seek the opinion that counts. I am praying that as you walk through your life and experience the world and all it offers, you will remember the warmth of the South and the things that you learned there. Don't always embrace every culture and every belief with all of their customs. I am not telling you to be unloving toward strangers, but just to be discerning and smart and true to yourself and your God.

On the funny side, having so many people moving to the South from other areas has made it more and more difficult to hold on to our dialect, our expressions, and especially our accents. When my daughter graduated from the University of Georgia and moved to Atlanta, I began to notice a change in her accent. And she began to notice my southern pronunciations! She lost some of her accent and I questioned mine. But I say, don't be wooed into thinking you should sound so correct in your pronunciations that when your words come out, they sound cold and hard. Embrace the uniqueness of this part of the country. Many people from all over have sifted into our midst in the big southern cities like Atlanta, and they must be taught how to talk! In all seriousness, don't lose your accent subconsciously trying to imitate theirs and all of its clarity. It's okay to say 'windah' instead of 'window.' Or 'pillah' instead of 'the pillow.' However, please try not to embarrass us all by saying 'windar,' 'warsh,' 'pillar,' or 'Panamaw' City! That would qualify you as a hick, not a southerner! Even though people who aren't from the South may think that our southern drawl and pronunciations mean we are not so smart, we certainly know better. Nothing could be further from the truth. So just keep that accent, because it becomes you!

I decided to include my own little collection of southern expressions here in hopes that they will not be forgotten. These are words that I have heard all my life, and they communicate, with amazing clarity, feelings that would otherwise be missed. Southerners use these sayings to decorate their speech in the same way a southern lady uses pearls to complete an outfit. The statement takes on more meaning and the conversation gets more interesting, lively, and much more fun.

Southerners Say it This Way

Hey, y'all!
How're y'all doing?
I'll have some sweet tea, please ma'am (meaning, tea with lots of
sugar, lemon, and ice in it).
This is heaven on earth.
If you can't say something nice about somebody, don't say anything at all.
Bless your heart! (This expression is used to communicate love, compassion and empathy,
but is also used often to communicate an insult, as in,
"You never learned to make corn bread, did you? Bless your heart.").
He knows which side his bread is buttered on (meaning,
he knows who he should be nice to).
Where there's a will, there's a way.
Don't sass your mama!
You're just being ugly.
You think you're a smarty pants!
You're too smart for your own good.
The apple doesn't fall far from the tree.
The apple didn't fall far from the tree, did it, y'all (an insult,
meaning the child is just like the also offensive parent).

Put your thinking cap on!
Tell it like it is.
You crack me up (meaning, you are so funny)!
You're beating a dead horse (meaning, too much has been said about the subject).
A thing of beauty is a joy forever.
Stop piddlin' around and get back to work!
That's a tough row to hoe (meaning, it's a big undertaking that is especially difficult).
She has a long row to hoe (meaning, she has a long road ahead of her)!
The handwriting is on the wall.
Land Sakes!
I'm sweatin' like a sinner in church!
She was pitchin' a fit!
You march to your own drummer, sweetheart, don't you? (an insult)
Yo (meaning, your)
Put your best foot forward.
Act like a lady.
He's drunk as a skunk!
Yo mama's gonna spank you!
Sho-nuf (meaning, sure enough)?
She let's everything roll off of her like water on a duck's back!
How's yo mama 'n 'em?
She's as tough as nails!
She's pretty as a peach!
He's three sheets to the wind (meaning, he's drunk)!
She's a tough old bird.
He is as stubborn as a mule!
She's cooked her goose (meaning, she's sealed her fate and she's in big trouble).
He's a dead duck!
Lord willin' and the creek don't rise.

Land Sakes Alive!

Well, I s'wanee (meaning, I swear).

They've buried the hatchet (meaning, they've made up or reconciled).

Who all's going to the play?

Let bygones be bygones.

She's feeling down in the mouth.

He's been robbing Peter to pay Paul.

It's not your fault, honey! You didn't know any better!

Act like a person.

I'm fed up with this (meaning, I'm sick of this)!

I'm trying to kill two birds with one stone.

I haven't seen you in a month of Sundays!

Don't let it ruffle your feathers!

Liar, liar, pants on fire!

He's as cool as a cucumber.

He's been moving from pillar to post.

Pull yourself up by your bootstraps (meaning, pull yourself together).

She was as pleased as punch.

You're a day late and a dollar short.

He's as poor as a church mouse.

Hop up, lazy bones!

These are my Sunday-go-to-meeting clothes.

We're about to have a little sit-to (meaning, we're going to have a little talk to straighten something out).

This is like old home week (meaning, there are very many familiar people or family members at a gathering).

She's a live wire!

We're kissin' cousins.

Beauty is only skin deep.

Be somebody.

Act like somebody.

You just need to get right back up on the horse (meaning, after you've been bucked off, it's best to get right back on so you won't develop a fear of riding, or of doing whatever has toppled you in life).

That's a nice how-do-you-do (a sarcastic way of saying, that's not very nice).

You can't see the forest for the trees (can't see the big picture).

A bird in the hand is worth two in the bush.

It's snowing down south (meaning, your slip is showing).

She was fit to be tied.

Pleg take it (meaning, plague take it)!

She's having a duck fit!

I'm about to have a hissy fit!

Gracious Sakes Alive!

What in the Sam Hill is going on?

That's the pot callin' the kettle black.

Y'all better watch y'all's selves!

All y'all been sick?

Y'all, don't be bad-mouthin' her now (meaning, don't talk ugly about someone).

Don't jump from the frying pan into the fire.

By hook or by crook (meaning, I'm going to do it one way or another).

I'm fixin' to go to town (meaning, I'm getting ready to go to town or I'm about to go to town).

I have a lot of groceries in my buggy (shopping cart).

Look over yonder (or actually, "yonda," meaning, *over there*).

He's as tight as a tick (meaning, he won't spend a dime on anything)!

He's as slow as Christmas!

Mind your manners!

Blood is thicker than water.

A Southern girl wouldn't be caught dead at the grocery store without her lipstick!
She's as brown as a berry (meaning, a person has very tan skin).
He has more than the law allows (tongue in cheek expression meaning, he has more money, or whatever, than should be legal).
She's just shugah-coatin' it (meaning, she's trying to make it sound better than it is).
I'm as hot as blue blazes!
What in blue blazes?
Dog gone it!
Dadgummit!
Dagnabit!
I'll be dog!
I'll be dog gone!
It's hot as hades!
Wait a nitpicking minute!
He's as rich as Croesus!
You're embarrassing the living daylights out of me, child!
I'd be ashamed (meaning, you ought to be ashamed)!
It smells to high heavens!
He is the cat's meow!
He's not the end all and be all!
She's as slow as molasses.
She was as white as a ghost!
The tincture of time heals all things.
Don't run roughshod over the daisies.
I'm could jerk a knot in his tail (meaning, I'm very mad at him).
Put a smile on your face!
Smile, and the world smiles with you; cry, and you cry alone!
Being impolite is the kiss of death for a southerner.
She's been run ragged (meaning, she's had way too much to do).

I'm caught between a rock and a hard place (meaning, I have no good options).

You're barking up the wrong tree (meaning, you're looking in the wrong place or asking the wrong person).

Don't hang me out to dry (meaning, don't put me in a bad position).

Gimme some shugah (meaning, give me a kiss).

The old gray mare ain't what she used to be.

She's just trying to butter him up (meaning, she's trying to get her way by flattering him).

Birds of a feather flock together.

He's up a creek without a paddle.

This isn't her first rodeo (meaning, she's done this before).

Early to bed, early to rise makes a man healthy, wealthy, and wise.

She was madder than a wet hen!

If I had my druthers (meaning, if I had my way).

Getting him to do something is like pulling teeth.

I 'reggen' or I reckon (meaning, I guess so).

I 'daclare!' (meaning, I declare, I am surprised, if only mildly so, or, you don't mean it)!

It's been a minute since I've seen Joe (meaning, it's been a long time).

I do declare!

He's just playin' possum.

I don't have a dog in that fight.

You're just splittin' hairs (meaning, you are being nitpicky).

Don't let it ruffle your feathers.

You're preachin' to the choir, sista (meaning, you're telling me something I already know all too well).

Hold your horses (meaning, slow down or be patient).

Don't you act ugly, now (meaning, don't be rude or mean)!

That dog won't hunt (meaning, the idea won't fly, or that won't work).

Don't buy a pig in a poke (meaning, don't accept a deal without examining it carefully first).

I got a mind to go dancin' tonight.
God bless you (after someone sneezes)!
Help, murder, police!
That picture is all catty-cornered (or catty-wompered).
I've got a hankerin' for some fried chicken.
It's a little wompy-jawed.
What's good for the goose is good for the gander (meaning, if it's good for you, then it's good for me).
There's more than one way to skin a cat (meaning, there's more than one way to get something done).
She's as cute as a button.
Scream bloody murder!
Oh my stars!
Heaven forbid!
She put up a good fight.
She fought it tooth and nail.
Oh shoot!
I'm gonna skin your hide!
I'm gonna tan your hide!
I'm gonna blister your bottom!
I think she's just feeling a little blue.
Phooey!
Heavens to Betsy!
She'll give him a run for his money!
Hush yo mouth!
He took off, lickety-split!
I'm going to the "buta parla" (beauty parlor).
Let me put on my face (meaning, let me put on my makeup).
He's like a bull in a china shop.

I've been running around like a chicken with its head cut off (meaning, I've been very busy).
He doesn't have two pennies to rub together (meaning, he's very poor).
Share and share alike.
Wet your whistle (meaning, have a drink).
Her tickle box has turned over (meaning, she can't stop laughing).
I haven't got one red cent!
A penny saved is a penny earned.
Oooh, I look like death warmed over!
That was ugly as sin!
Absence makes the heart grow fonder.
Everything's gonna be alright, so straighten your face up!
The apple doesn't fall far from the tree.
I can't call her name (meaning, I can't remember her name).
Howdy do.
Howdy doody.
Sugah Bear, Sweetie, Sweetie Pie, Cutie Pie, Doodle Bug, Lady Bug, Sugah Pie, Chickadee, Prissy Pants, Missy Prissy, Miss Priss, Prissy Tail, Monkey Tail (terms of endearment used for children).
I think they're in cahoots together.
Holy moly!
He had to eat crow!
Somebody got up on the wrong side of the bed (meaning, they aren't happy)!
You're makin' a mountain out of a mole hill.
Laws a mercy (meaning, Lord, have mercy)!
He's got one foot in the grave.
Don't cry over spilt milk (meaning, don't get upset over little things).
You could hang meat in here (meaning, it's so cold).
Keep it in the road (meaning, keep things under control).

Give him an inch, and he'll take a mile.
I'm gonna wash your mouth out with soap.
It doesn't amount to a hill of beans (meaning, it's not important)!
The early bird gets the worm.
I'm worn slap out.
A rising tide lifts all boats.
She'll be doin' that 'till the cows come home!
Don't count your chickens before they're hatched.
Don't put all your eggs in one basket.
There're too many cooks in the kitchen.
I saw lightning bugs for the first time this summer (our word for fireflies).
These were our old stompin' grounds.
He's about to make me lose my religion!
You're the spittin' image of your grandfather.
The squeaky wheel gets the grease.
Don't judge a book by its cover.
It's blowin' up a storm!
They are like two peas in a pod.
You can lead a horse to water, but you can't make him drink.
She's as good as gold.
He's as good as dead!
She was doing something to beat the band (meaning, she's doing something *fast*).
She was going to town (meaning, she was dancing or talking fast or a lot).
She was going ninety to nothing (meaning, she was doing something or talking fast).
Don't throw the baby out with the bathwater.
If you don't rest, you won't be worth shootin'!
She's the redheaded stepchild (the opposite of fair-haired child).
They're kissin' cousins.

She's just kowtowin' to him (catering to him).

Don't bow and scrape (sarcastic way of saying you're treating someone like a king for some unfounded reason).

He's dumb as a post!

I just call a spade, a spade!

Whatever floats your boat!

Drunk as a coot!

He's the black sheep of the family.

I haven't seen you in a coon's age!

Moses sakes alive!

Don't be mealy-mouthed.

That doesn't mean squat (that doesn't mean anything).

She can't do squat (meaning, she can't do anything right).

He's poor as a *haint* (haint means ghost).

You hit the nail on the head.

She's pitching a fit.

He was on him like white on rice!

You're cutting off your nose to spite your face.

Hop to it (meaning, get busy)!

They're like oil and water (meaning, their personalities clash).

Things roll off of her like water on a duck's back (meaning, nothing bothers her).

Put the pedal to the metal (meaning, go fast)!

He's as dead as a door nail!

He was cuttin' a buck! (meaning, he was having a fit and acting very badly, usually relating to a child)

Let's go while the gettin's good.

Pretty is as pretty does.

The horse has been let out of the barn.

He's as crazy as a bedbug!

Two heads are better than one.
Hottameeta! (a word my father made up, and as close as I can tell, means, watch out or oh my goodness)
I'll give you a ring later today (meaning, I'll call you on the telephone later).
Strike while the iron's hot.
He's green around the gills (meaning, he looks sick).
It's raining cats and dogs.
You're puttin' the horse before the cart.
I've got more than I can say grace over.
She was all decked out.
Don't try to get on my good side.
She was dressed to the nines (meaning, dressed to perfection).
If you keep making that face, it might stick that way.
She's on cloud nine.
You can take it to the bank.
She's old as dirt!
She can spot trouble a mile away.
I'll give you nine-to-one that's what happened.
That's a whole *nuthah* thing.
He took the whole nine yards (meaning, everything or the whole lot).
He's gettin' too big for his britches.
He looks like he's been rode hard and put up wet (he looks really bad).
He's as old as Methuselah.
I don't want to wear out my welcome.
He doesn't know when to come in out of the rain.
They're livin' high on the hog.
I'm waitin' for my ship to come in.
Your room looks like a pigsty (meaning, it's a mess).
It's like herding cats.

There's bad blood between them (meaning, they've had run-ins or conflicts in their history).

Sleep tight. Don't let the bedbugs bite.

I'm fat as a pig!

See you later, alligator.

I love your pocketbook (meaning, purse)!

It's six of one; half a dozen of the other.

He doesn't know when to come in out of the rain (meaning, he's not too smart)

He calls a spade, a spade (meaning, he tells it like it is)!

In a while, crocodile.

Get off your high horse (meaning, stop acting so haughty).

That doesn't ring a bell with me (meaning, it doesn't sound familiar).

She can really cut a rug (meaning, she can really dance).

Don't look a gift horse in the mouth. (You say this if someone to whom you've generously given something attempts to refuse it, saying things like, "I can't accept that—you are too nice! You shouldn't have done that!" It used to be that when a horse was being considered for purchase, the buyer would look at the horse's teeth in order to determine his state of health. Hence, if someone is giving you a gift, you don't examine it or question it.)

This is more than I can shake a stick at.

Beggars can't be choosers.

Christmas gift! (On Christmas morning, when the telephone rings, you should answer by saying, "Christmas gift!" Whoever says it first is supposed to receive a Christmas gift from the other person.)

You're in high cotton now (meaning, you are financially successful). This originated in the antebellum pre-Civil War South and meant that the crops were very good and the person was making a lot of money; hence, he was living a very comfortable life.

Be sweet (bidding farewell expression, especially to children)!

Bye, y'all!

Eufaula, Alabama, where I grew up, had its own language. My mother's pronunciations were

different from any of those I've heard in any other part of the country. Her dialect made her sound like she was almost speaking a different language. For the most part, the language was sweet sounding, but we would all laugh about those words that were so mispronounced. For instance, she said "caughtaflower" for cauliflower, and "boofay" instead of buffet. And oh yeah, who can forget her enunciation of the word Hawaii? It was "Hi-wah-ya." It sounded like she was saying, "How are you?" Mammy must have had roots in France because she pronounced "menu" "main-you." It sounded very French to us. All of us say things like "beauta parla" instead of beauty parlor. We often drop r's. For instance, I recently attended the funeral of a friend whose name was Martha. The preacher pointed out that she did not like to be called Martha and instead wanted to be called Mahta. In the South, "Martha" is just incorrect, and anyone who says that is just ignorant, basically, because it doesn't sound refined. It sounds too harsh.

As I grew up, I began to notice the difference in the way a word was supposed to be sounded out and how we pronounced it, and I became familiar with the rules of grammar. Since English was my interest, I found myself greatly irritated by the misuse and mispronunciation of words. But I actually never mastered grammar, learning all of its many rules, so I don't know why I *evah* thought I should be the one to judge anyone else. I've definitely caught myself butchering the king's English, saying things like "That's a whole *nuthah* thing," or instructing my dog to "lay" down. I'm not even sure why I want everything to be correct since I love the relaxed southern way of speaking so much. However, there *is* a big difference between having that southern-sounding elegance and sounding like a hick or a hillbilly. And although I don't think any of you sound like a hick, there are commonly misused words and phrases that we all need to be aware of. Your children need to know enough about the rules of grammar and elocution to avoid those subtle and not so subtle mistakes and incorrect pronunciations that will make them sound like uneducated southerners. A pure southern accent reflects a gentility and an elegance that few people in other areas of the world seem to possess.

When my granddaughter, Caroline, was two years old, we were all eating Christmas dinner together, and she announced that she was "done." My sister, Kim, attempted to correct her by saying, "You mean you are finished?" Caroline replied (thinking she was actually helping Kim), "Kim, 'done' is just another word for 'finished'!" We laughed and laughed about this! Caroline was so smart to be able to articulate this to Kim in such a grown-up manner, but she was wrong. The two words are not exactly interchangeable, at least not in this instance. Many people use the word *done* incorrectly to say they are finished with something. However, this word should really only be used to reference the completion of food that is cooking. For instance, "The chicken is done." If you are through eating, you should say, "I'm finished," "I have finished," or "I'm through." A common English phrase is used to clarify this: cakes are done, but people are finished. If your children say they are *done* after a meal, it sounds just a little wrong (because it is) and may make them sound uneducated and unpolished. And not simply too southern.

Another mistake that people often make is in the use of "I" and "me." One should say, "Caroline, Clara, Georgia, and I are going swimming." Always say the other person's name first. You wouldn't say, "Me and Caroline, Clara, and Georgia are going swimming." And the way to decide whether to use I or me at the end of the sentence is to leave out the other person and see if you can say the sentence using "I." For example, if you are saying, "Jonathan and I went to the circus." You know you cannot say, "Jonathan and me went to the circus." How do you know this? Simply because you cannot say, "Me went to the circus." Leave out the other person or people and try to say it that way. If it doesn't work, you know it is wrong. In other words, if the sentence is, "He gave the flowers to Katherine and me," you can check it by trying to use "I" without mentioning the other person. "He gave the flowers to I" does not work. So you then know you cannot say, "He gave the flowers to Katherine and I."

So, since you are setting the example, make sure you understand this. Don't let yourself become lazy and say these things incorrectly. The children will never adopt the correct way of expressing themselves if you don't model it for them. Their teachers will try to teach them the correct grammar rules, but they will have an uphill fight if you are not reinforcing it at home. If they don't learn it, they will sound uneducated to anyone who has paid a bit of attention to proper English. And in business, especially, they will need to sound intelligent.

Never say, "Me and Clara are going to go to the zoo." Equally wrong is "Clara and me are making a cake." You should not say, "Him and I are going somewhere." It should be, "Clara and I are going to bake a cake," and "He and I are going to a concert."

"Lie" and "lay" are commonly misused words. The general rule is that you can often use "lie" and be correct. For years I would instruct my dog to "lay down." That *was* wrong. It should have been "Lie down, Lily." In the present tense, to use "lay," you must have an object. You "lay" a *pillow* on the bed. You "lie" on the bed. But then comes the rub. The past tense of "lie" is "lay"! "Lily lay down in the grass enjoying the sunshine yesterday." The past participle of "lie" is "lain." So you would say, "Lily has lain on the grass for four hours." The past tense *and* the past participle of "lay" is "laid." "I laid the pillow on the bed last night." "I have laid the pillow on the bed numerous times."

Let's get this straight! It's this way, not that!

I lie down.
I *lay* down yesterday.
I *have lain* on the bed for days.
And then for the word "lay," it's as follows:
I *lay* the pillow on the bed.
I *laid* the pillow on the bed yesterday.
I *have laid* the pillow on the bed.

A few more words to keep straight are "swim," "sing," "may," and "can."

I *swim* in the river.
I *swam* in the river yesterday.
I *have swum* in the river.
I sing a song.
I sang a song yesterday.
I have sung a song in the past.
Use "may" to ask for or grant permission.
May I have I drink of water? Yes, you may.
Use "can" when expressing ability
She can swim.

There are many other word usages and sentence structures to consider, but I will leave those to your own diligence. Just please don't let your children ignore the important rules of English and sound like an unrefined hick. If you're reading this and laughing, just remember that your speech and your vocabulary may just be the very things that people use to judge your qualifications for a job, your degree of intelligence, and your communication skills as a possible friend. And if you're not from the South, you will have to work even harder to teach your children proper English. Don't forget to soften those words!

This brings me to the most southern thing (or person) I know. Daisy Davis. Daisy, as I mentioned earlier, was my mother's housekeeper and my childhood nurse. Her southern word usage was quite a bit different from ours, but we all somehow understood one another perfectly. I guess it was actually her dialect that was different, and we loved it. She was like a second mother to me, and I adored (and still adore) her. She started working for my grandmother when she was probably only fourteen or fifteen, and she is now eighty-five years old. After being under the tutelage of Lulu (Mammy's cook, Mary Lou, who dipped snuff and called it chocolate) for one or two years, she came to work for us at age sixteen. I admire her more than most anyone I know, so I'd like to share a little about her, right here on these pages.

It's not just Daisy's language that is southern. It's her simple joy and love for anyone in her path. It's the hard life that she lived, that never hardened her. It made her sweeter and more fun and one of the most grateful people I have ever known. To those who, in so many ways, had command over her life, she said, "Yes'um" and "Noam," and did everything with a smile. I'll always remember her happy countenance. There was no pretense. She was genuinely happy. She still smiles and laughs with contagious abandon, as if she has never experienced a single bad thing in her life, and she loves us all so deeply that she prays for all of us, *on her knees, every morning.* When she told me this, it shamed me. I knew that I had never committed myself to be on my knees every day for anyone. Not even my own family. The humility that I feel when I ponder this is inexpressible.

I could have no more respect and love for anyone than I do for Daisy. In all of my sixty-two years, I have never met another human being who possessed more of all of the things one would want to possess than Daisy. And yet, of the world's wealth, she possesses very little. But she, *herself*, is a real treasure to me. And that's the thing; you can be a treasure in spite of whatever befalls you and whatever your lot in life might be. The positive influence she has had on my life is beyond measure.

Daisy and Her Brother, Henry, Ready for One of Mammy's Infamous Parties

Daisy's father made her quit school in the first or second grade in order to work in the fields. I'm sure that life was not easy for him, and stress makes people do things they wouldn't otherwise do. She and two of her siblings picked cotton in her daddy's field, and when they were finished with his field, they boarded a bus and were taken to another man's field to work. They were allowed to go into this man's store to pick out their lunch (potted meat, etc.), the cost of which would be garnered from their pay. She and her sister would sometimes take their money (before they had to give it all to their daddy) and buy themselves shoes. She never learned to read or write, and she looks back on that now and asks God why He didn't let her get an education. But she made sure her children did. Her childhood was far from easy, and her adulthood was as challenging, I'm sure, though you would never have suspected it if you knew Daisy. Just thinking about this makes me cry, because although we loved her dearly, we never could have imaged the difficulties she faced in her life. Her world was very different from ours. But we lived in a time and a place where those things were just accepted, and no one would have known exactly how to rectify the situation even if they had thought about it. Daisy was somebody I loved, and that's all I knew. Oddly, those days were better in some ways. People's character was honed by facing difficulties and surviving them, and I think those people were better for it. People didn't feel victimized if their worlds weren't perfect, and it seemed that resentment was less common, at least in the folks I knew. Gratefulness and graciousness were big parts of all of our lives, no matter the hand we had been dealt. We looked into each other's eyes and we loved each other.

Daisy has worked hard all of her life. She worked for our family five or six days a week and stayed late many a night while my parents were out socializing. People in Eufaula entertained a lot. From what I remember my mother saying, I believe Daisy cleaned all of the bathrooms every day. She cooked at least one meal for us every day. She ironed and watched the children and polished silver and whatever else had to be done. She had a full day of work every day. Her husband and their five children lived in a one-bedroom house that belonged to my grandparents, and Daisy walked the short distance to our house and back to her home every day. Her mother, who lived to be 101, took care of Daisy's children while she was at work. I have never heard Daisy complain about her life. *Not once.* She doesn't dwell on what she doesn't have. She is, instead, thankful!

In our antebellum house we had sixteen-foot ceilings and a staircase with the most beautiful, wide, mahogany banister I've ever seen. It was also the longest banister I've probably ever seen. Daisy and I still giggle like school children when she tells me about the day she secretly slid down the banister. I used to dream that I was falling off of that banister, and just before I hit the floor, I would wake up!

Daisy and I had fun doing things that would never entertain a child today. One of our favorite things to do was to sit in the rocking chairs on our wide front porch and play a game we called 'counting cars'. Daisy would get to count the cars coming from one direction on Country Club Road, and I the other. When the game ended, whoever had counted the most cars won. Simple times. We played in the sand, looking for 'Doozem Bugs' while Daisy sang a song to the bug. 'Doozem Bug, Doozem Bug, where are you? Your house is on fire and your wife is ….' All the time she was stirring the little well in the sand with a stick, looking for the elusive bug. I have never figured out what bug we were looking for. She and her brother, Henry, who grew the most beautiful roses I have ever seen in all my life in my grandmother's rose garden (and as an adult, I have searched to no avail for one to compare), pushed me nearly to the heavens in a swing that hung from the huge pecan tree beside our house. Under that same tree we found pecans to crack and we ate them with reverence as though they were a rare delicacy. Daisy watched my siblings and I as we rode the child-sized (but very exciting) metal roller coaster in our backyard. She welcomed the other neighborhood nurses, in their neatly pressed uniforms, when they came with their charges to our backyard for tea parties of graham crackers and orange juice. She watched one day as my sisters and I climbed to the near tip top of a Magnolia tree in our front yard, and when my horrified mother came home, she found Daisy standing underneath the tree ready to catch us if we fell. And Daisy was there, too, when our neighbor's yard man carried me home covered in blood after I had been knocked out cold from a limb that was being sawed from a tree next door. She was a huge part of our lives!

Still, she managed to raise five amazing children of her own who are literally some of the most well-spoken people I have ever met. One day, I received a letter from one of them and could not believe how polished it was. A text from another daughter was classically written and reflected a gentle person far above average in their communication skills. That makes me so proud. They are smart and gracious and kind. One of her girls began nursing school but had to drop out for reasons unrelated to the challenge it presented. One of Daisy's sons is a policeman *and* a preacher. All of her daughters are precious, and her sons impressive. They have held together families and marriages, which rates very high in my book. So few people accomplish this all-important thing anymore. Above all, they adore Daisy, and they make sure she knows it.

I'm including this in my parenting book because she is so much a part of my southern experience and because her story can serve as an important lesson for my children and grandchildren and great-grandchildren. Hard times of some sort will come to every one of us, and when they do, they will reveal what we're made of. Daisy proved that she is made of pure gold. She passed through the fire and came out smiling and laughing and caused us to do the same. If you know Jesus, which Daisy does, your joy will be irrepressible. That old southern heat will destroy you if you choose not to look up. You have to let it drive you to seek the one who can make you strong in the face of it. The outcome is your choice. A decision to grab hold of the strength of Almighty God will make all the difference. By being faithful and trusting in a loving God, Daisy was able to take what might have been considered by some to be a pile of scraps and make it count for so much more. The key, too, is that she is grateful for everything she has, and that gratefulness turns everything else upside down, shakes it up, and turns it into joy. This is such an important lesson to learn. Count your blessings one by one. Daisy says that she needed God, and He showed up. And through Daisy He blessed our family.

Now, you are going to want some of Daisy's southern recipes because she can cook, and because you are going to want to make sure your children get a taste of real southern cooking as it was before we were invaded by the food police and were enlightened! Here are just a few of Daisy's recipes, but look for our forthcoming cookbook. We are not claiming that any of these delicious recipes are good for your children's bodies, but they may just be good for their souls! These recipes are recorded just as Daisy described them.

Hoe Cakes or Johnnycakes
Crispy and sometimes Lacy Cornbread Patties

White Cornmeal (package has a scarecrow with a hat on it)
Water
Vegetable Oil
Cast-iron Frying Pan (or other heavy frying pan)
Cookie Sheet lined with Paper Towels to drain patties

Butter

Jelly, Jam, Preserves, or Honey

Coat the frying pan with thin layer of oil to coat. Turn the eye to medium-high heat. Mix the cornmeal with enough water to make it the consistency of pancake batter (or a little thinner). When the pan is hot, pour the batter into the pan like you would a pancake. According to Daisy, it will tell you when to turn it! Daisy also said, 'When it starts browning, slap it over!'. If it seems to be sticking, let it keep cooking a little longer. Add a little oil for each new patty or set of patties. Drain on paper towels. Slather the patty with butter and preserves. Yum.

Fried Chicken

Chicken Breasts (bone in, with skin), Thighs, or Legs (Drumsticks)
*Lawry's Seasoning Salt (optional)
Salt and Pepper
Ziploc Bag
All-purpose Flour
Vegetable Oil
Cast-iron Frying Pan or Dutch Oven
Cookie Sheet lined with a Brown Grocery Bag or Paper Towels

Wash the chicken. Pat dry. Sprinkle liberally with Lawry's and salt and pepper. If time permits, cover and put in the refrigerator for an hour or overnight. Put the flour in a Ziploc Bag and drop the chicken in the bag, seal, and shake to coat with flour. Put about 2 to 3 inches of vegetable oil in the frying pan (preferably cast-iron) or Dutch oven and heat on medium high. Be sure to watch the oil carefully, as the oil will catch on fire if it gets too hot! When the right temperature is reached, the chicken will sizzle when it touches the oil. Carefully place about three pieces in the oil. Cover and cook until brown on the bottom, then turn. Cook sort of slowly. You don't want to cook the chicken so fast that the skin burns and the inside does not cook. Uncover to crisp the last 10 minutes or so. Total cooking time is around 25-30 minutes. The internal temperature at thickest part of chicken should be 165 degrees.

*I'm sure Lawry's was not part of the recipe when I was growing up, because it was not available. So you may want to use only Salt and Pepper, which you will need a lot of!

Baked Chicken

Chicken Breasts (bone in, with skin), Thighs, or Legs (Drumsticks)
Lawry's Seasoning Salt
Salt and Pepper
1 Stick of Butter, melted
Worcestershire Sauce
Kitchen Bouquet

Wash the chicken and pat it dry. Season the chicken with Lawry's and salt and pepper. If time permits, cover the chicken and place it in the refrigerator for one hour or overnight. When you are ready to cook the chicken, preheat the oven to 350 degrees. Place the chicken in a Pyrex dish and pour up to a stick of melted butter over the chicken, depending on how much chicken you are baking. If you are cooking only two or three pieces of chicken, use much less butter. Cover with foil. Cook until almost done (thickest part of the breast should register 165 degrees), then add a little Worcestershire Sauce and Kitchen Bouquet for color. Remove the foil and allow the chicken to brown.

Pickled Cucumber and Onion

1 Cucumber, Peeled and Sliced
1 Small to Medium Onion, Sliced
A Few Shakes of Salt and a Shake or Two of Pepper
1 Heaping Tablespoon of Sugar
1/4–1/2 Cup Vinegar **and** at least Twice as Much Water

Combine all and place in refrigerator overnight. This is great with green beans or by itself.

Turnip Greens

Fresh Turnips, washed, trimmed but with some stems, or Frozen Turnip Greens with Roots
Fat Back (probably half a package) or Bacon Grease Drippings
Salt

Fry the fat back. Fill the pot one-third to one-half full with water (enough to cover turnips, but not too much). Add fried fat back and the rendered fat (from the frying). Add the turnip greens and roots, if desired, to the water. Daisy doesn't use the roots, except when using frozen turnips that have the roots diced in them. Salt to taste. Cook a pretty good little time, probably two to three hours. If you've never tried Ketchup on turnip greens, try it!

Cabbage

1 Head of Cabbage, green outside leaves separated from the lighter colored leaves
Fat Back (about half a package) or Bacon Grease Drippings
Salt and Pepper

Fry the fat back. Add a small amount of water to the pot. Put in fat back meat and rendered fat *or* the bacon grease. If the cabbage has dark green outside leaves, cut those up and cook them first because they take longer to cook. Add cabbage to the boiling water. Reduce heat to simmer. Cook until just about done, then put in roughly chopped white cabbage leaves. Add salt and pepper to taste and cook till tender.

Squash Casserole

Squash, Peeled (Peeling optional)
1 Medium Onion, Chopped

Worcestershire Sauce (a few quick shakes—you don't want to add so much that your Squash turns brown)

4–8 Eggs (depending on how much Squash you are cooking)

1 1/2 Cups Extra Sharp Cracker Barrel Cheddar Cheese (at least this much Cheese, maybe more, depending on how much Squash you use)

Saltine or Ritz Crackers, crumbled (enough to thicken Squash)

Salt and Pepper to taste

This recipe, like all of Daisy's recipes, has no real measurements. The good news is that you really can't go wrong. I use the same ingredients, except that I have never peeled the squash, and I only use one egg and a little onion. So just adjust the recipe as it appeals to you. You will need a good deal of salt and pepper. Slice the squash and place it in the pot with the onions. Add just enough water to cover. Bring this to a boil. Turn the heat down to medium and boil the squash and onions until tender. Drain well. Preheat the oven to 350 degrees. Use a potato masher to mash the squash. You can leave chunks or make it smooth by beating with a mixer, if desired. Combine everything, reserving some cheese for the top. Cook 30–45 minutes until bubbly. Sprinkle the cheese on top and put it back in the oven for a minute or two to melt the cheese.

Daisy's Corn Bread

2 Cups White Cornmeal with Buttermilk (I actually use Yellow Hot Rize Cornmeal)

Buttermilk (add a Little Tap of Soda if using Buttermilk) or Sweet Milk

2 Eggs

1/4 Cup Vegetable Oil, plus some Oil to coat the Pan(s)

Cast-iron Pan or Muffin Pan (6 large or 8 small muffins)

Preheat the oven to 400-450 degrees. Put a little oil in the pan to coat, *plus just a little* (do the same if using individual muffin cups). Mix together all ingredients, adding enough milk (or buttermilk, which is what I use) so that the batter is the consistency of pancake batter (or even a little thinner). Heat the pan(s) with oil until hot. You can test it by carefully dripping a little drop of water into the oil. If it sizzles, it's ready. *But be careful!* If you let it get too hot, the oil will splatter and pop. And be sure not to let it get too, too hot because it will smoke and catch on fire! Pour the batter into the pan(s) and let the corn bread cook about 20 minutes or until slightly browned. Remove from the oven, and use a knife to go around each muffin or outside of big pan to loosen the corn bread. If muffins, lift up on one side and leave standing in muffin cup to cool a little before eating.

Butter Beans

Lima Beans (1 Package frozen or 2–3 Cups Fresh)
1/2 Stick of Butter (adjust if cooking fewer Lima Beans)
Salt and Pepper

Put lima beans in a pot. Don't put a heap of water in the pot—just enough to cover the beans so they won't stick. Add half of a stick of butter, salt and pepper to taste. Bring the water to a boil, then reduce the heat to simmer. Cover. Cook until tender, stirring occasionally and adding water when necessary.

Fried or Stewed Corn

6 Ears of Fresh Corn (preferably Silver Queen), shucked
Water
Milk
½-1 Stick of Butter
Flour
Sugar
Salt and Pepper
Bundt Pan

Carefully cut the kernels off of the corn cobs with a knife. To make this easier, use the center hole of a Bundt pan to hold the corn while you cut the kernels off of the Cob. The kernels will fall conveniently into the Bundt pan. Scrape the cobs with a knife to get the *milk* that is left on the cob. Pour the kernels and the milk into a large frying pan. Add enough water so that the corn won't stick to the pan (you can add more as it cooks). I always add a little bit of milk, but it's not necessary. Add the butter (you may want to add more than ½ stick of butter, perhaps ¾ stick), a good bit of salt and pepper (to taste), and a pinch or two of sugar, depending on how sweet the corn is and how sweet you want it. Cook until tender, about 15–25 minutes. Daisy thickens it with a teaspoon or so of flour (which has been mixed with a little water to avoid lumps). I've never done this, but this *is* Daisy's recipe! Adjust ingredients to suit your taste.

Black-Eyed Peas

Fresh or Frozen Black-Eyed Peas
Water
Salt Pork
Salt and Pepper

Cook the salt pork in water until tender. Add the black-eyed peas, salt and pepper. Cook until tender, about an hour. If you've never tried ketchup on your black-eyed peas, you might want to try it. Believe it or not, it's awesome! And if you're really brave, add some diced raw onion, which takes it to a different level. This combination is good with fresh green beans too.

The Best Peach Ice Cream You'll Ever Put in Your Mouth

This is actually Mammy's recipe, and we have been making this Peach Ice Cream every summer for at least sixty-two years!

1 Quart Half & Half
1 Pint Whipping Cream
Small Amount of Fresh Squeezed Lemon Juice to prevent Peaches from turning brown
2–3 Cups Sugar

About 9 Medium to Large Ripe Peaches (preferably cling-free, Georgia), Peeled and Cut into bite-size pieces
Ice Cream Salt
Ice
Electric Ice Cream Maker

Peel and cut up the peaches into various bite-sized pieces, making sure there are some sizable chunks to bite into. In other words, you don't want it to be pureed. The peaches and the juice from the peaches go into a large bowl. Squeeze a Little lemon juice over the peaches and mix it together so that the peaches won't turn brown. Add a lot of sugar to the peaches (probably a cup), so that the peaches are really sweet. They should seem *way too* sweet to you. They will lose sweetness when they are frozen. About 30 minutes to an hour before freezing, mix the Half & Half and the whipping cream together in the ice cream maker's canister. Add about 1 cup of sugar and stir till dissolved. Store in the refrigerator until it's time to freeze. When you are ready to freeze, mix the peaches and milk mixture together in the canister. Turn the ice cream maker on, and let it mix the milk and peaches together a minute or two before adding the ice and ice cream salt around the outside of the canister to begin the freezing process. You will never taste anything better. Pure bliss! At least once every summer, you *have* to make this heavenly, homemade Peach Ice Cream!

I will end my little southern salute, and in fact my letter, by saying that I hope you hold on to the good things about the South—that is, if you were born in the South. If not, we southerners will gladly share what we have with you. A softer language and approach, gracious hospitality, and a warm smile. You can win your children's hearts with just these three things. But more importantly, I hope that as Christians and as Americans, my children will look back to consider the convictions of a different day in America, when those things that should matter really did. Hold on to the faith of our founders and question the validity of each new philosophy that presents itself. Think about what was considered good and right in our country for two hundred years, and what made our country such a gem that it drew the world's attention and envy. Don't be swayed or persuaded by the changing cultural winds to walk away from the solid foundation of the Gospel of Jesus Christ, which defined America. Be ready to defend those truths even though the world now says they are old-fashioned and no longer relevant. Stand firm, and don't try to be part of the crowd when the crowd is walking down the wrong path. Show your children the narrow gate that leads to life, because it is inevitable that everyone else will be beckoning them to choose the wide gate that leads to destruction.

Be sure that you have a clear understanding of what God says is right and wrong. I have learned from your father, who is such a straight shooter, that there really aren't any gray areas. Either it's right or it's wrong, and either you are moving closer to God or you are moving farther away from Him. Very few people subject themselves to such a standard. As a Christian, you are no longer bound by the requirements of the Law, which Jesus fulfilled. Rather, you now live under the Law of Christ; of grace. Loving God with your whole being and others as you love yourself is what now motivates you to live a life that excels the limits of the Law. God's love has transformed your heart, and now you desire to do those things that God loves.

You will have to turn your back on the ways of the world nearly every time they come hurtling your way. To do this, your convictions will need to be rock solid. You are passing down truths to your children about the ways of the one true and living God, so you need to be aware that the prince of this world would love to trip you up. Don't fall for his lies and don't take your eyes off of the goal. Remember this, that all things are possible with God. And remember that your daddy and I love you more than is possible for you to know.

> Behold, children are a heritage from the Lord, the fruit of the womb a reward.
> Like arrows in the hand of a warrior are the children of one's youth.
> Blessed is the man who fills his quiver with them.
>
> Psalm 127:3–5 ESV

CHAPTER 18

A Letter To My Grandchildren

To Caroline, Clara, Georgia, Nico, Margot, and All of Our Precious Grandchildren and Great Grandchildren to Come.

Please Remember What Gigi has Told You!

I love you. Jesus loves you. Your parents love you. Love God with all your heart and mind and soul. Love your friends. Love your enemies. Be kind to animals. Always be willing to forgive. Mind your manners. Girls, cross your ankles. Ladies, cross your legs. Cherish your own name and your own reputation. Be upstanding. Be outstanding. Say, "Yes, ma'am" and "No, ma'am," "Yes, sir" and "No, sir," "Please" and "Thank you." Never do drugs, not even once. *Nevah, evah* smoke cigarettes. Don't drink alcohol, at least not until you are twenty-one, and then only if you are old enough to understand that even one drink can be dangerous. Always treat your body, both inside and out, like the temple of the Holy Spirit, which it is. Eat food that is healthy for you. Watch your figure. Don't overeat. Think twice before you let someone talk you into a tattoo. Unless they are discreet, they aren't very pretty on a young bride with a beautiful white wedding gown on! Or a fifty-year-old woman with wrinkly skin. Be careful! Don't ride in the car with a person who has been drinking alcohol or taking drugs or who is a daredevil. When you're feeling blue, look around and count your blessings, one by one. Be wise. Be moral. Marry a born-again Christian. Be thankful for everything you have. Follow the Ten Commandments. Hate the sin but love the sinner. Be discerning. Don't fall for the schemes of the devil. Know that fifteen and sixteen and seventeen-year-olds make decisions based on the trends of the day and the opinions of their friends, not always taking sound advice. Instead, *you* be smart! And know that the media and the trend setters and the marketers would love to turn your head, while your parents will do everything they can to keep your head on straight, because they love you more than anyone else. Don't live a life that leaves you with regrets. Always put your best foot forward. Be thoughtful and kind, gracious and grateful. Be sweet. Be a blessing. Let your light shine! Stand up straight with your shoulders back and head up. Carry yourself like a queen (or a king, if we finally have some grandsons!). Let the words of your mouth be pleasing to God. Be true to yourself. And never pass up an opportunity to be beautiful.

Fall 2024 in Highlands, NC

Walking on Majestic Shores
Gigi, 2018

Come cuddle close, my little one.
Your precious life has just begun!
I want to tell you of the love
That brought you here from up above.
The light that shines through you to me
Is beautiful for all to see.
It's heaven's glow that glistens still,
Around your face, your world to fill.
Take my hand and play with me.
Let's sit together under yonder tree.
What fun you'll have; just wait and see,
Riding horses upon my knee.
You are mine, and I am yours,
Walking on majestic shores.
Grand it is with you, my grand,
As I watch you learn to sit and stand.
Walking farther down the road,
You'll say, "Look, my Gigi, how it has snowed!"
Or maybe call me on a starlit night
To tell me of your first real fright!
And I'll be there to laugh and sing,
Remind you of the joy He brings.
You are His, and He is yours,
Walking on majestic shores.

About the Author

Georgia Adams West is from a large extended family whose roots run deep in the southern towns of Eufaula, Alabama and Columbus, Georgia. She received a journalism degree from the University of Georgia, and has since worked as a writer for a major insurance company. She is married to the love of her life, Joe, and together they have three children.

Joe and I Celebrating My 61st and His 65st Birthdays at Bijoux in Destin, Florida

www.ingramcontent.com/pod-product-compliance
Lightning Source LLC
Chambersburg PA
CBHW051401070526
44584CB00023B/3243